Cory Everson's
life balance

Cory Everson's life balance

The Complete Mind/Body Program for a Leaner Body, Better Health, and Self-Empowerment

Cory Everson

with Greta Blackburn

A PERIGEE BOOK

Before beginning any dietary or exercise program, always consult with your doctor. The exercises in this book are intended for healthy people. People with health problems should not follow these routines without a physician's approval.

A Perigee Book
Published by The Berkley Publishing Group
A member of Penguin Putnam Inc.
375 Hudson Street
New York, NY 10014

First edition: October 1998

Published simultaneously in Canada.

The Penguin Putnam Inc. World Wide Web site address is
http://www.penguinputnam.com

Library of Congress Cataloging-in-Publication Data

Everson, Corinna.
    Lifebalance : the complete mind/body program for a leaner body,
better health, and self-empowerment / by Cory Everson with Greta
Blackburn. — 1st ed.
        p.   cm.
    ISBN 0-399-52444-4
    1. Women–Health and hygiene—Popular works.   2. Physical fitness
for women—Popular works.   3. Reducing diets—Popular works.
4. Body image—Popular works.   5. Reducing exercises—Popular works.
6. Mind and body—Popular works.   I. Blackburn, Greta.   II. Title.
RA776.5.E94   1998
613'.04244—dc21   98-26664
                                                                              CIP

Printed in the United States of America

10 9 8 7 6 5 4 3 2 1

CONTENTS

Contents

INTRODUCTION

Each day, as I sift through correspondence sent to me from all over the world, I'm reminded how many women are unhappy with themselves no matter how much weight they lose, inches they diet off, or hours they slave away at the gym. We live in a land of tremendous opportunity and abundance, yet many are more unhappy than ever before, or so it seems. We live in an era in which family problems and personal pressures burden and incapacitate us with a type of poverty generations before never had the luxury of worrying about.

Americans are obsessed about physical appearance. We focus on our looks like artists creating living sculptures. We obsess about our waistlines, breasts, and bottoms as we spend billions of dollars on liposuction wonder wands, bust-line-building Wonder Bras, and miracle weight-loss pills, powders, and potions. We equate looking good with having a good life.

As a former top bodybuilder, I understand all too well what it's like to focus compulsively on this or that body part and to try to mold each into "perfection." At times in my life I, too, have been a slave to the quest to build a better butt, but I've learned what this physical obsession costs not only to the wallet, but to the psyche as well. The time, energy, and money wasted trying to be competition-ready year-round, fashion-model thin, or movie-star perfect could be better applied doing what makes us feel good—not bad—about ourselves. After all, how many of those we emulate, those who have made it to the top, are really leading satisfying, fulfilling lives? Not many, when you consider the reports about them in substance abuse clinics, divorce courts, and even jails! Why do we want to emulate the supermodels, rock stars, and Oscar winners, given that they usually have little to teach us about creating a happy life?

And what has all the worry, disappointment, and focus on our looks gotten us? Given that 60 percent of American women do not match the cinema ideal and are size twelve or above and nearly half of American women (49 percent) are size fourteen or above, our obsession is probably not getting us much more than disappointment and frustration. Most of us are simply not genetically programmed to be waiflike, and I believe the stress of trying to meet the unrealistic standard actually keeps us stuck right where we are, since stress causes our bodies to store fat and makes motivation more difficult to maintain. The payoff for all the obsession is ironic: 33 percent of the American population is overweight today, compared to only 25 percent nearly twenty years ago. If you don't think that 32 percent increase sounds like much, think of it this way: Were it to show up in your bank account, it would be considered a big improvement, but if that dividend were "invested" in your bottom or body fat count, it would be most unwelcome.

Shockingly, many women would rather be fashionably thin than healthy! *The Wall Street Journal* asked both men and women, "Would you want to weigh fifteen pounds less or live five years longer?" A majority of the men wanted to live longer, while a majority of the women wanted to weigh less. So many women are dissatisfied with their bodies, and are carrying that dissatisfaction around with them every day, that it's distorting not only their self-image, but their relationships with friends, family, and coworkers.

Following are excerpts from a few of the letters I've received in recent years, which serve, I think, as good examples of some of the issues that underlie female self-loathing. The women who wrote these letters share the unhappiness and many of the same problems, misconceptions, and negative self-images that abound in so many others today. Happily, they also show the hope and willingness to change that can be used as a foundation for future health and happiness.

Dear Cory,

I have a goal to shed this weight that is my safety—my wall of protection. I want to be strong, healthy, and fit and to start living for the first time in my life. To be proud and not sink into the background. It's funny, no matter how smart or kind or funny we are, if we don't look good, we feel 'bad.'

Dear Cory,

I just wanted to tell you what an inspiration you have been to me. I'm really going to try to not make this too corny or soppy. I'm twenty-one years old and I've been working out since I was fifteen. I play college tennis at [name of institution]. When I was about four I was molested by my grandfather. I've never told anyone in my family about this. I guess I just didn't want to disappoint anyone that I love. But when I was about eight years old I started cutting myself. I guess I was punishing myself for what had happened. I never tell people about that because I don't want them to think I'm a weirdo. When I was about fourteen I saw you win your Ms. Olympia title. And I wanted to be like you. Well, obviously I haven't quite achieved your physical stature yet but I started exercising every day then and I've kept it up till now and it has really helped me to get through that experi-

ence that happened to me and instead of cutting myself now I try to exercise instead. This is the first time I have seen you in person and it makes me so happy to see what a great person you are. I really relate to a lot of the things you are saying about how you have to love yourself for others to love you. Now my goal is I would like not to look like you on the outside but to be like you on the inside. I really feel I owe you a great deal, I feel like in an indirect way you have saved my life or at least helped it to be the quality it is now. I sometimes have a hard time telling people I love them but I can truly say I love you and thank you.

Dear Cory,

Thank you so much for your phone call and words of love, encouragement, and support. I cried when I heard it. You are such a wonderful and truly spectacular person. I also got and appreciated your tapes and note. Cory, my life has become nothing but days of total obsession [with] food and exercise. I was at one time a very fit and muscular and healthy young woman, full of energy and life. Anorexia took a vicious grip on me, but you gave me hope. Just this past week I decided and committed to give up and start eating to live again. I have gained fifteen pounds in six days. Your tapes have been such an inspiration and motivating tool to help me deal with feeling "fleshy" or human again.

Cory, you have helped me more than you know.

I work out religiously five times a week and eat healthily, but everyone is [so] obsessed with conforming to the magazine model image that it is almost sickening. Many times I fall into the same trap.

I am twenty years old and used to model. I was underweight (as expected of me) and unhealthy (both physically and mentally) because of the modeling. I went through stages of starvation or crazy diets and bulimic tendencies. All of this to keep my weight below the norm. This went on for a couple of years and now my metabolism is way out of whack. I still drink laxative teas and don't eat like a normal person.

My friend Susan (not her real name) is typical of those searching for more substance in their lives. As she puts it, she wants to connect with what she calls "something bigger than just little me—something with real meaning." She just doesn't know how.

In search of a spiritual tune-up, she once took a half day off of work and went to a local metaphysical center for a special day of meditation. The next day I called to ask her about her spiritual exploration. Her response was less than enthusiastic. "It was weird," she told me. "They had a photographer there from a big newspaper and he kept snapping off photos and flashing his strobe light during the meditation. The camera noise and lights were distracting and I was unable to really get into the meditation because all I could think of was "Is he taking pictures of me and how do I look? It made it all seem so . . . commercial and superficial. I felt as though my personal moment was being exploited or something." Susan's search for the mystical and magical had devolved—in her opinion—into just another commercial photo opportunity.

She told me, disheartened, "I guess even churches and spiritual centers need to balance their beliefs with good advertising or they'll go out of business, but it seemed strange, somehow." Susan had experienced firsthand the balance necessary for that organization to stay in business. We all need balance between what we want (or think we want) and what we really need to manage the business of our lives. The one thing that can bridge the two is balance.

WHERE'S THE BALANCE?

I've found that life is a constant teeter-totter between extremes of all kinds. Do you, like me, find that many (if not most) areas of life require this balance? In order to build healthy relationships and strong family units we *do* have to do battle with a society that doesn't always support such priorities. We have to fortify our feelings, hopes, and desires for long-term relationships against the onslaught of messages that invalidate relationships and promote only the quest for cosmetic perfection and the search for the Bigger, Better Deal. Leading a happy life becomes a balancing act between how we're told we should look, do, and act and what we know to be true for ourselves. When we fail to perform this balancing act, we can set ourselves up for illness and unhappiness.

Experts on the mind/body connection tell us that just as *suppressing* anger can cause illness, *expressing* too much anger can, too. In other words, an imbalance at either end of the spectrum and we're in trouble. The same balance is important for us in our efforts to get more healthy, more thin, more whatever. Too many women, in their quest for a better self-image, fall into the trap of working out either too much or too little. Their health suffers and their results are limited. In seminars, workshops, and public appearances all over the world, I've found that one of the most difficult acts we women have to perform is achieving a balance between the conflicting messages about our health and our bodies we get from medical authorities (espousing healthy food intake and not fad dieting) and the media (telling us on film and in photos that scary thin is in). After all, the popular slogan notwithstanding, it's pretty difficult to be too rich, but it's certainly possible to be too thin!

If you think of health and well-being as a tripod with a "self-image camera" attached, you'll get an idea of the balancing act required of you as a woman in the '90s. How well you balance the tripod will determine how well you "see" yourself through the lens. Imagine that each leg of the tripod represents a different aspect of your whole being. One leg represents all the health and fitness activities you do for yourself, including diet, travel, and vacations. Another leg represents your everyday life, including work, family, relationships, education, and responsibilities. The third leg represents the ways you nurture your inner self. All must be in balance for a "picture" that is in "focus." Unfortunately, that balance is missing for most women and their self-image is horribly out of focus.

What women need are ways to correct the imbalance that underlies the insecurities, bad eating behaviors, and lazy exercise habits, because this imbalance leads to an unhealthy self-image, which in turn leads to more symptoms: addictions; alcohol, sex, and drug abuse; and emotional problems. If you take your vitamins regularly, watch the scale, exercise, limit fat and sweets, but still don't get results, it's probably because you haven't hooked up the mind with the body so that the two work together efficiently. Only when they work together as a mind/body force will you achieve lasting health and fitness results.

Sound difficult? It's not. Making a mind/body connection isn't a long, arduous process. It's not like so many other goals you may have set in the past, ones that required years and years of practice or hours and hours of training. For example, entering the New York Marathon every year, but running only one mile each time, starting where you left off the last time, does not make you a marathoner. On the other hand, becoming adept at making the mind/body connection, unlike many sports or aspirations, can take place in small increments—starting today. There is no measuring, rating, or scoring. If you can sit still for one minute today and just quiet your mind, you're on your way to being a winner. You can be on your way in a day!

TURNING ICE INTO STEAM

Many people are frozen solid—stuck in the activities, habits, and attitudes that they've had for years, but can't let go of, even though they don't work. Well, I'm here to turn up the heat and get you moving! I wrote this book to show you the shortcuts to *life*Balance that will enable you to turn ice into steam without going through the liquid stage—because in water you either sink, swim, or drown! If you are up to your knees in fitness tips and techniques and sinking fast, or if you feel as though you've lost control over your life, I'm here to prevent you from going under one more time. I know all too well how much time, money, and energy can be wasted on crazy tricks, wacky supplements, and ineffective self-improvement techniques. I've weeded out what doesn't work—the activities and attitudes that destroy instead of create balance—and included here only what does work.

You're going to learn what Arnold Schwarzenegger always called "shocking the muscles," creating change in the body by surprising it with a completely different workout from time to time. I believe in using that technique for the body, but we're also going to shock your mental muscles, too, and enlist them to work powerfully with you as you create balance. Along the way, you'll learn ways to simplify your training routine and fitness program as you generate power and satisfaction in your life.

This isn't just another motivational book—although I will give you some tried and true secrets for motivation—but a course for jump-starting a new life, particularly if any of these are true:

- You've wasted a lot of time in the past listening to—or complaining with—bitter bitchin' buddies. (You know the ones I mean—those who waste hours of your time with their excuses or whining.)
- You've become bored with your own or someone else's pity patter—the endless shoulda, woulda, coulda conversations.
- You've grown tired of seeing your good intentions go down the drain and your motivation poop out just when it had got going again.

Copy the following sentence and hang it on your wall, fridge, or mirror today. As you work through this book the meaning will grow clearer, day by day:

With moderation and balance I can find the Real Me and move power-fully into the new life I begin to create for myself today.

ARE YOU LIVING OR JUST SURVIVING?

Too many people look at life as a punishment, a sentence that must be endured until something better comes along. I believe that life is indeed challenging, but that the challenges are stepping-stones in the creation of who we really are. I've had my share of challenges—anyone who's been told they would never walk again, as I was when suffering from a life-threatening blood clot, knows about challenge—but I don't view the challenges, as many do, as some sort of punishment. Challenges, believe it or not, can sometimes even be fun.

Life is an action-packed adventure that is best enjoyed when you feel great about yourself and you live, not endure, life. In my opinion, most people are very good at surviving, but not very good at living!

I believe with all my heart that if you develop a healthier lifestyle and find a way to experience joy and satisfaction—and don't allow depression and dissatisfaction to rule your inner world—you will live a longer, healthier life. I believe that each and every one of us is capable of creating moderation and *life*Balance in our lives.

I like to remember the quote I heard once from a woman whose name I've now forgotten. When she was interviewed on her hundredth-plus birthday, she said something like this: "Yes, I lived a long, happy life. I drank the occasional glass of wine, I stayed up late a few too many times, I ate my bread and olive oil, and I enjoyed the occasional piece of chocolate cake. Most of all, I had fun."

This book is dedicated to the healthy, happy centenarian in all of us.

one

WHY WHINE, WALLOW, OR JUST SURVIVE—WHEN YOU CAN LIVE?

More and more we've become a nation of people who whine or wallow. If there were a Top Ten chart for complainers, it would look something like this. See if you're guilty of any of these most frequently heard whines and wallows:

"I'm just too tired to do any more than I'm already doing."

"I have way too much to do."

"You don't understand; I was a neglected child and didn't get enough attention from my parents."

"I never catch a break."

"I'm just not lucky."

"I don't have what it takes to succeed."

"I'm a loser."

"This is the best that I can do."

"Life is hard."

"We live in screwy times."

I've done a lot of traveling around the world and I've found that the planet seems to be made up of two groups of people: those who live in countries where there is such abundance that they have plenty of time to whine, wallow, and complain and those who live in underdeveloped areas where the people spend each day trying merely to survive with the bare necessities.

Why is it that those lucky enough to live without the fear of daily hunger, war, or poverty spend so little time living joyfully and so much time fixated on imagined problems and obstacles? I believe it's because we seemingly fortunate ones are so focused on the external life (the shape of our body, the size of our home, the contents of our bank account) that we neglect our internal life (which is the source of lasting happiness and contentment).

BREAKTHROUGHS AND OTHER GROWING PAINS

Ever have one of those flashing light bulb experiences? You know what I'm talking about: in the comic strips when a character has a sudden idea or insight, a little flashing light bulb appears over the character's head. I had one of those experiences not long ago. It was a blistering winter day in Southern California—the temperature soared close to one hundred degrees and the humidity was nearly as high. I was being interviewed for a magazine article announcing me as "the Fittest Woman in Hollywood." The interviewer had asked all the requisite questions about what it's like to compete as a bodybuilder and how it feels to appear on magazine covers and in television shows and movies. We were doing the standard public relations interview when the conversation veered off to more personal, intimate, nonfitness or showbiz matters. "What was your mother like, Cory?" the interviewer asked me, seemingly from left field. I was momentarily at a loss for words.

My mom was (and still is) the most amazing female I've ever met. She's been an incredible influence on my life. In fact, a very dear friend of mine met her once and later told me, "Now it all makes sense. Now I know exactly why you are who you are. Everyone should have the chance to meet [your mother] just once in their life." Physically, she could outdistance, outsprint, or outlift me until I was well into my teens. Emotionally, she has always been a strong, rocklike foundation for the entire family, but especially for me.

My mom was truly SuperMom!

My mother, Christa Elizabeth Schmidt, grew up strong, solid, and brave in wartime Bad Konigsophen, Germany. Like me, she was the middle child, born between her older sister, Huberta, and her younger brother, Udo. Her father, Andreas "Opa" Schmidt, was a forest ranger. Because of Opa's occupation, the family had a variety of exotic pets running through their home: wild boar, deer, birds. (That's probably where I get my love of animals!) Dorothea "Oma" Schmidt, my grandma, was also one of the strongest women I've ever known—probably because she, like Mom, had to be.

This is a sketch someone did of my dad during his gymnastics days

They lived in a country torn apart by war. There simply wasn't room for weakness of the body or spirit. To make matters even more difficult, Opa died in a Siberian prison camp when Mom was only twelve years old.

I told some of Mom's story about life during the war to the interviewer, although I forgot a few details. I didn't mention that my Mom probably would have trained for the Olympics had the war not broken out or that when I was in high school and already a regional state champion in track, Mom beat me in a race in Florida!

I truly grew up with SuperMom, but didn't even know it at the time. She raised three girls, worked full-time driving a school bus, put food on the table and clothes on our backs, and found time to do all the landscaping on a five-acre yard. Oh, yeah, she also built the majority of the furniture in the house, as well as the exterior fencing and stone wall borders. I never realized till years later that other kids' moms didn't just pick up a heavy wooden picnic table with one hand and sweep under it with a broom in the other hand. I didn't know that most people bought their clothes, toys, and other household goods at stores, since my mom always made whatever we kids needed with her own two hands, often recycling cast-off goods she found in the streets or picked out of Dumpsters! (No, she wasn't a bag lady—she just didn't see the sense in buying something new when there was perfectly good stuff to be found everywhere, for free.)

My dad had an equally grueling life, yet remains one of the sweetest, most affectionate and optimistic people on this planet. He was a rescue pilot by the age of sixteen and was later captured and placed in an American POW camp in France. There, he taught the American soldiers Ping-Pong as he stayed in shape by practicing his beloved gymnastics, for which he had a real talent.

To this day, Dad remains a gentle, loving spirit who is more likely to be found nurturing a sick bunny back to health with a tiny eyedropper than complaining about life's iniquities. I thank Dad for giving me my love of animals and the gentle, affectionate side of my nature.

The magazine interviewer scribbled much of what I shared with her in her notepad, capturing and recording my thoughts with astonishing speed. That's when the light bulb went off. I realized in an instant that in all my years of doing magazine, book, television, and radio interviews I had never been asked much about who Cory Everson really is on the inside—underneath the muscles and athletic ability. The interviewer noticed something in my expression.

"Anything wrong?" she asked.

"Not at all!" I responded. In fact, I was intrigued by the implications of my new insight.

Yes, I thought, I love telling people about my incredible Mom and about other, more private aspects of life, but I rarely do, because Cory Everson is considered strictly a physical entity. I'm always "Cory Everson: The Bodybuilder" or "Cory Everson: The Athlete." Even "Cory Everson: The Workout." The focus has always been on the lean, muscular bodybuilder who can pose, run, or compete with the best of the field. Like most people in the public eye, I have been pigeonholed into a category: in my case, fitness celebrity or bodybuilding expert. Yet, my success in bodybuilding, acting, writing, whatever, all came about not as the result of just my physical gifts, but as a result of my body's innate physical talents coupled with less visible, but equally important inner resources. A strong inner connection is responsible for most of my accomplishments, yet I have publicly explored only one dimension of my capabilities. In doing so, I realized, I have shortchanged not just myself, but those who look up to me for advice, guidance, or direction. I thought of the thousands of letters from women all over the world who want me to help them reach their personal goals.

My mind was racing as I left that interview. By now the light bulb moment had grown into a full-blown mental explosion. The powerful inner connection, which I now call the mind/body/soul connection (or MBS for short) affects territories in me that can't be limited by simple definitions like "bodybuilder" or "actress" or "celebrity." I am who I am (and you are who you are) in so many more ways than just the labels we—or the world around us—give ourselves. What my light bulb moment illuminated is that there are new ways to communicate the key to my success and to teach others how to duplicate it.

The MBS connection is not something I created in that lightbulb moment. It's a process that is based in *scientific* fact and available to everyone. It can improve the quality of your life and help you reach your goals, but the secret to learning to use this process is to approach your life on both a physical and a mental level—not just a cosmetic or surface one. What I, as a fitness expert, have to share can no longer be taught from a strictly physical point of view. I need to show you how I, like you, must focus on the "internals"—which are crucial to achieving success—as well as the "externals" that are so important to all of us. I realized that I had been pigeonholed and stereotyped not just by others, but by myself as well. I had fallen into a classic trap.

THE TWO-DIMENSIONAL TRAP

We Americans tend to see things two-dimensionally. All around us the world is made up of many different dimensions that create the one incredible whole, yet most of us persist in seeing things in black or white, good or bad, all or nothing. We've built a nation of specialization, where divisions, departments, and niches rule. Let me give you an example.

Doctors used to be general practitioners who made house calls to fix just about anything that ailed us. Now doctors aren't simply doctors, but *specialists* like OB-GYNs, internists, or ear, nose, and throat experts, most of whom have staffs ranging from answering service operators to receptionists to nurses who buffer them from time-consuming contact with patients. In the old days a doctor knew a good deal about his or her patient as a whole, but today's specialists know little outside of their area of expertise.

As individuals, we look at ourselves as a conglomeration of divisions all operating independently of each other. Most women would agree that their hips and thighs seem to have a life of their own, separate from the rest of their body. We tend to think of our health and wellness as one "department" and our weight, shape, and appearance as another. This two-dimensional thinking dominates how we view our bodies and we seem to thrive on contradiction and counterintuition regarding them. We have a love-hate relationship with our bodies, seeing them as things we have to control ("Gotta keep that weight down," "Need to *kill* my appetite") or delight in (by taking them away to exotic locations or feeding them exotic cuisine). This extreme of viewing the body as a source of pleasure as well as the root of conflict carries over into the way we talk about it. We get moralistic about our bodily appetites, saying that eating chocolate is "sinful" and admonishing others by saying, "How could you eat that?" In the next breath we may talk about a great sexual experience that was "to die for." Take a look at the best-seller lists at any time: cookbooks (about different ways to eat and prepare food) are right up there with diet books (about different ways to stop eating food). We can't seem to decide whether we want to reward or punish our bodies.

These extremes exist not just in the way we think about our bodies and appetites, but in our attitudes toward work, play, and school. The dichotomies are everywhere! The work week continues to increase and we work to a much later age than ever before, yet we spend increasingly more time going mindless in front of a television. (We have the second longest work week—after Japan—and the second highest rate of TV viewing—also right behind Japan.) Our second most common leisure activity is shopping. It would appear that we work ourselves into oblivion and then we watch TV until we turn into zombies or we shop till we drop.

Today's college students are, now more than ever, not only full-time at school, but full-time at work, too. They work and go to class all day, then study and work all night. We go to extremes in nearly everything we do, becoming workaholics, TV-aholics, shop-aholics, and choc-aholics. We have 5 percent of the world's population, but participate in 50 percent of the illegal drug use of the entire planet. Sexually we swing back and forth from repression to overexpression. The proliferation of twelve-step programs attests to our proclivity toward extremes of all kinds and our inability to manage them on our own. Most of us have no balance in our lives.

Romy, a human potential counselor, is a perfect example of someone who has been unable to achieve balance. Romy works ninety hours a week and travels all over the country teaching individuals and corporations how better to optimize their creativity and potential. Ironically, her own productivity has been affected by all the travel and restaurant food, which has begun to take its toll on her. She has gained excess weight, which is bad not only for her health, but for her professional image as well. Her biggest obstacle to taking back control over her body is, as she puts it, "seeing [myself] as more than just this brain. I don't think of myself as a body, but as a mind. It's hard for me to focus on my body." She admits that she is unable to make a meaningful mind/body/soul (MBS) connection. She, like so many other women today, needs to create *life*Balance, which is the one surefire way to stop living a life dominated by stress or frustration.

We lose *life*Balance when we buy into two disempowering myths:

> *The mind and the brain are the same.*
> *The mind and the body are separate.*

THE BRAIN VERSUS THE MIND

The brain is a complicated system of from 10 to 100 billion specialized cells called neurons. Yet, it's so compact that it can fit into the palm of your hand. (Talk about microcomputers!) We've always thought of the brain as the main command center of the body. Inside, connected to this command center, are the controls that regulate body temperature, hunger, physical energy, movement, and more. The brain has the ability to maintain all these actions. Yet, recent discoveries about how the mind affects every cell in our body are changing the way we look at the power and capabilities of the brain. It seems that it requires more than just neurons, cell connections, and the physical "stuff" of the brain to run the entire bodily network. Without a "manager" (the mind) none of the machines in this powerful but compact control room work properly. Without direction from the mind, the brain and the body cannot perform optimally.

THE MIND AND THE BODY

Leading researchers from many fields of science have been grappling with the mind/body debate for years and are finally beginning to see the light at the end of the tunnel. What they've proven recently is the absolute "oneness" of the mind and the body. We can no longer think of the mind and the body as separate, because researchers with titles like biopsychosocial professionals, psychoneuroimmunologists, and biological psychologists are hot on the heels of exciting new discoveries about how the mind, the brain, and the body work together to fight off disease, create health, and help us to function.

Nearly half of all office visits to doctors these days are for mind-related issues rather than body issues, but 95 percent of what doctors learn in medical school is about the body, and only 5 percent of medical studies concern the mind. In our search for health and well-being we often turn to crazy, costly gimmicks. We believe so strongly that the answers to all of our problems lie somewhere outside of ourselves that the goofy gimmicks often work due to the placebo effect. Studies have even shown that placebos work even better when they have a higher price and are of a certain color! Advertising dollars pay off because we'll pay much more money for stuff that looks good and is packaged in a snazzy color. The millions and millions of dollars being spent daily on wacky remedies for everything from weight loss to stress to insomnia clearly illustrate the fact that many of us are ready to make the MBS connection and find *life*Balance.

Some of you may be thinking, "Whoa, Cory, I'm reading this book because you're a fitness expert, not a guru. I just want to lose a little flab, not discover my inner child or anything like that!" Don't worry, this book is indeed about fitness and about you reaching your ideal weight and being healthier. And yes, it's about helping you look and feel better than ever before. But it's also about helping you reach your goals in other areas of life with an exciting inner technology that will help you power up all the different dimensions you possess as a human being.

You'll learn how to take full advantage of the fact that you're one amazing whole: mind/body/soul. This technology, using the MBS connection to find *life*Balance, is not like any other you may have tried in your efforts to lose weight, get in shape, or otherwise improve yourself. It won't feel like work or hardship or deprivation, like so many other programs you may have tried. You won't be working out harder or longer. You won't have to feel the pain to get the gain. You won't be starving yourself or depriving yourself. You won't be caught in a struggle with your body. You won't be trying as you have in the past.

Creating *life*Balance will enable you to relax about who and where you are right now, at this stage of your physical or emotional development. Wherever you are is OK and once you accept that, almost immediately your health will improve as your stress goes down. You'll have more time for family and friends, as well as for yourself. You may discover a renewed affinity for childhood hobbies or interests and you'll discover "the Real You" (more about her later!). All aspects of your life will be affected positively, not just your physical shape. Don't be surprised if you make a career change, move to another city, recommit to your romantic relationship, find inner calm, and yes . . . lose weight. I promise that you'll feel better and become more fit and energetic than ever before.

YOUR PART OF THE DEAL: A *LIFE*BALANCE JOURNAL

I've given you my promise and now I'm going to ask you to make me a promise. Promise me (and yourself) that you'll keep a journal as you read the rest of this book—and for at least one month after you finish. For some of you, this promise will be difficult, particularly at first. After all, what's a journal anyway and who's got time for one? If keeping this promise sounds difficult, relax. A journal is a valuable tool that can help you sort out your feelings, reflect on your day, or vent anger and frustration. It can also be a place to write down goals, hopes, dreams, and accomplishments. It can serve as a record of your program as you find your way to *life*Balance.

It's been proven in many fitness studies that people who keep a daily workout log get better results than those who don't. Experts have said that the simple act of keeping a record of the day's physical activity and nutritional intake seems to help people stay focused on their goals. I think the success of these workout logs has more to do with the inner process that takes place when we just slow down long enough to quiet the chatter in our mind and touch base with our inner self. That, I believe, is what makes a workout log or journal work and powerful change happen. Mental bookkeeping can help keep you on track and give you amazing personal power. Plus, studies show that expressing emotions gives us mental and physical resilience, and your journal allows you to express your emotions in a safe way and begin to free up any emotional blockages that can stop the flow of good feelings into your body and mind.

For those of you who suffer from recurring depression, journaling will be doubly beneficial. Depression is *not* an emotion, it's a state. I've personally used my journal as a way to get very clear about feelings and thoughts that might otherwise clutter my mind and cause depression.

How to Keep Your Journal

For your journal, get something special that you'll be happy to see and open every day. It can be loose-leaf or bound, small or large. It doesn't have to cost a lot to become special. The least expensive notebook at the drugstore can be made meaningful simply by pasting a favorite photograph on the cover or adding a few personal designs, sketches, or cutouts. Your journal can be whatever suits you—as long as you use it. I'll lead you through some fun and easy exercises to get started, but as we go along and when you're ready, begin to make other daily journal entries along with the exercises I give you. I suggest finding a time—even if it's only ten minutes a day—when you can sit quietly, without disturbances, and just allow your mind to wander. You can begin to create *life*Balance by taking time for reflection—each and every day—in the journal. Start by taking a few minutes to write down random thoughts. What you write in your journal isn't important, only that you do it. What you're developing is not necessarily a great writing style, but a good way to pay attention to the thoughts that rule your mind! Each time you write in or read your journal, you'll reinforce your commitment to the new you. Your new journey and all its promise will always be within arm's reach. Your goals and dreams will be closer to you, making them more real. Ever notice when you write a love letter to a boyfriend how much more clear your thoughts and feelings become when you write them down? When you put pen to paper you can figure things out, you begin to see what your real needs are, and everything becomes a little more clear. Writing promotes thought, acts as a reminder, and helps to create a clear picture. Believe it or not, your decision-making abilities can improve.

LifeBalance JOURNAL EXERCISE: "WHAT I WANT"

Let's try something right now to help get you started. Find a piece of paper and pen or pencil. At the top of the page write: THE DREAM ME. Then, write down thoughts about what you would like to do and achieve in life. Pretend that you can have anything you want, go anywhere, do or be anything. Be creative! Be wild!

After you've completed your dream list, go back and examine each item. After each, write down what keeps you from doing or having that dream. Write down the up side and down side of actually attaining that dream. Be honest. If, for example, you've written "I want to be thin," you might write, "If I were thin I would like myself more." The down side to being thin might be, "I'd have to deal with something other than my weight for a change and that frightens me," or, "What will I have to complain about then?" Be sure to list the good results of having your dreams come true and the scary parts of having what you really want. Use this opportunity to get in touch with what you really want out of life right now. You might be surprised by what shows up for you in this exercise.

Congratulations! You've just completed the first page in your *Life*Balance Journal. Now that you've begun to travel inward, the empowerment that comes from harnessing your inner energy makes it impossible for your life ever to be the same. Your journal is a good place to start this journey, since the first step in finding *life*Balance is to discover ways to quiet the busy brain and get in touch with the inner calm and power that reside in each of us.

LifeBalance JOURNAL EXERCISE: "THE MIND VERSUS THE BRAIN"

Hopefully, by now you have personalized a notebook or folder to make your own *Life*Balance Journal. Write your name and the date at the top of a page. (This is day one of your MBS connection!) Now, just sit back and think about your health and fitness goals. This list will be more specific and immediate than your dream list. Focus on what it is you want right now—what you want to get out of this book and what you'd like to accomplish for yourself in the next few months. When you first try to do this, it might be difficult, especially if you're busy, stressed, and have been outwardly focused for a long time. Stay with it. Just sit quietly and allow your mind to wander. Put this book down and come back to it when you're done thinking.

Did you have a hard time staying focused on the subject? Did your mind wander back and forth to different topics? If you're like most, it did. Don't worry, that doesn't mean you did it "wrong" or failed.

Now, starting in the middle of the page, at the top, draw a line from the top all the way to the bottom. You should have two big columns. Write "B" at the top of the left-hand column of the page. In this column, jot down what you thought about. Whatever the thoughts were, just briefly make a note of them. It's perfectly OK if you wandered off the topic from time to time. We all do. Write down whatever you remember. Did you think of some goals? Write them here. Did you think about things you have to do or have other random thoughts? Write these down, too.

Now, at the top of the right-hand side of the page, write "M." Below this, I want you to write down what the little voice inside your head had to say about what you were thinking. If you're not sure what little voice I mean, it's the same one that just said, "What little voice? What is she talking about? I don't hear a little voice in my head." For example, did you at any time during this exercise think, "This is silly" or "Why am I doing this?" Write down those comments. They're all from the little inner voice. It might even have said, "Cory Everson has lost it—why is she having me do this?" or maybe, "You'll never make it to your goals, who are you kidding?" Sometimes the little inner voice offers encouragement, like, "Perhaps you can do it this time!" Don't worry, whatever the thoughts were, they're perfectly OK and normal. Each and every one of us possesses this extremely vocal inner observer who is always there to put in her two cents' worth. Your brain rallies up all its resources to stay on topic, but your mind has its own agenda and will drive you crazy if you let it!

Now let's examine your page. You should have two very different columns. The left column represents your brain, its ideas and thoughts. The right column represents your mind and what it thinks about these thoughts. Here's an example of what your page might look like:

"B"	"M"
I have to lose weight.	Who are you kidding?
I have to pick up the kids at school later.	This is stupid.
I'm going to work out every day.	I'll never have thin thighs.
What movies are playing now?	Uma Thurman has thinner thighs than I.

Can you see the difference between the two columns? Your brain contains all the facts, logistics, plans, and concrete information you need to get through the day. Your mind is the observer who is always there to comment, cheer you on or drag you down, and constantly offer its own opinion. Your job is to create an environment where your mind becomes your secret weapon, working in harmony with your brain and your body to empower you to reach your goals.

THE BUDDY SYSTEM

I love it when something I instinctually and intuitively believe is proven by science. Bodybuilders know the value of the buddy system for training. There's just something about having that pal there, day after day, that makes all the hard work seem easier. I used the buddy system when I trained for the Ms. Olympia and other competitions because there were often days when I didn't want to train and my buddy was always there to help and encourage me to dig in and do it. On those "off" days, the buddy system is very helpful.

I would never have won the Ms. Olympia contest—not once—if it hadn't been for my training partner, Darcy. She would smile, laugh, tell jokes, and support me at tough times. When I was anxious or scared, she was always there to help me pull through—just as I was for her during her off days. My lifelong "buddy" is my sister Cameo. We have always relied on each other to help stay motivated. You'd be shocked at how out of shape each of us gets when the other is out of town. I depend on our talks during long, brisk walks. The emotional healing, venting, and expression that we engage in when we walk together is so valuable to me!

I've always trained better with a buddy, and I use the same principle to get through tough times in life by depending on the support and concern of family and friends. Now science has proven my belief that the buddy system works not only in the gym, but in life.

Two hundred seventy-six people participated in a study in which purified cold viruses were sprayed into their noses. People who had good relationships in their lives had a four times less likely chance of contracting a cold. The evidence, reported in the *Journal of the American Medical Association,* points to the importance of having friends, family, and others to improve one's health. The experts further concluded that with each added relationship one has, the less likely one is to become ill. In other studies, women with support systems and good friendship networks were shown to have lower fetal cancer rates, less problems with PMS, fewer miscarriages, better health during and after childbirth, better recovery from illness, and reduced stress on the body! Family and friends can be your own germ-fighting buddy system!

Because social support is a key factor in health and well-being, I suggest that you find someone with whom you can share some of the work in this book. Working with a buddy can be an important step toward creating health and well-being. I'm going to give you *Life*Balance Exercises that are geared to help you alone and I'll also give you some exercises that require a friend's or relative's help to do.

My sister Cameo and I use the buddy system for support.

You can choose to do these partner exercises now, later, or not at all, but it might prove very effective to team up with a buddy and work through parts of this book with her.

Use the buddy system, where appropriate, to help you in your mind/body journey. It'll supercharge your efforts. Plus, you'll have fun with your buddy during some of the exercises.

THE GOOD, THE BAD, AND THE DRIPPY

If you're like I was before learning about *life*Balance you probably don't have a lot of time to think about much more than the seemingly infinite items on your daily "to-do" list ("Did I drop off the shirts at the cleaners?" "Should I stop at the gas station before or after the grocery store?"). Face it, it's the little things that consume most of our day, and for those who work with charitable organizations, social clubs, school or church activities, the daily to-do list gets even bigger as time gets even scarcer. When you factor in the mental self-abuse many of us engage in ("How badly did I eat today?" "Do I really have the nerve and the legs to wear that new miniskirt to dinner Friday?"), you've got a mind that's verging on overload.

We all waste time on mental garbage. It's normal. I've been known to spend days buying a new rug, then returning it and deciding to keep an old rug after all! I got so involved in one of these rug adventures that I reached the point where I couldn't train until I had my stinking rug problem handled. I wouldn't go to the gym for days while I went back and forth on a simple decision about a rug. The day before I travel I'm really obsessed by mental garbage. I act like I'm leaving for three years as I clean my entire house, file all my papers, order office supplies, go grocery shopping, do the laundry, and fill the refrigerator for my fiancé (like he can't go to the store for himself!). Oh, yeah, and I also bathe the dog and wash the car before I allow myself to leave town with a clear conscience. I go a little nuts myself at these times as my mind gets really busy with silly stuff. What I've learned, though, is how to balance crazy days with cool ones. I've learned how to create enough *life*Balance so that I can battle the enemy most of us face every day, an enemy that causes many people to turn to unhealthy food, alcohol, drugs, and other self-destructive behavior. It's harmful and often it goes unnoticed, doing its damage almost undetected. This enemy? Stress.

two

STRESS: YOU CAN'T STOP IT, BUT YOU CAN SURVIVE IT

Stress causes the body to respond less effectively to good diet, training, and health efforts. It diminishes the immune system and the emotions and even encourages the body to become better at fat storage! Stress can turn even the most high-octane efforts into cheap low-grade fuel as it acts like a huge filter blocking much that is nurturing, powerful, and positive. Before we learn more about what creates *life*Balance, we need to understand more about this enemy that prevents it. Let's take a good look at just how pervasive, destructive, and disempowering stress can be.

STRESS AS COMMON DENOMINATOR

Like many of us, I come down with a mild case of the flu from time to time. The symptoms are usually the same: runny or stuffy nose, watery eyes, scratchy throat. I visited a doctor last winter when I was spending much of my time in planes traveling from one end of the country to the other doing personal appearances for a charity with which I'm involved. I had begun to feel that telltale tickle in the throat that often means the beginning of *something*.

After a preliminary exam, the doctor asked, "Do you have any stress in your life?" and I burst out laughing.

"No, Doc, I'm from Mars. We don't have stress there!" I jokingly replied.

Then I asked him how many of his patients reported no stress in their lives. He thought for only a split second before he conceded that none of them did.

I guess they came up with that question in medical schools years ago when life was very different. Today, for most of us, stress is a constant daily companion. It's something that we all have to deal with every day of our lives, from birth until death. Like earth, wind, and fire, stress is part of our environment. Whether in physical or emotional form—or both—it's there. That wasn't always so.

The Stress-Free Life

Roseto, Pennsylvania, is still a small town, but in the 1960s it was even more so. Back then, researchers found that the heart disease rate there was 25 percent of what it was in the rest of the nation. In the tight-knit little Italian community only one out of a thousand people died of heart attacks. Few had ulcers. There was little or no senility or Alzheimer's. This little town got a lot of attention, even back then, in the less health-conscious sixties. When word of the healthy people of Roseto reached medical authorities, they decided to pay a visit.

What the experts found there was unexpected. The healthy residents of Roseto were not fitness nuts or exercise fanatics. Many of the people smoked and even more were overweight due to the popularity of rich Italian meals. Few of the town's residents exercised. These were people who loved their oils and butters and cigarettes, yet still enjoyed good health. Why? The experts conducted exhaustive studies and polls and when all the information was in, the results were surprising.

In the 1960s, there was a close cultural structure in Roseto, Pennsylvania. This supportive cultural environment encouraged families to house the elderly in the family homes, not in nursing homes. When people ran short on money, they turned to family and friends for financial help. This nurturing environment not only kept family and friends together, it helped them all stay healthy.

In the late sixties, the young adults and teens of Roseto decided they wanted the Bigger, Better Deal. They moved out into larger houses and bought more "stuff." They stopped going to church or attending family-oriented functions. Guess what? The heart attack rate for people under the age of thirty-five rose dramatically in Roseto!

Today most Americans live in a much different atmosphere than that of Roseto during the 1960s. About 60 to 90 percent of the time we go to the doctor, it's for stress-related problems. Sadly, most of our attempts to get relief from stress fail, since the remedies and treatments doctors use have little effect on stress and its related diseases. Thirty percent of Americans surveyed said they experience high stress every day. Frustrated, they spend upwards of $13 billion dollars on alternative therapies.

The Stress-Filled Life

A very close relative of mine recently went to the doctor complaining of constant fatigue. The doctor told her, "You've been in here off and on for the past three months for this fatigue problem. We've done blood tests, physicals, and metabolic rate exams. You're 100 percent normal according to the tests."

My relative was alarmed, not comforted, by this diagnosis. "I'm not imagining this fatigue, Doctor. I'm really, really tired all the time. What can it be?"

Her doctor thought for a moment. "Are you PMS'ed?"

"Not for three months straight!" she replied.

"Are you sad? Has anything happened to anyone close to you?" he asked.

To make a long story short, the stress of financial problems and child-rearing difficulties had taken a huge toll on this otherwise healthy young woman's health. She didn't have chronic fatigue, thyroid problems, or a metabolic disorder—all possible explanations for her symptoms. What she did have was a ton of stress.

The physical results of too much stress can be devastating. Often people ignore the physical symptoms, attributing them to other causes. Stress-related symptoms include:

- irritable bowel syndrome
- chronic stomach pain (Stomach disorders occur most frequently in women who were abused, either physically or sexually, as children.)
- diarrhea
- mitral valve prolapse (This is a heart condition that gets more severe during very emotional periods of life. It occurs twice as frequently in women as in men.)
- TMJ (Temporalmandibular joint syndrome affects the joint attaching the jawbone to the skull and can be very painful. Ten million people have it, 80 percent of them women.)

During my divorce from Jeff Everson, whom I had known since college and who had been a huge part of my life for most of my adult years, I was sure that I had contracted throat cancer. I couldn't swallow even the smallest bits of food without a lot of pain. My chest hurt. I went to the doctor, sure that he would find a tumor in my throat.

The doctor guessed right away the cause of my symptoms and asked me, "Are you experiencing any emotional upset?"

Upset? You bet I was upset! My body actually hurt from the anxiety and emotional upset from the divorce, which was breaking my heart.

Years later, during a long, drawn-out, and expensive legal dispute with a former business associate, I contracted TMJ from the amount of stress involved. The TMJ was very real, very uncomfortable, and disappeared only when the legal problem did.

Stress, which can be exacerbated by emotional roadblocks I call Negative

Emotional Connectors (explained in chapter 7), is a major factor in many diseases today. Researchers found that women with a high incidence of cancerous lymph nodes were those who didn't complain much, didn't have a lot of social support, and didn't participate in many of life's activities. Those with fewer cancerous nodes were active and involved in life. Negative emotions and stress may affect how women's immune systems respond to cancer.

When we are chronically stressed, our body may turn against us and become our adversary instead of our ally. We feel tired, then depressed, and eventually we get ill. The hardest part of assessing stress and its effect on our lives and health is that it's hard to separate the actual causes of stress from lifestyle responses to stress, such as cigarette smoking, overeating, drinking, and obsessive behavior. It becomes like the chicken and the egg: which came first? I suspect that at the root of many women's problems with food, drink, and body image are stress factors that must be cleared up before progress can be made in their quality of life. By creating *life*Balance we can survive the various types of stress modern life deals us and remain healthy and centered.

THE THREE TYPES OF STRESS: ACUTE, CHRONIC, AND INVISIBLE

As explained by psychologist Hans Selye, stress is "the reaction of the body to any demand placed on it."

Acute stress is the kind you can clearly see and experience. When you're in a car wreck, no one needs to tell you that the experience has been stressful. It's obvious. You don't have to be a psychiatrist to know it exists. That is acute stress.

Chronic stress is much more sneaky. It's hidden in the little things you have to deal with every day which take an emotional and physical toll without you even knowing it. Traffic, constant environmental noises, even a coworker's irritating cigarette smoke—all are forms of chronic stress. If you're having relationship problems and the communication channels with your partner have closed down, you're probably suffering from chronic stress. If you're overweight and less able to move around comfortably, chronic stress may be sneaking up on you.

When Negative Emotional Connectors (NECs) are present, they misdirect information headed to your mind and reinterpret it in a way that is destructive and stressful. This causes the most lethal stress of all: invisible stress. Invisible stress hides within NECs, polluting your belief systems. It disguises itself as disillusionment, insecurity, and pessimism. It does its damage undetected until its effects show up in the form of illness, overeating, or lethargy. By getting into *life*Balance you can turn off the NECs (I'll show you how in chapter 7), stop the invisible stress, and give yourself a break.

STRESS CAN BE GOOD

Selye also made a distinction between *distress* and *eustress*. Distress is the debilitating kind of stress we've been discussing. Eustress, on the other hand, is positive stress, like that which occurs when a person wins the lottery. Even scary transitions like a career change, home relocation, or dissolution of an important relationship can be stressful but enlivening. They can help us become better people. Lifestyle changes like deciding to lose weight or become healthier, while stressful, can also lead to positive change. Stress can cause mobilization for healthy change in the person who has developed *life*Balance. It's not just the events that occur in life or the stresses we face—it's how we deal with them that affects us.

It's possible to survive and thrive in stressful environments. Leading a happy, peaceful life isn't limited only to those who live in bucolic, peaceful, small towns (like Roseto in the 1960s). In fact, the well-adjusted, hardy person who lives a fast-paced life may be healthier and better able to handle stress than his frustrated, small-town counterpart living in isolation.

People who are overworked are not necessarily those who will suffer the most stress-related illnesses, either. Hard work in itself is not stressful. It's the reasons we work hard that make it stressful. When you are obsessed with the thought, "He'll leave me if I don't get that big promotion," or, "I need to lose thirty pounds to get a date," the stress can be damaging, because the pressure created is enormous. When stressful reasons push us to do too much at work, at home, or in our social lives, it's our negative thoughts and feelings about our own self-worth that's at the root of the disease-causing stress. It's not the long hours, the hard work, or the dress size. The secret is to recognize when you are under a lot of stress and learn to handle it in a healthy way.

LifeBalance EXERCISE: "AM I STRESSED?"

Circle the items that have applied to you in the last twelve months and total them.

THE STRESS SCALE

Death of spouse	100
Son or daughter leaving home	29
Divorce	73
Trouble with in-laws	29
Marital separation	65
Outstanding personal achievement	28
Jail term	63

THE STRESS SCALE (*continued*)

Wife begins or stops work	26
Death of close family member	63
Begin or end school	26
Personal injury or illness	53
Change in living conditions	25
Marriage	50
Revision of personal habits	24
Fired at work	47
Trouble with boss	23
Marital reconciliation	45
Change in work hours or conditions	20
Retirement	45
Change in residence	20
Change in health of family member	44
Change in schools	20
Pregnancy	40
Change in recreation	19
Sex difficulties	39
Change in social activities	18
Gain of new family member	39
Mortgage or loan less than $100,000	17
Business readjustment	39
Change in sleeping habits	16
Change in financial state	38
Change in number of family get-togethers	15
Death of close friend	37
Change to different line of work	36
Change in eating habits	15
Change in number of arguments with spouse	35
Vacation	13
Christmas	12
Mortgage or loan over $100,000	31
Minor violations of the law	11
Foreclosure of mortgage or loan	30
Change in responsibilities at work	29

This classic scale in stress research (often called the Social Readjustment Scale) has been used for thirty years for a variety of purposes. It's been used to correlate the number of injuries athletes suffer at a particular time with the amount of stress in their lives. (As stress levels rise, so do the number of injuries.) A score of over 200 on the scale can mean that you are more likely to incur illness, injury, or accidents. People with scores over 300 are those with a significant number of physical illnesses, heart disease, accidents, and emotional problems.

I know just how devastating an accumulation of stress can be. While I was in college I had a life-threatening blood clot that was so severe doctors told me that if I lived I would probably never walk again. The blood clot developed during a very stressful and emotionally difficult time in my life. I was going to college part-time and working full-time in downtown Chicago. My job required a ninety-minute commute each way by train and my fiancé lived in a different state, so to see him I had to travel a long way also. I was spending a lot of time traveling. On top of that, I was training and dieting to compete, trying to take my beloved art classes, and attempting to have a regular life—all at the same time! There is absolutely no doubt in my mind that the blood clot was caused by stress. If I had taken the stress test at that time, my score would have been off the chart.

I still have to battle stress accumulation. As recently as 1995, I was going through another very frantic time in life as I worked on a television production. I was writing and coaching the talent, and at the same time I was finding directors, choreographers, and sponsors. My back went into a spasm that wouldn't quit. The pain hit when I didn't have time to stop—or so I thought. I pushed through it until it went from really bad to worse. Finally, on the advice of my coworkers, who couldn't stand to see me in pain any longer, I went to a chiropractor. During the adjustment and examination he discovered that I had slipped two discs and fractured my spine! Here I am, the fitness expert who should have known better, with a stress-induced injury!

How about you? Was your score on the scary side? Take heart. The Social Readjustment Scale may tell you how much stress you have in your life, but as I've already suggested, it's not just the amount or type of stress you encounter, but how you handle it that makes the difference in how it affects your life.

FIGHTING STRESS IS YOUR JOB

Unfortunately, when it comes to alleviating stress, you're pretty much on your own. Blue Cross, Blue Shield, Medicare, and Medicaid won't pay for nutritionists, social workers, or other professionals who can help you with stress problems. Our medical system doesn't recognize alternative treatments, which have been proven effective for thousands of people. Insurance companies will cover doctors' bills, medicine costs, and symptomatic treatments, but often consider chiropractors, herbalists, bodyworkers, and acupuncturists to be "quacks." Sadly, this attitude affects many who look to the establishment for guidance in medical and health matters. When the experts fail to give their seal of approval to alternative methods, many fail to receive help that might be very beneficial. The good news is that there are ways to fight stress that aren't costly and are available to all of us.

Not Just for the Rich and Famous

One of the most unfortunate aspects of the mind/body movement is that for many years it was deemed accessible only to a rich and famous few. When many of the women I've talked to think about yoga, meditation, or biofeedback, they think of rich ladies at cushy resorts. As one woman told me, "Yes, women like Julia Roberts or Elizabeth Taylor can afford to get away from it all, relax, and unwind. I have to work for a living!"

But de-stressing doesn't have to take place at an expensive retreat and the cost of not doing so is enormous. Eliminating stress is of utmost importance to each and every one of us and it's not something you need a big bank account to get rid of. De-stressing isn't some mystical experience for a sophisticated few. It's a way of simplifying life, finding empowering, and handling stress better.

The Hardiness Scale tells you how likely you are to be able to handle the stress in your life.

*Life*Balance EXERCISE: "CAN I HANDLE STRESS?"

THE HARDINESS SCALE

Write down how much you agree or disagree with each statement by placing a number following the statement. Use the following scale:

> 0 = strongly disagree
> 1 = mildly disagree
> 2 = mildly agree
> 3 = strongly agree

A. Trying my best at work makes a difference. _____
B. Trusting to fate is sometimes all I can do in a relationship. _____
C. I often wake up eager to start on the day's projects. _____
D. Thinking of myself as a free person leads to great frustration and difficulty. _____
E. I would be willing to sacrifice financial security in my work if something really challenging came along. _____
F. It bothers me when I have to deviate from the routine or schedule I've set for myself. _____

G. An average citizen can have an impact on politics. _____
H. Without the right breaks, it is hard to be successful in my field. _____
I. I know why I am doing what I'm doing at work. _____
J. Getting close to people puts me at risk of being obligated to them. _____
K. Encountering new situations is an important priority in my life. _____
L. I really don't mind when I have nothing to do. _____

To score yourself:

These questions measure control, commitment, and challenge. For half the questions, a high score (like 3, "strongly agree") indicates hardiness; for the other half, a low score (disagreement) does.

To get your scores on control, commitment, and challenge, add and subtract the numbers you've written beside each statement, according to the formulas shown below. To get your score on "control," for example, add together your responses to statements A and G; add together your responses to B and H; and then subtract the second number from the first.

Add your scores on control, commitment, and challenge together to get a score for total hardiness.

A total score of 10 to 18 shows a hardy personality; 0 to 9 shows moderate hardiness; below 9 shows low hardiness.

Total of A and G	minus	Total of B and H	=	_____	*Control Score*
Total of C and I	minus	Total of D and J	=	_____	*Commitment Score*
Total of E and K	minus	Total of F and L	=	_____	*Challenge Score*

Control + Commitment + Challenge = *Hardiness Score*

The Hardiness Scale distinguishes between hardy individuals, who cope well with stress, and nonhardy individuals, who are adversely affected by stress.

If your Hardiness Scale score is low and your Stress Scale score is high, you *must* learn ways to handle the stress in your life.

USE THE THREE Cs!

Experts have determined that three factors can help you manage stress: control, commitment, and challenge.

Control is the tendency in an individual to feel and act as if she's influential rather than helpless about the events of her life. People who have a sense of control believe that the things that happen to them are not foreign, unexpected, or overwhelming. They're optimistic rather than depressed about life's events.

Commitment is the tendency on the part of someone to fully involve herself in whatever she's doing or encountering. The woman with the ability to commit to life approaches it head on, rather than avoiding it.

Challenge is the belief that change, rather than stability, is the pattern of life. Anticipate change as an incentive to grow rather than as a threat.

We have opportunities to use the three Cs in big and small ways every day. I was driving down the street to an important meeting one day when I ran into a roadblock. A road crew was doing some construction and there were signs directing motorists onto another, much longer route. My first reaction was to get upset. I muttered some not so nice words under my breath. I pushed my foot down hard on the brakes. I felt my face flush as I started to really fume.

"This shouldn't be happening," I told myself. Then, I realized how silly that was. It was happening. There was nothing I could do about the delay, except deal with it.

Once I calmed down a bit I started to look around and realized I had never driven on that street before, even though I drove near it almost every day. I saw a quaint little Italian restaurant that I had never heard of. There were cozy tables on the sidewalk and it had the look of an authentic Italian café. I made a mental note to check it out some evening.

When I arrived at my appointment I was in good spirits and only a few minutes late. A few weeks later, I visited the little Italian restaurant and had a wonderful meal with some friends. We had a delightful time and have since returned for equally pleasing times.

The roadblock enabled me to honor my commitment to having my life be better each and every day. The challenge it represented gave me an opportunity to control my reaction and find the positive in the situation.

Last summer I had a similar experience when I was en route to a speaking engagement at the *Ms. Fitness* magazine FITCAMP in Malibu, California. I live in the San Fernando Valley near Los Angeles and the camp is held at the beach, not far from my home. A road connects the valley with the beach, but at the time, unbeknown to me, the connecting road was washed away and the road was closed.

I was driving along—with plenty of time—when I came to the detour. It took me by surprise, but I didn't let it throw me for a loop, even though it was clearly a more time-consuming and lengthy way to reach the camp. I decided to simply enjoy the new, unfamiliar route since I had no alternative. Rather than get upset by the detour, I put on my favorite CD and cruised to the beat.

When I got to the camp I discovered that the schedule had been pushed back, since all the seminar leaders were encountering the same detour and all were late. I was early! If I had freaked out, driven like a crazy person, and possibly had a wreck, it would have been for nothing! My commitment to enjoying life would have folded under the challenge had I allowed negative emotions to assume control of my day. I don't always keep my cool—but I do so more than I used to and I continue to try to follow the three Cs.

Some people's first instinct about a change is to resist it at all costs. "Do we have to change this? It's always worked before, why do it differently?" they seem to say. How many people do you know who complain constantly about where they live but would never dream of actually moving?

By learning to use control, commitment, and challenge, you can begin to alleviate some of the stress in your life. You can also begin to handle stress better by viewing it in a different way. People typically look at stress in one of three ways: personal, global, or catastrophic. If you can begin to change the way you view stress, you can begin to remove it from your life.

THREE VIEWS OF STRESS

Stress Scene One: You and your significant other of two or more years have an argument—one in a long series of disagreements that have taken place almost since the beginning of your relationship. Your natural tendency is to think:

(Personalizing) "It's my fault. I did it."
(Globalizing) "My whole life is ruined!"
(Catastrophic) "We'll never get through this. I'm going to throw all his clothes and CDs on the porch."

Stress Scene Two: You are invited to a big party. You try on your favorite cocktail dress, but it's now too small. You say to yourself:

(Personalizing) "I can't stick to a diet."
(Globalizing) "No way can I go to the party now."
(Catastrophic) "That's it. I'm never going out again."

Think about your scores on the Stress Scale and the Hardiness Scale to know how much stress you're currently under and how likely you are to be able to handle it. Then, notice which of these three ways you view stress when it enters your life. Begin to make the adjustments that can help you create *life*Balance. (I know that my initial reaction is the catastrophic one. Then, I tend to personalize.) Those who personalize need to build up more Power Connectors (explained in detail in chapter 9) to rely on when stress hits. Globalizers need to find ways to accept change and be more flexible. They, too, can use Power Connectors related to past positive change in their life. Catastrophic types need to learn more inner calm and reason when they are faced with stress challenges. They, in particular, should begin to practice mind/body exercise (like the *Life*Balance Yoga Flow in chapter

12) to help them handle stress. Remember, the adaptive species are the ones that survive in this world!

Knowing how much stress you have and how able you are to handle it is good information. It can provide motivation for healthy change. What is also helpful, however, is being able to recognize the early warning signs of stress so that you can take action early.

LifeBalance EXERCISE: "BODY SCAN"

Close your eyes and remember the last time something really frightening happened to you or a family member. This exercise works for me when I remember the pain and fear my dog Bolero had to endure when we discovered cancer in his leg and he had to undergo a bone graft. It was horrible for me as well as for him. You might remember a family member who had an accident or injury or another time when you were really fearful about something. If you have a fear of flying, remember the last bumpy flight you took. Pick an incident that was memorably scary in some way. Next, focus on your feelings as you experience a total inability to stop the incident from happening or stop the pain and suffering occurring. Concentrate on these images and feelings for at least three minutes. Notice your body's reactions to your mind's imaginings.

Where did you feel the fear (stress) in your body? Did your shoulders tense up or your neck ache? Were your legs shaking? This test helps you see how you're wired for stress and where it hits in your body. Knowing where stress begins in your body and what it feels like can help you to know when you're stressed. Learn these signals and become even more aware of them—and others!—so that you begin to *feel* the warning signs of stress. This can be a valuable step toward alleviating some of the physical symptoms of stress early on, before they become full-blown and potentially harmful. Some of these stress warning spots are hard to pinpoint because they have been activated so frequently that you have gone numb to their pain, but with time you will become familiar with your own Achilles heel.

I feel my stress points very clearly whenever I see a dead animal in the road. First, I get very nauseous thinking about the fear the poor little thing must have experienced and the loneliness the creature may have felt dying without anyone there to hold and love him or her. Next, my inability to help the animal in any way causes me a lot of emotional distress, which shows up as a piercing headache that is so intense it can bring me to tears. Inevitably, these road encounters happen and I hate them, but I've used them to learn more about my body and where it holds stress. So whenever I'm going through hectic times, I recognize the very first signs of stress and make sure I do some deep, healing breathing before my back goes out or TMJ strikes. If I have the opportunity, I practice yoga or mindful walking to control the stress. I take steps to avoid further physical problems once I recognize the precursors (nausea and headache).

If you're not handling your daily dose of stress well, you know how hard it can be to find the time and energy to get started on a health and fitness plan. Learn how to handle your stress and you'll be on your way to creating *life*Balance. Proper breathing, yoga, using quiet time with your journal, and other techniques will help. We'll learn more about these anti-stress methods as we continue the work in this book.

But if you're having a hard time believing that you'll ever be able to de-stress, create *life*Balance, and still achieve your fitness goals, it could be that you have bought into one or more of the ten stupid myths circulating about diet and exercise—and we need to dispel those right now.

three

TEN MYTHS THAT KEEP YOU BEHIND THE EIGHT BALL

More and more of us—people of all sizes, shapes, and sexes—are working out, yet more and more of us are gaining weight. What's wrong with this picture? According to "Tracking the Fitness Movement" (a 1996 study from the Fitness Products Council), "the number of Americans aged 6 or older who participated regularly in one or more of 40 different sports, fitness or outdoor activities increased 31% between 1987 and 1995—while the population rose." Many are following the advice of authorities like the acting Surgeon General, who suggested, in the "Report on Physical Activity" issued in July 1996, that exercise be propelled into "the front ranks of essential health objectives." We're hiking, biking, running, swimming, even climbing walls and yet we're still losing the battle of the bulge as we try not to become one of the three hundred thousand deaths each year related to diseases caused by poor diet and inadequate physical activity. And yet, we aren't getting any healthier.

I believe that the fault lies in popular myths about diet and exercise which too many people have bought into lock, stock, and barrel. By my count, there are ten stupid myths about diet and exercise which can keep you behind the eight ball. These myths prevent many people from making an MBS connection and attaining *life*Balance as they tilt the scale away from health and wellness and toward obsessions, compulsive exercise habits, and disease. Let's take a good look at them to see if any of them pertain to you.

Stupid Myth #1: If a Little Exercise Is Good, Then a Lot of Exercise Is Better

When I was training for the Ms. Olympia, if anyone had told me, "Cory, you can train less, eat more, and get better results," I'd have thought they were dumb or lying. There was no way I would even have entertained the thought of listening to anyone who told me to do less, back off, or take it easy. I was absolutely certain that when it came to workouts, there was no such thing as too much or too long. I was from the all-or-nothing school of thought and had been since I was a young girl, when I went straight from my hometown in Illinois to the University of Wisconsin. I was this little muscular hick with a ton of natural talent who made the track team while on a full academic and athletic scholarship. In no time at all I was moved from individual events like the shot put and long jump to the pentathlon. I even made Nationals and won the Big 10 title while a freshman. My philosophy then—and after, when I started competing in bodybuilding—was "If one hour of training is good, then four hours are better." This no-holds-barred, take-no-prisoners mentality served me well as a young competitive athlete, but as I got older it began to take its toll. After all, the body can take only so much abuse before it starts to rebel!

My training partner for bodybuilding, Darcy D'Mitrenko, and I would get together in the morning before weight training and figure how much to cheat each day: not by doing less than we were supposed to—but by doing much, much more. We would sometimes do as many as one hundred sets for legs during one training session. We were nuts, but truly believed that there was no such thing as too much exercise. We prided ourselves on our training style, which could only be called over the top. Little did we realize that we were doing way more than necessary and could have trained much less and gotten the same—maybe even better—results. I know that now because I currently train for many fewer hours, have fewer injuries, and get great results—all without the pain and overwhelming time commitment required when I was training over the top.

Fitness Addicts and Training over the Top

Deborah couldn't believe what was happening to her. For years, she had been the envy of all her friends. She had a seemingly endless supply of energy for work and play. She excelled at any sport she tried and she participated in many. She trained rigorously twenty hours a week and rarely missed workouts. Suddenly, at age thirty-one, she began to be plagued by colds, infections, and other ailments. Worse, she no longer had all the energy in the world, which really bothered her. Instead of being able to go! go! go! all day long, she felt listless and tired most of the time.

When I met her, I asked if she had changed any of her workout or diet habits. I asked her to think about anything in her lifestyle that might have caused the recent changes in her health.

"Not really," she replied. "I mean, I train about the same as always—although I have less energy and endurance now. My diet has always been, and still is, good. Nothing has really changed, Cory," she told me, the desperation clear in her voice.

Later, I learned that while her exercise and diet hadn't changed in any significant way, she had overlooked other dramatic lifestyle changes. She had recently gone through a messy, acrimonious divorce. She had moved to a new town and changed jobs. Exercise had always been her ally; now, coupled with the increased stress load, it had turned against her. The new stressors she faced in her personal life and career demanded that she adjust her habits. She needed to create a balance by making some adjustments in her workout regimen—but she didn't know it.

Deb needed to refocus her workouts and include some mind/body work, which would contribute to her well-being during this stress-filled time in her life. I suggested that she cut back on her weightlifting and eight-mile-a-day runs and de-stress with plenty of deep breathing, stretching, and long, mindful walks. I explained to her that with all the added stress of the divorce, the job change, and the move, her old workouts no longer empowered her in any way. She acknowledged that she (mistakenly) believed that her emotional problems could only be overcome by pushing herself to exhaustion physically. She, like so many fitness addicts, believed that she could cover the emotional pain with extreme physical pain.

Typically, we think of couch potatoes (more than half of all Americans fall into this category) as the ones with bad attitudes about physical fitness. But fitness addicts like Deb also have bad fitness attitudes, particularly when they fail to heed the body's need for moderation at certain times in life. Exercise addicts are as unbalanced in the way they look at fitness as those who do nothing at all physically.

If you tend to work out over the top, remember that too much exercise puts the body through biological paces that can be very harmful. Pushing the body too hard with excess exercise is not unlike being in a car wreck as far as the body's responses are concerned. During excessive training, extreme demands are placed on the body as the heart rate rises, blood pressure soars, and blood pumps furiously. The fitness addict further damages herself because the overwhelming need to work out harder and longer steals valuable time away from family, friends, and career. (Deb admits that her exercise habits were a major bone of contention in her former marriage. "He always nagged that I spent more time at the gym than with him," she admits now.)

Even though they often do physical damage to themselves, fitness addicts usually go undiagnosed by medical professionals, since most doctors don't recognize the symptoms—joint problems, chronic colds and flu, and infrequent or nonexistent menstrual cycles—as being related to exercise addiction. Even if a doctor were intuitive and observant enough to recognize a patient as a fitness addict, any treatment would be symptomatic, since the underlying causes of exercise addiction are psychological and result from an emotional imbalance. Fitness addicts only feel good about themselves when they push the envelope until it (or muscles, tendons, or ligaments!) tears apart.

Stupid Myth #2: Follow Trendy Exercise Fads because if Everyone Else Is Doing It, It Must Be Good

I call the women who believe this myth the Willing but Misguideds (WBMs). WBMs are those who have a desire to get fit that is outweighed by their own intelligence and intuition. Many of these types are very smart and motivated, but have heard about and believed fitness misconceptions, not facts. These women know enough not to believe stupid myth #1, but waste plenty of time just the same following fads that contribute very little to their health and well-being. They participate in activities that can be very beneficial for some, but may not be for their individual body types or fitness goals.

Rachel: Too Much of the Wrong Thing

Rachel runs a small business and is a capable, intelligent woman. She is also a good example of a WBM who never could seem to get on the right track with a fitness program. She had a naturally lean body, but wanted to add some muscle. When fitness classes became popular at a nearby gym, Rachel signed up and made it a point to try every aerobics class on the schedule. She eventually settled in to daily boxing classes because she had seen a television special highlighting boxing aerobics as the exercise choice of her favorite supermodel.

Rachel approaches each new workout trend with enthusiasm tempered with due diligence. She began to study everything she could get her hands on about women's boxing classes. She was careful to perform the moves correctly so as not to injure herself. She began to eat four to five small, high-protein, lowfat meals a day. She took supplements recommended in a magazine article she had read. After about three months of this circuit work, however, Rachel found that she hadn't put on any muscle. She had lost a little more body fat, but she had failed to add any mass. Her arms and stomach got pretty lean and ripped and her legs became even more toned, but she actually looked skinnier than when she began the classes—not more dense, which is what her goal had been.

With the boxing, as with other trends she had followed, Rachel failed to get the result she wanted because she didn't match her goal to the right workout. She followed programs designed for women with far different body types and metabolisms than hers. Rather than jumping on the aerobics bandwagon, which is appropriate for a great number of women who primarily want to lose body fat, Rachel would have fared much better doing aerobics two to three times a week (for shorter periods of time) and more work with free weights. She needed to tune in to the demands of her body type and not just join the latest fitness craze.

Rachel, like many other WBMs, over-the-top exercisers, and even those who can't seem to get motivated to do anything at all, spent a lot of time wondering why the fitness equation (time spent working out + desire = results) didn't add up for her.

Many women, like Rachel, really have put forth a good effort to get into terrific shape, but failed. They've starved themselves or aerobicized themselves almost to exhaustion. They've made a commitment to change and haven't gotten results. I'd be an incredibly wealthy woman if I had a nickel for every time someone has told me, "But Cory, I've tried. I really have. I can't do it," or, "I just can't lose weight or stick to a diet and get results." Look out, Donald Trump, if I ever start collecting those nickels!

Lydia: Frustrated with Fitness

I'll never forget Lydia, a beautiful young mom who couldn't lose ten bothersome pounds of body fat no matter how religiously she stuck to her latest diet program.

"I can't quit now. This diet has got to work. All my friends lost weight on it!" she practically shrieked when I suggested she try the *life*Balance plan. "I'm following this diet to the T," she proudly proclaimed. "I eat some carrots, a piece of dry toast a day, two protein drinks, and I never cheat," she explained. "The only thing is, nothing's happening," she complained.

I couldn't resist a little sarcasm. "Gee, Lydia, you're on a diet that makes you miserable and gets you absolutely no results, but you stick to it because a bunch of people you know have used it to starve themselves. No wonder you don't want to try something new!" I told her.

She laughed and so did I, but I understood her skepticism about trying another plan. Heck, as far as she knew, I might have wanted her to give up one of her carrot sticks!

When we began to discuss workouts, she was equally hesitant. "I don't want to learn a new workout, I like the one I'm doing now!" she begged off. This surprised me, since earlier she had told me that her workouts took up too much time and energy, left her drained and depressed at the end of the day, and weren't doing a darn thing for her body. I almost asked her, "You're right, why mess with success?" but held my tongue. After all, she had spent a lot of money on a six-months' supply of special pills and powders that went with her starvation diet and she desperately hoped that her investment would eventually pay off. I had to commend her for her commitment but I wouldn't let her off the hook until she had learned to invest her energy more appropriately. With a little more coaxing, she finally agreed to follow my *life*Balance suggestions, and she began to get results. She couldn't thank me enough for hanging in there with her.

Another drawback to following fads and trends that may have worked for others is the disappointment that can set in if your results don't match theirs. Never compare your achievements with others'. You need to do what it takes for you to see results. Everyone is different. Your body is in a constant state of fluctuation and responds differently at different times of the month, when stress levels change, or even when the weather changes. You need to change with it, not with the trends. Everyone responds differently to different programs. Do what is appropriate for you.

Stupid Myth #3: You Need a Lot of Money to Get in Shape

Many women postpone their workout plans because they believe this myth. They think that to get their fitness act together they need a trainer, a fancy-schmancy gym membership, and a nutrition consultant. They find it hard to believe when I tell them that I know plenty of women with memberships at expensive gyms they never use who pay for professional advice they never heed.

You can go for walks for free. You can buy exercise videos—or rent them—and not pay an arm and a leg to get your arms and legs in shape. You can buy a book about nutrition and study it. By relying on yourself you can save not only money but time. That way, if you can one day join a gym or hire a trainer, you're way ahead of the game because you've already been exercising at home. Take action—even on the strictest budget—and see what can happen.

Stupid Myth #4: If You've Tried Many Times Before and Failed, You Probably Have a Metabolism Problem—Give Up!

Sorry, but very few people have the type of medical condition that inhibits fat loss. If you think you might really be one of those few, check with your doctor. Have her perform the necessary tests to determine whether or not you have a problem.

Just because you've tried to lose weight and diet before—and been promised fitness heaven while being taken through fitness hell—doesn't mean you'll fail this time.

"I'll never get this *life*Balance thing right," one woman whined to me in frustration after having tried (and failed) everything from four-hour-a-day boot camp workouts to food combining, juice fasts, and, finally, dairy-free/wheat-free dieting. She had purchased aerobic steps, slides, and saucers to work her body. When she finally came to me for help it was after she had once again yo-yoed up nearly twenty pounds in weight. She was unable to get excited about getting in shape *one more time* because of NECs (Negative Emotional Connectors, which we'll discuss in chapter 7) she'd developed around her past fitness failures. I told her what I tell hundreds of women with the same frustrations: *very few get it right on the first try!* Remove the NECs about past diet or exercise attempts by appreciating your past efforts as ones that have only brought you closer to the fitness finish line.

Stupid Myth #5: For Exercise to Work It Must Be Boring and/or Difficult

Many women think about exercise as punishment. They've got it all figured out. Here are some of the objections I've heard on a regular basis:

Exercise hurts.
Exercise is boring.
Exercise isn't fun.
Exercise is for others.
Exercise makes me hungry and then I eat like a pig.

If any of the statements listed above ring true for you then I'm going to ask that you begin to think about exercise much differently. If you're ready (or you need) a breakthrough in your beliefs about exercise, then start by replacing the old ideas—like the statements above—with new ones like these:

Exercise is fun.
Exercise is exciting, not boring.
Exercise feels great.
Exercise is for everyone.
Exercise allows me to eat more food and still weigh less.

Sound hard? That's because sometimes breakthroughs require breaking the "rules" and for some of us, that's hard to do.

LifeBalance JOURNAL EXERCISE: "WHEN YOUR BELIEFS ARE WRONG"

This test doesn't take much time, creativity, or effort, but it's a great way to prove to yourself that it is possible to see things in entirely new ways and throw out the old rules—in an instant.

Copy into your journal what's written below, exactly as you see it here. Next, study what you've written and see if you can make sense of it, then get ready to answer a single question about it. Here's the text:

STRC PRST SKIRZ KRK

Copy it down. Study it briefly.

Now, think carefully and answer the following question:
Is the text above a sentence?
Write "yes" or "no" on the page.

Most of you probably answered "no" without much hesitation. If you did, guess what? You're wrong! STRC PRST SKIRZ KRK is indeed a complete sentence. It means "Stick your finger through your throat" in the Czech language. Most of you probably would have bet your high school grammar books that any bunch of "words" resembling those above couldn't possibly be a sentence. The letters certainly don't look like they belong to any words. Our English rules of grammar tell us that every word has a vowel, don't they? But there's more than one way of looking at a group of letters, more than one way to string a sentence together, and more than one set of rules about just about everything.

If "STRC PRST SKIRZ KRK" is a sentence (even if it isn't in your native language), then is it possible that maybe, just maybe, exercise is something other than what you think it is?

If you think exercise isn't fun, maybe it's because whatever form of it you've tried hasn't fit your idea of what "fun" is. But what if exercise suddenly fit your definition of fun? What if enjoying exercise simply meant learning a new "language" in which exercise and fun were synonymous? What if exercise meant participating in activities that are not only fun, but that bring you satisfaction and pleasure, not pain? Think of the payoff in terms of health, fitness, and lowered body fat! Think about what it would mean to your health, fitness, and well-being if you were *wrong* about what exercise is.

When I was deep in my Bionic Woman mode—running, jumping, training, competing—I got so hung up on doing better and better each day that training became a constant grind for me. Each day I was obsessed with doing more than I had done the day before. I think many women share this tendency to lose sight of what exercise is all about. Yes, it's for health and fitness and it's an important necessity, but it's also for fun and play. Too many of us have forgotten the importance of exercise as refreshing physical play.

There's a deeper meaning to exercise than just providing health benefits to the body. Your definition of exercise should also include play—something that can help us maintain our sanity in crazy times. Too many have become gym rats who do what they have to just to stay healthy and never for the fun of it. Begin to play again and see how quickly the world around you begins to look like a friendlier, less frantic, and more enlivening place. In chapter 10 we'll learn ways to rediscover play.

Stupid Myth #6: If You Weren't Athletic as a Child, You Won't Be Now

That's a sad statement for the playful athlete who resides deep within all of us. Too many believe that the realm of exercise and play belongs to those people who excelled at sports as kids and who later became fitness competitors or big-time pros. Those who weren't jocks as children frequently lose their appreciation and respect for healthy play and evolve into disgruntled members of high-tech gyms and bored users of modern fitness equipment.

Anthropologists say that the games we play reflect who we are as a culture. Games mirror society. The same values, codes, and rules will be found in the games as are found in rules governing any society. The 1980s were go-go times, the "Me" decade. Team sports mirrored this type of thinking as they emphasized everything from sneaky fakes (basketball) to physical annihilation (football) to compulsive scoring and record-keeping (all sports). We practiced high-impact, fast-paced sports. Women all over the country aerobicized themselves with high kicks, bone-jarring step workouts, and knee-cracking lunges. The '90s continue to build upon that legacy, even though increasing numbers of injuries to aging baby boomers have forced most people to take a serious look at low-impact activities, which do less physical damage to the joints.

We're told, "Look at your workout as a daily need, just like brushing your teeth or visiting the dentist regularly." It's no wonder so many people view exercise as a chore. This negative indoctrination about exercise starts early. If you were a bookworm or just not athletic as a child, don't let that stop you from enjoying sports play now. Some of the best middle-aged athletes are those who sat on the sidelines during their school years. We all know a popular former school cheerleader who stopped bouncing around once she hit twenty and never did another high kick.

Stupid Myth #7: Exercise Is Fun Only for "Athletic" Types

I can't even count the number of women who have told me that the reason they hesitate starting an exercise program is that they fear looking like an uncoordinated fool—like they did back in grammar school! For the child who wasn't chosen to play on a school team or who didn't do well in gym class, anything having to do with exercise can hold all kinds of negative connotations. That's no surprise. Phys ed classes in schools are about dress codes and showers more than anything else. Classes are run like the military. Competitiveness and one-upsmanship are applauded while sincere effort often goes unrewarded. Kids are taught that only the best players get the accolades. Making the team becomes an obsession for kids and parents alike. Ironically, all the energy that goes into these early athletic efforts is wasted when the majority of the participants do not go into professional sports and do not learn skills that contribute to their future health and fitness. In fact, many kids who were jocks find themselves with injuries and disabilities down the road which severely limit their ability to enjoy sports later in life.

We first get set up to play the "bad body image" game when we're excluded from school sports because of body type. Of all the body types that exist, how many are represented at any Olympics or professional sports events? The emphasis on being physical is, from the start, for the very few.

For those who didn't do well in school sports, the long-term ramifications can be incredibly damaging. Sometimes I have to reeducate these women in their thinking about sports, play, and athletics. I have them imagine an entirely different childhood experience with athletics. I ask them, "What if gym class hadn't been about making a team or being picked by the other kids or about anything competitive at all? What if you had learned about things like exercising to lower your body fat percentage and been taught noncompetitive ways to have fun at sports? What if the focus had been on your unique physical abilities and not your lack of sports-specific talents?" This kind of thinking can help remove mental roadblocks and open up a whole new way of looking at fitness.

For those who did do well at school sports, but who have become fitness challenged (how's that for a euphemism?) later in life, I suggest finding new ways to get excited once again. I tell them how lucky they are to have such a wealth of stored muscle memory and coordination for sports. Their job is to find a sport, game, or exercise that's fun to do and fits into their current lifestyle.

If we taught children specifically what they need to become healthier—good nutrition and healthy workout habits—we'd be giving them skills that would serve them for a lifetime and not set them up for fitness failure later in life. We could involve them in a program that's about getting in touch with their body, instead of making them compete for places on teams and practicing drills they'll never do again in their lives. If we focused on instilling in them a sense of the fun and the play around sports instead of a loathing of mandatory showers, we'd be doing them a big service. We wouldn't have a nation divided into over-the-top exercisers, WBMs, and couch potatoes. All of us would have spent our childhood not in competing for places on teams in sports we'd never play again, but in discovering our natural talents and the sports that utilize them best over the course of a lifetime.

Stupid Myth #8: The Statistics Lie—You Can Lead a Healthy Life Without Proper Diet and Adequate Exercise

Can you say *denial?* Many of us know the three-pack-a-day cigarette smoker who refuses to follow the medical community's recommendation to quit puffing away, because he or she believes that chain-smoking has no effect on health. Healthy eating and regular exercise keep you healthy. End of story.

Stupid Myth #9: Exercise Makes You Hungry

There's a famous study by a physiologist which shows that as people become more sedentary and less active, the appestat (the inner gauge that tells us if we're hungry or full) goes crazy. Sedentary people crave food. In fact, the less they exercise, the more they eat. We pig out as we become lazy pigs. If you've used this excuse to stay out of the gym, give it up right now and get moving.

Stupid Myth #10: Make Exercise Your Top Priority because if You Have a Perfect Body, You'll Have a Perfect Life

I have a pet theory, which I think disproves this myth pretty thoroughly. I call it the Fourth of July theory. Here's how it goes:

Alexa (not her real name) trains like an animal each and every day. She rarely takes a day off. Her diet is squeaky clean. Her idea of a cheat day is to eat half of a baked potato—with absolutely nothing on it. When Alexa goes home at night she is so physically fried that she can barely move. She has no energy for friends, socializing, family, or any other kind of fun. She moans and groans with every move because her muscles are so sore and full of lactic acid at any given time that to lift the telephone receiver causes her excruciating pain. Between her tanning, training, massage, and chiropractic sessions, and her clients (she's a personal trainer), she can barely manage to find time to shop for all the special supplements she ingests almost hourly or to prepare her six perfectly bland and tasteless daily meals.

Alexa lives a very disciplined lifestyle that rarely allows her the luxury of time for rest, relaxation, or enjoyment. Except, that is, for a few days every summer. When summer comes Alexa is in her glory. She puts on a teeny-weeny halter top and a pair of cutoff jeans and gets a ton of attention everywhere she goes. She's the redhead you see walking next to the street during rush hour who nearly stops traffic. She's the woman on the beach in the thong bikini whom you love to hate.

Come the Fourth of July, Alexa is queen. That's the day she shows up at the beach in her star-spangled sequined bikini to party. Everyone's jaw drops. The men want to get her phone number and the women want to slip some half-and-half into her sugar-free nonfat decaf iced café au lait. (She never cheats on her diet—not even at a party.) Her quads, abs, and biceps are the center of attention on the sand. She basks in all the attention as she flexes ever so slightly with every move. When the party's over, however, Alexa goes back to her regular life and the daily workout grind, deprivation, and starvation that allow her to forever look like she stepped off the cover of a muscle mag.

Alexa has a very big problem, however. She has no life. Her entire year, her every workout, her every waking moment are about that one day on the Fourth of July when she can strut her stuff and (finally!) feel good about herself. That's her one moment in the sun and it comes only once a year. Alexa is a very lonely, insecure lady who misses out on a lot in life. The price it costs to keep that body cover-shot ready is enormous. The payoff? That one sunny day in July.

Exercise for the Health of It!

Women like Alexa have bought into the idea that fitness is about an aesthetic ideal and nothing more. They don't do it for the health or the fun of it. They do it to fill up an inner void, which they think will disappear once they have attained the pluperfect physique. If Alexa could get off the emotional roller coaster and find *life*Balance, she would never again be willing to pay the price she pays for the life she leads. If she could get in touch with the power of play, she would never again be happy exercising on autopilot.

Too many people don't ever get to know the wonderful feeling that comes from doing exercise for the fun of it. If they did, hospitals would be emptier and advertisers would have to sell products for goods other than back remedies, headache cures, digestive aids, and the like. More people would stick to their fitness routines because they would be more like fun and less like drudgery.

These ten stupid myths about exercise serve no useful purpose for any of us. They can only keep us stuck and disempowered.

EMPOWERMENT IS AN EQUAL OPPORTUNITY EXPERIENCE!

Empowerment is what has allowed me to continue on my own personal path and remain consistently excited about life, while making choices that move me toward my goals. It makes magic happen—whether it's losing those last five pounds, getting excited about building a healthier body, or making positive changes in other areas of life. Its magic is like a chemical reaction that occurs when you finally decide to make choices that give you power, rather than ones that leave you a victim to the whims of other people or to old memories, expectations based on the past, or a lack of faith in yourself and your capabilities.

Everyone remembers the Vince Lombardi quote, "Winning isn't everything, it's the *only* thing." I like another quote attributed to him even better. It goes something like this: "The Green Bay Packers have never lost a game. The time clock may have run out before they attained a lead, but they've never lost."

Do you take your vitamins religiously, watch the scale, exercise regularly, watch your fat intake, and still not get results? Do you feel as though the clock has often run out on your personal relationships before it should have? Has being a player in your chosen field become a boring drag? Well, that can all change once you discover empowerment, the big word packed with important meaning for all of us.

EMPOWERMENT: WHO HAS IT?

What does it mean to have empowerment? According to *Webster's New World Dictionary*, to empower is "1. to give power to; authorize 2. to enable." Women who are empowered have given themselves permission to be at the top of their game in all areas of life and are actively engaged in leading amazing, fulfilling lives. They don't let past obstacles, negative thoughts, or self-sabotage flavor their life in the present or as they move eagerly into the future. They don't sit around waiting to feel everything is OK only when: someone else makes them feel good about themselves; or the planets are in correct alignment; or everything in life is going smoothly and perfectly, with absolutely no challenges or problems.

Women who are empowered have found ways around the obstacles and detours that inevitably show up in life. When a challenge arises they find ways to rise up, deal with it, and conquer it. They welcome the responsibility that comes with creating a successful life and consistently search for ways to make life even better, rather than relying on luck, chance, or fate.

Women who lack empowerment often experience the following symptoms:

stress
anxiety
feeling out of control, powerless
physical ailments
bad eating habits
inconsistent (or overly obsessive) exercise schedule
lack of sexual or other healthy desires
lack of self-esteem
inability to stick to *anything* for very long
lack of interests

According to a report in the *Journal of the American Medical Association* in the early 1990s, tobacco caused about 30 percent of all cancer deaths and 21 percent of cardiovascular disease deaths in 1990. People who were sedentary were linked to 23 percent of deaths from the leading diseases. Misuse of alcohol caused between 3 percent and 10 percent of all deaths. Clearly, unhealthy lifestyle choices are killing us and I firmly believe that a lack of self-empowerment is to blame. When people value themselves more and make healthier lifestyle choices, they'll experience less disease and live longer, happier lives.

An article in *Parade* magazine on April 17, 1994, listed the following top causes of death for Americans:

1. Heart disease (33.2%)
2. Cancer (23.7%)
3. Strokes (6.6%)
4. Lung diseases (4.2%)

Many of these deaths were due to lifestyle choices—choices that could have been avoided. Again, I believe this is the negative result of being out of *life*Balance and having no self-empowerment.

Empowerment, and related concepts, has become the gospel of the '90s, crossing all sex, gender, and demographic borders. Most people know they need it, but don't have a clue how to get it. Unfortunately, if you're like Emmy, a housewife from New Mexico, empowerment is a four-letter word. She wrote to ask me what all the hoopla was about.

"Dear Cory," her letter began, "I don't know why people keep talking about this empowerment stuff. Who's got time for it? I have three kids—all between the ages of 2 and 10. By the time my day ends, the only thing I really need is a good night's sleep!"

Another woman wrote to tell me, "I feel like I'm always putting things off because I'm not fit. I put off going to Europe, going out at night, gosh, I pretty much put off everything for 'someday when I'm thinner and I deserve it.'"

For many, empowerment is something they'll begin to seek when the bills are paid, the house is cleaned, the body is back in shape, and the kids have gone off to college. It's an option that one can afford to think about *after* (as in, "*After* I get through these next few weeks at work I'll ask for that raise" or "*After* I can fit back into a size 8 dress I'll take those tennis lessons"). Empowerment, however, is not just some future goal, but a tool that can be used *now,* not *after,* to make all of your goals, dreams, and personal visions a reality. You can begin today to create a life that is uniquely rich and rewarding, a body that functions with vitality and wellness, and a fun-filled, optimistic outlook. What you need is a way to make empowerment a reality, not a future goal, fantasy, or pipe dream.

Those of you who are overworked, megastressed, and on the verge of personal or professional meltdown are probably thinking, "Jeez. Just what I need, another celebrity telling me that I need to empower myself to *do* more, *be* more, *get* more out of life. The last thing I want in my life is more pressure."

Or, as one busy mother told me, "Face it, Cory, it's not that easy for real people who have to deal with real life." You might even be saying to yourself, "I don't want to hear any psychobabble stuff from anybody. I want to get in shape and I want to get there *now.* Just teach me the magic that'll make my body fat go down and after that we'll talk about something else."

I wish I could wave a magic wand and give everyone exactly the body, lifestyle, relationship, and financial success they dream of. Then, maybe, no more hard-earned dollars and human time and energy would be spent looking for immediate, hocus-pocus solutions. Haven't we all had enough of the magic pills, powders, potions, and programs that promise the world and deliver zippity-do-dah?

Magic bullets don't work because too many people jump on these fads and the fitness bandwagon for the wrong reasons. Fads can't work because they're built on rocky foundations. Health, fitness, and longevity aren't found in a "quick fix." They're found in the realm of empowerment, which, once discovered, creates *life*Balance.

BEGIN TO *SEE* IT

My favorite saying, one that I tell myself every single day when I wake up, is "As we imagine so can we create." It's been proven time and time again by those who have gone from rags to riches and beyond (hello, Horatio Alger!) that we are the sum total of our thoughts and not our circumstance. Forget about being born into royalty, inheriting a genius IQ, or living under a lucky star. There is nothing as effective as your own mind as a tool for creating empowerment and forging a brilliant future for yourself.

Empowerment can be created in many ways: through visualization, meditation, certain forms of mind/body exercise, and even prayer. You don't have to be a saint to get empowered, nor do you have to be a genius or a mystic. Empowerment isn't some esoteric, intellectual technique that requires a degree in rocket science. It can be attained by all of us. It inevitably shows up when you take the time to slow down, quiet your mind, and listen to something other than your mind or your brain. Remember the "Mind versus the Brain" exercise in chapter 1? I ask that you now begin to listen for a third voice—one that is loving, supportive, nurturing, friendly, and always there to guide you. That voice is the voice of empowerment and it will guide your visualizations, meditations, and prayer. By hearing its message, in addition to the others, you make an MBS connection and create empowerment and *life*Balance.

LifeBalance JOURNAL EXERCISE: "HOW I SEE MYSELF TODAY"

Let's see how you really see the current you. Time to let down any defenses and allow your playful, childlike expression to surface. Forget about being judged—especially by yourself!—and use a full page in your journal as a canvas on which to draw a picture of your body. Don't worry about the artistic merit of your work. This isn't art class. You won't be graded or criticized on your artistic talents. If you can doodle, you can draw, so don't worry about what style of drawing you make. It can be abstract, realistic, whatever. Try to remember when you were a child and you had fun spending time by yourself with just a crayon and a pad of paper, then have some fun as you sketch what you think your body looks like. Use crayons (if they're handy) and your nondominant hand (the one you don't write with). Your nondominant hand is more closely related to your creative, imaginative self. Your dominant hand is linked to the logical you. So let's experiment with the part of you that isn't run by expectations, rules, and logic and allow the more fanciful you to surface. Come back to the book when you've finished.

Now, take a look at your body sketch. Your drawing can provide terrific access to understanding where you lack empowerment. Again, keep in mind that there is no right or wrong way to have drawn this picture. We're looking for insight here, not artistic awards. Make notes beside the picture about what your picture tells you. If you drew a flabby stomach, make a note that you think your tummy needs a little work. If you gave yourself a great head of flowing hair, note that you like your hair. Just write a few quick words about what your picture "says" about you. Other than specific gripes or good parts, three general areas can be illuminated by your drawing.

First, did you draw a stick figure or a more fully detailed picture? If your picture lacks any realistic, lifelike detail, you might want to begin to take more time getting in touch with who you are and what it is you really want out of life. The first step toward empowerment can be as simple as taking time to think about what it is that is truly meaningful to you and then taking small steps that will move you toward your goals. There's power in true self-knowledge, and it's available to everyone. Begin an investigation into who you are today and where you want to go in the future.

Second, did you include a head, or, like many, did you neglect to include this important part of you? If your drawing lacks a head, you may be one of those women who separate the mind and the body. Neglecting this important connection will inhibit the creation of *life*Balance. Use this book to forge a strong mind/body connection.

Finally, did you draw any of the internal organs? For example, did you put a little heart in the middle of your chest or genitals down below? Most people don't—so if you didn't, you're among the majority. Overstressed, busy people often neglect key areas of life—including sexual expression, love, and other emotions. This neglect can lead to illness and other limiting physical manifestations. If your drawing lacks these details, ask yourself, "What have I sacrificed emotionally that might not only be affecting me physically, but which might be cutting me off from my power?" A fully self-expressed human being is not lacking in empowerment. Begin to express yourself fully in all areas.

Such a self-portrait can be a pretty good indicator of where each of us stands in relation to *life*Balance. If you only drew a sketchy, headless outline with lots of negative margin notes, don't be discouraged! You're going to get a lot of benefit from the work we'll do in this book. After all, if your drawing represents just the cosmetic outline of your body, think of all the wonderful organs, muscles, and working body parts that you will now begin to include! These are all important parts of the balance needed for health, happiness, and well-being.

CREATING EMPOWERMENT

Empowerment is a powerful formula for change that you will begin to create today. This book will lead you through the necessary steps to attain it, step-by-step.

These include some creative visualization (like that in the following exercise), the removal of old Negative Emotional Connectors (chapter 7), Mental Trash Compacting (chapter 8), and the use of Power Connectors (chapter 9). As you learn each step you will experience more and more empowerment and begin to reclaim your power from wherever you've given it. You begin by *visualizing* your dreams and goals, then you take the next steps and, before you know it, you'll be *realizing* them!

LifeBalance JOURNAL EXERCISE: "ME IN THE FUTURE"

Use another full page for this crayon drawing. This time, use your dominant hand as you draw yourself in the future. Incorporate any changes in your body, hairstyle, or personality as you create this image. After you draw it, write some margin notes—like you did in the previous exercise. Jot down any emotions you think you'll be feeling in your "new life."

Did you find this picture easier to create? Did it take less time? If so, it's probably not due to the fact that you were using your writing hand; it may be because most of us have a clearer idea of what it is we want in the future than of how we are today.

This type of visualization is important because it helps us create impressions for the purpose of change. Take time each day to mentally picture yourself as you'd like to be. Draw more pictures of this image, if it helps. As you begin to create positive mental pictures of yourself through visualization or drawings you'll begin to know a new you. With this knowledge will come empowerment through learning about this person you will begin to accept, like, and hopefully even love.

MOTIVATION AND HOW TO GET IT

How many times have you hated your body and wanted to change it? I know I have. As a child growing up I was often laughed at for my slanted eyes and high cheekbones. I was called Pocahontas or Sitting Bull more times than I care to remember because of my protruding German facial structure. I didn't look like the girl next door, but I desperately wanted to. The kids would ask me, "Are you Oriental or Indian?" I spent hours in front of the mirror pushing my cheekbones down with the heels of my hands. While I did my homework I pulled the corners of my eyes down in the desperate hope that they would tilt down at the edges instead of up. I couldn't bear to be called any more names by my classmates and I was willing to try anything to change the way my face looked.

My body was different, too. In grade school I was commonly referred to as Frog Legs because my legs were muscular and looked like those of a frog. I wore long pants so that the other kids would think I looked "normal." In high school I was nicknamed the Bionic Woman because of my strength. In college they called me Boomer when they referred to my muscular butt. Eventually, I wore big, baggy clothes and kept my body under cover in the hope that no one could see it.

I had such a rotten self-image from all the teasing that I spent my time and energy trying to camouflage who I really was. I got straight A's so that people would like me. I began to collect sports titles. I became a cheerleader and became a pro at putting on that pretty, smiling, happy face that I thought I needed to have to be accepted. Underneath it all, I was dying. All the trying and putting on the happy front and working so hard for positive attention was killing off my ego and my self-image.

It wasn't until sometime during my college years (around age twenty-two) that the tables finally turned and I began to like the way I looked—a little bit. Luckily for me, I met someone who believed in me enough to stick with me through a difficult learning process as I slowly came to love myself. It took years and a trusting, caring, honest individual (my ex-husband, Jeff) before I finally became comfortable with and proud of and able to accept myself. I realized for the first time that I was the best me that I could be and that's all I or anyone else should ever need.

I started wearing track shorts instead of sweatpants. I cut my hair so that I no longer hid behind bangs. I even started accentuating my almond-shaped eyes with makeup! I said good-bye to all the tricks I had resorted to in order to feel OK about myself and accepted the attributes that were unique to me.

I am often amazed at the lengths to which women will go in their attempts to look like the women on the covers of fashion magazines. Often, we succeed at our attempts to change our body only to see it revert back to its former, pre-diet shape. Although our body may change and our size may vary from year to year— for better as well as for worse—what remains constant is not our dress size or body fat count, but who we are and how we experience life. Doctors frequently report about patients who have undergone drastic weight loss, only to continue to see the world through "fat eyes." When we motivate ourselves to make our life experience better, rather than only to reduce our weight, it's a much wiser energy investment.

MOTIVATION FOR ALL THE WRONG REASONS

Too many women are motivated by a desire to change the outward appearance of their bodies. They exercise just to look a certain way or fit into a certain size and they spend more time being unsatisfied with themselves than not. When your reason for exercising is not just about looking good or becoming a size two, you'll find that you can remain motivated longer and feel good about yourself no matter what the scale says.

Carolyn M. Doherty, M.D., is one of the top facial plastic and reconstructive surgery professionals in Beverly Hills, California. She creates amazing physical transformations for men and women every day at her chic Bedford Drive office, particularly for those wishing to look younger (face-lifts) or slimmer (liposuction). Often, the results dramatically change peoples' lives. Some patients, however, regardless of any dramatic physical change through surgery, continue to self-criticize themselves. "Plastic surgery—or any other 'cosmetic change'—won't fix a bad relationship or correct an underlying lack of self-esteem. It won't get you the job that you wanted. It can make you feel great if you do it to feel better about yourself, but not to change your life," Dr. Doherty explains. "The motivation has to be coming from the right place."

Motivation in the Molars

Dr. Steven Donia is a man who helps people who are motivated to make a change in their molars—or any other teeth, for that matter. He practices cosmetic dentistry in his Encino, California, office. Cosmetic dentistry can create a much different impact than plastic surgery. Studies have shown that the first thing a woman or man initially looks at when meeting a member of the opposite sex is the smile.

"Your smile is the connection between you and your friends, relationships, or business partners," Donia explains. "It's the bridge that connects two cities. If you have a beautiful, inviting smile you can conquer the world, even if you are fifty pounds overweight and have a huge nose. We can change the shape of our bodies through exercise and diet, but we have no control over our teeth. Some of us spend years wearing braces or covering our mouth with our hands to camouflage our stained or crooked teeth. Most people don't realize that in only four days they can erase an entire lifetime of insecurity or avoidance of intimacy."

Donia believes that people who come to him for veneers or other cosmetic dental procedures are often driven by very positive motivation.

"I've seen men and women unable, or unwilling, to get into relationships because they were self-conscious about their teeth. Within a very short time, after having some corrective work done, they would tell me that they had gotten engaged. That's my greatest sense of accomplishment, being able to bring a dazzling smile into someone's life."

Garth Fisher, M.D., another top Beverly Hills plastic surgeon, concurs. "Plastic surgery is a solution for those honest enough with themselves that they know they would like improvements in their superficial structure. It is not a solution in itself for negative emotions or depression."

I Don't Know about Too Rich, but You Can Be Too Thin!

Karen is a model who eats a fairly clean, healthy diet. She has to stay slim in order to continue to work in her profession. Even though she stays away from fats, sweets, and even caffeine, she finds that her energy level is low and her body fat percentage higher than she'd like. When she strides down the runway in designer gowns, she looks pretty good. It's only when she dons a bathing suit or lingerie that her lack of muscle tone is apparent in the wobble of her legs and the dangle of her upper arms.

Karen, and many women like her, believed that all she needed to do was stick to an extremely low-calorie diet and her health, energy level, and emotional well-being would fall into place. She thought that if she stayed away from certain foods and ate very little she'd be healthy and have a lean, toned body. She learned the hard way that the fashion model diet mentality may give you a thin, size two figure, but it doesn't guarantee health or fitness. If you look closely at the skin and bones in fashion magazines, you'll also see relatively high body fat counts. As many emaciated women have found, you can be skinny and fat at the same time.

With proper nutrition and exercise, you can add tone and lean muscle mass to a scrawny body, but ultrathin women (women on the verge of eating disorders) can get very anxious when told to eat more—even when it's healthy, nutritious food. I encouraged Karen to find the time to incorporate some mind/body work-outs (like those in chapter 12) into her daily routine to lower her anxiety levels. Next, I encouraged her to eat regularly during the day and to balance her diet to include grains, pastas, and some lean white meats. Her body got firmer and her *life*Balance improved.

"I was always afraid of bulking up with a lot of muscle. I never realized that exercising and building muscle would help me," she now says. Once she under-stood that muscle tissue uses so many more calories (than fat) to keep the body going and that fit people have higher (fat-burning) metabolisms than sedentary people, she began to incorporate exercise into her life. She found that she could eat regularly, have the occasional food treat, and stay slim. I told her, "If you add some exercise to your day, you can also add some scones (her favorite) to your diet." She also found that yoga and walking—the *life*Balance fitness choices she made, according to her fitness mode (chapter 10)—afforded her a mental calm that made every assignment seem more fun and every day a little more satisfy-ing. She found a balance!

MOTIVATION BEGINS WITH GOALS

The solution to Karen's problem was the same as it is for many of the women I meet in my travels. She needed new goals. Karen's old goal was to starve her-self down to be as thin as possible. Now, her goal is to be healthy, toned, firm, and full of energy. She's still slender, but there's less jiggle and more jump in her runway moves.

Developing motivation that lasts means establishing new, realistic, and authentic goals that take into account the Real You (chapter 15), the total pic-ture of who you really are, rather than just who you want to look like or think you'd like to be. When goals are unrealistic or unhealthy, they are doomed to fail-ure, so why set yourself up for frustration? Is it your goal to look like the girl in the swimsuit ad in the fashion magazine? That may not be a healthy, realistic goal for you.

What are realistic versus unrealistic goals? Let's use the example of the short, muscular woman who wants to look like a model, not a gymnast. She needs to look honestly at herself, her mom, her dad, her brothers and sisters. (Don't forget that genetics play an important role in body types.) If both Mom and

Pop have short legs and heavy thighs and are under five-foot-four, don't expect to be mistaken for Elle MacPherson's sister—unless, of course, you were adopted. Your weight is to some degree genetically programmed (although not set in stone) so you may have to readjust your idea of your dream body. Readjust this dream image to what is actually possible to achieve and work within realistic expectations. If you're short and stocky, concentrate on developing a great set of abs and strong, muscular arms. Show them off. (One tall, lanky woman I know would give almost anything for a big set of calves. She's got the longest legs on earth and all she wants are well-rounded calves!)

Choose realistic, healthy goals that contribute to *life*Balance, not detract from it.

Motivation and Commitment: The Chicken and the Egg

Motivation and commitment are like the chicken and the egg because if you're truly committed, then you've got plenty of motivation and if you've got plenty of motivation, then the commitment part is easy. One is a better starting point, however—and I believe commitment is where it all begins. Get committed and you'll get motivated.

Make sure that you are 100 percent committed and not just talking the talk. If you're not ready, you probably won't be honest with your attempts. Walk the walk and don't just drive yourself (and others!) crazy talking about what you need to do or are going to do. I have never seen someone honestly put out the work effort, eat a clean, healthy diet, and *not* stay motivated and make progress.

Stop the "I Don't Have Time" Whine

"Cory, I don't have time to exercise or meditate or do yoga or fit one more thing into my day," busy women tell me time and again. To them, I reply, "You don't have time not to!" One of your most important jobs in life is to create the healthiest physical environment possible for yourself. Without that, *life*Balance is impossible. Those who cling to this excuse may be truly busy, but more likely they have become resigned about their ability to lose weight, regain their health, or feel better about themselves.

Prioritize for Motivation

We've all had a friend call us to say, "Where have you been? Why haven't you called me?" We've all let someone down when we've promised to do something and then didn't. Haven't we all used the excuse "I didn't have time to do it?"

sometimes? What we often mean when we say we didn't have time, however, is that we didn't *make* the time for the phone call or for the favor or whatever. It just wasn't a priority for us—but the truth is that unless you're hooked up to an IV in the emergency room or crossing the Sahara Desert on foot, you've got time. When you say you didn't have time to make the call, do the favor, or finish the job, it's because something else was more important to you. You were motivated to do something else you'd given a higher priority.

Ever notice how much your subconscious mind loves to help you prioritize your day? Your inner critic loves to get her two cents' worth in—about nearly anything that will rob her of her negative power. "Go to the gym for a workout after the day you've had? You've gotta be kidding! Don't you have work to do?" she asks you, hoping that you never get enough self-empowerment to ignore her negative comments. "Forget about that aerobics class, babe, you've had a rough day. How about a quick treat?" she pipes in, knowing that her power over you is completely dependent on keeping you dependent. It's your job to nip these subconscious objections in the bud—right at the source—and create your own (appropriate) priorities.

Remove the Reasons That Stop Motivation

Forget about the real reasons that keep you busy—the kids will always need to be fed and shuttled about, your boss will always want more hours from you, and the house will always need to be cleaned and stocked. Those things won't change. But there are things that can.

For starters, choose a workout program that fits into your lifestyle, is fun, and isn't too difficult to maintain over time. You'll soon find that getting away from it all to do something for yourself is no longer such a problem. Let's take a look at a few "problems" that stop motivation, but which can be solved.

· "My gym is so far away. It takes too much time to get there every day." If your gym is far from home or work, or has crowded parking areas, it's no wonder you miss workouts. Your mind can have a field day making excuses for you not to get to the gym! If you can't join a closer gym, then make sure you find a way to work out which doesn't require travel. (Walking, video workouts in the living room, and bicycling the neighborhood are all good.)

· "My workout is no fun. It's boring." Finding the right workout means finding the one that's fun and engaging for *you*. If the latest, most popular fitness craze doesn't interest and entertain you, then there's no way you'll stay with it. Do what's fun for you and you'll find yourself looking forward to, not dreading, workouts.

· "Working out is too hard. It's too much work." Don't ever give your subconscious a chance to shoot you down. If your workout is too complicated or too hard or too distant, the odds of your doing it get lower. Find a type of exercise that provides healthy benefits, but doesn't leave you needing medical attention. It doesn't have to kill you to cure you.

Remove the obstacles and you'll find your motivation.

BURNOUT KILLS INITIATIVE

Burnout at work, in relationships, and in nearly any aspect of life occurs when a person perceives that he or she is giving more than he or she is receiving. In a relationship, burnout can destroy passion, affinity, intimacy, and joy. The woman who believes that she is carrying all the responsibility for making her marriage or relationship work is not likely to be motivated to act playful and romantic when she's with her partner. If she's experiencing too much stress and responsibility and not enough nurturing from those she loves, she may not be motivated or feel empowered to find ways to nurture herself. In the workplace, burnout can lead to nonproductivity, sloppy work habits, a lack of creativity or follow-through, and dread. Most people find it difficult to stay motivated about their work when they feel that they put in too many hours for too little pay or feel that their efforts go unnoticed. The negative emotional balance that results from giving so much of one's spirit to a partner, job, or workout program that disappoints can be devastating. Burnout can cause all sorts of other problems, including physical ones. Headaches, ulcers, eating and sleep disorders, and immune system susceptibility are just a few of the side effects of job, relationship, or fitness burnout. I can't count the number of relationships I've seen suffer within the bodybuilding community because someone was too burnt out to give to loved ones.

Do you suffer from burnout? Take the Burnout Quiz below to see if you're a candidate for illness, negative emotional imbalance, and lack of motivation. Answer "yes" or "no" to each question.

THE BURNOUT QUIZ

1. Do you care less about how you look to others? (Have you gotten sloppy in your grooming habits?)
2. Are you missing workouts or eliminating them entirely?
3. Are your eating habits, sleeping habits, or energy level(s) out of whack?
4. Are you cranky and quick-tempered?
5. Do you do either too much or too little at work (job) or at home (housework)?

6. Are you bored, sad, anxious? Are you experiencing more than your normal share of emotional ups and downs?
7. Are you getting sick more often?

If you answered "yes" to more than three questions, you may be suffering from burnout. Focusing on your goals, finding motivation, and beginning your new program today could make the difference between being a success story and being a burnout.

Fight Burnout

I am a world-class authority on burnout. As they say, "Been there, done that." Take my advice and, as they also say, "Don't go there!" Cut burnout off at the pass with the following Eleven Commandments of Cory—developed in my personal trials by fire! They're guaranteed to help you fight burnout and clear the way for motivation:

CORY COMMANDMENT #1: *Just say no. Speak up for yourself. Be assertive.*
(OLD CORY: *Only the weak say no to anything. Be a good Samaritan to the lowliest of pond scum and drop whatever you are doing at any given time to help someone you don't even know. Never put off until tomorrow something you can do in the middle of the night.*)

CORY COMMANDMENT #2: *Get centered. Sort out what* is *important from what is* not *important .*
(OLD CORY: *Don't be a fool. Everything is important. Worry and obsess as much about the little things as you do about the big ones! "What color should I paint my ceiling? Think I'll spend twelve hours thinking about it."*)

CORY COMMANDMENT #3: *Practice moderation. Learn to find a balance at home, at work, at the gym, and conserve your valuable energy.*
(OLD CORY: *Balance is for people who burn incense in their navels. Face it, only the strong in perpetual motion survive! I think it's cute that Steve, my fiancé, calls me PMM: Perpetual Motion Machine.*)

CORY COMMANDMENT #4: *Be kind to yourself. Eat healthy foods. Get plenty of rest, water, and fresh air.*
(OLD CORY: *Keep pushing the mind and body to their limits and never give them a minute's rest. Plenty of time for that when you're dead!*)

CORY COMMANDMENT #5: *Set boundaries. Make your work, family, and fitness goals doable by refusing to take on so many of others' projects or demands that you no longer have time for your own. Protect your time and your emotions.*

(OLD CORY: *You don't need boundaries. You can do it all!* "If the Bionic Woman can do it, so can I. After all, she's only a TV weenie, I'm six-time Ms. Olympia—no special effects here!")

CORY COMMANDMENT #6: *Delegate. Rescue yourself and your time, energy, and goals by learning to detach (appropriately) from certain needs and responsibilities of others.*
(OLD CORY: *Never put off to someone else what you personally can do at midnight!*)

CORY COMMANDMENT #7: *Don't take on too much at a time. Set do-able goals for yourself and slowly work toward them. Don't get bogged down by other people's problems. Take time for yourself.*
(OLD CORY: *Be everything to everyone. Take on not only your own problems and anxieties, but those of virtual strangers! Take on all the problems of your friends and make life easier for everyone but you!*)

CORY COMMANDMENT #8: *Lighten up. If areas of your life are really intense and stressful, find ways to relieve the pressure. Don't be so hard on yourself.*
(OLD CORY: *Don't ever lighten up. Intensity is good. Push yourself to the max at all times!*)

CORY COMMANDMENT #9: *Don't be afraid to change. Try new things. If your workout, your relationship, your job, or anything else is not working in its present state, make the appropriate, healthy changes.*
(OLD CORY: *If something is not working, keep at it anyway. Beat your head against a brick wall if necessary.*)

CORY COMMANDMENT #10: *Listen to your body. Admit when you're too tired, weak, or sick to go to work or the gym. Workaholics push themselves to mental as well as physical burnout and workout-aholics injure themselves!*
(OLD CORY: *Ignore your body. What does it know, anyway? There's never a reason to miss a workout. [I used to work out until I practically went unconscious. In fact, I actually did go unconscious once and woke up to my dog licking my face to revive me!] If you're a family- or career-oriented woman—or both—never, ever let something like illness or extreme fatigue keep you from your responsibilities and don't rely on anyone else to help you, even if you're on your death bed.*)

CORY COMMANDMENT #11: *Get a buddy. Renew an old friendship; develop a new one. Take advantage of all the good benefits you get from this type of support.*
(OLD CORY: *Lock yourself in the gym (or office) alone and train (or work) for*

hours. After all, if anyone sees you training, they might steal your workout (or project)! If you do train with a partner, make sure you train so hard that you make your buddy throw up! Make sure that you drive your coworkers and family to extremes so that they, too, will be world-class burnouts!)

UNTIE THE *NOTS*

Another important step toward motivation is to learn to remove certain words from your vocabulary.

LifeBalance EXERCISE: "DO *NOT* THINK ABOUT PINK ELEPHANTS!"

Try this: Right now, right here, do *not* think about pink elephants. Understand? Good. Do it.

My guess is that the only thing you can think about right now is big, fat, thick-skinned, pink mammals with long tusks and big ears. Am I right? Of course I am! Wanna know a secret? Your brain doesn't know what to do with the words *not, no,* or *but.*

The Mind Cannot Process Certain Words

When your motivation is *not* being fat, you might get fatter than ever. There is no picture for the word *not* in your mind. "I will *not* gain weight over the holidays." Your brain hears the command, but it doesn't know what to do with *not.* You're programming your body to gain weight! A more effective motivation would be a more balanced message that avoids using the word *not.*

Instead of saying, for example, "I'm on a diet so I don't look like a cow in my new dress," or "I'm not eating fatty foods anymore," you can say, "I'm going to eat healthier to enjoy a longer life," or "On the fifth of February I will shift to eating healthier foods." Notice the negative slant in the first two statements and how positive the last two sound. Positive phrasing is a much better motivational tool.

Next, remove the qualifiers "I've tried," "I can't," and "I won't" from your speaking. They suggest a finality to your fitness goals which is incredibly disempowering. Always remember that it ain't over till the fat lady sings—and if she follows this plan, she won't be fat anymore!

If you wanted to learn to golf you wouldn't be upset if you didn't get a hole-in-one your first day out. You'd keep taking lessons, practicing, and playing the game until you got it right. If one method didn't work for you, you'd try another type of swing, a new club, or another golf pro until you found a way to learn which clicked for you.

Do you think I stayed with the very first, second, or even third workout program I ever tried? No way! I've had to make my own mistakes, travel down the wrong roads, and *fail big-time* before I found what works. "Tried," "can't," and "won't" are for those who have given up.

REMOVE THE LABELS

Lack of motivation often hides behind other labels. Flush it out into the light of day if it's been running your life under any of the following assumed names:

Unwillingness: We all know people who stubbornly resist any change in their life or way of thinking. These types don't want to rock the boat or shake up the status quo. Getting more out of life scares them and they're unwilling to step up to the plate and go to bat.

Overwhelmed: Some people don't like to think of themselves as unmotivated. They prefer to think that they're just too darn tired, overworked, or hassled to do anything to improve their life. They want things to change and are open to it but they simply lack the commitment to do so.

Fear: Like laziness, fear may stop even the most willing people. Sarah is a woman who wants to change and knows that life can be better. Her fear of the unknown keeps her from trying anything new. Yes, she admits, her life is in need of drastic restructuring. She's more comfortable with her unsatisfying life, however, than she is with her fears of all the horrible things that could befall her if she changed. Fear can become almost like a superstition for many people who desperately want to change but are scared of the possible negative consequences.

Insecurity: Often when people hear terms like "empowerment" or "mind/body awareness" they run for cover. They think these words are for people far more intelligent, "together," or sophisticated than themselves. This intellectual insecurity keeps them from being motivated to explore avenues that might enrich their lives.

None of the labels are real; they're just ideas you or those around you have created to try to explain why you lack motivation.

SECRETS OF MOTIVATION

If you've removed the nasty qualifying words from your vocabulary, studied the Cory Commandments, resolved any burnout problems, and recognized any label you might have been hiding behind, you're ready to get on the inside track to motivation.

Motivation Secret #1: Exercise for Yourself

A study reported in *Self* magazine found that women who exercise regularly had taken charge of their own bodies. They had a strong sense of self-worth. Instead of looking to others for direction, they "had transferred authority for their health and bodies from an external source, such as a celebrity role model, boyfriend or parents, to themselves." When women exercised because someone told them they should—or because they wanted to look like someone else—they invariably dropped out.

Another *Self* magazine survey found that "most women who exercise regularly like it for the way it makes them feel—not for the way it makes them look." What's really important is "the sheer pleasure of doing it," as *Shape* magazine recently put it.

Discovering that "sheer pleasure" is a main component of doing for yourself, not for others. The impact is immediate and personal. I compare enjoying the process of exercise to enjoying the process of sex. Think about it: isn't the excitement of having sex more motivating than the orgasm itself? The orgasm, the product, is soon over. The process, however, is where all the fun happens and it can go on for much longer than the actual climax.

What will motivate you to do it for yourself? When you figure that one out, you'll have solved a whole truckload of problems. Start today to do a mental inventory and find what might work for you, then try it on for size. Does self-empowerment ring the bell for you? A sense of well-being? Use what works.

*Life*Balance JOURNAL EXERCISE: "WHAT MOTIVATES ME"

Place a check mark next to any of the following statements that apply to you. Be honest. None of these statements is "bad" or "wrong," just how things seem to you.

1. My life is out of control. _____
2. Things never go my way and I never get a lucky break. _____
3. After I lose ten pounds, find the right partner, or get the right job I'll feel better about myself and then be able to be more happy and satisfied. _____
4. I'm going through a very difficult time and it's really hard for me to imagine having any joy, happiness, or satisfaction in my life until things turn around. _____
5. No matter how hard I try—and I really have tried hard—I just can't seem to get my life to be the way I'd like it to be. _____
6. I just want to be the best me that I can be._____

7. Losing ten pounds, being in a great relationship, and having the perfect career are all nice, but I'm not waiting for all of them to fall into place before I can be happy. _____
8. Even though I've failed in the past at dieting, relationships, or job satisfaction, I know that I can still succeed at any or all of them. _____
9. My life is pretty good right now. _____
10. Life is tough right now but I'm OK. _____

If you checked off more of statements 1 through 5 than of 6 through 10, you will probably find self-empowerment a great motivator. Your responses indicate that you're probably not living fully in the now, but are waiting for life to begin sometime in the future, when things are "better." You'd like to feel more in charge of your own life and less at the mercies and whims of others. Can you imagine what it would be like to enjoy your life right this instant, just as it is? Those who live in the here and now feel good about themselves and often find it easier to stay on track at home, on the job, or within a relationship. They don't feel powerless, because they have a sense of control over their life.

If self-empowerment is a stretch for you, maybe you'd like to have feelings of well-being. A sense of well-being doesn't mean that you don't want improvement, it just means that you no longer beat yourself up if your life doesn't fit some perfect picture. You are able to enjoy your life now. Creating a sense of well-being might be a great motivation for you if several or all of statements 1 through 5 apply to you.

If you checked off more of statements 6 through 10 than of 1 through 5, you are probably clear that your life doesn't depend on the winds of fate or the whimsy of others. You already recognize your personal responsibility in making life happen. Self-empowerment and self-improvement are probably equally good motivators for you, because they will give you even more access to health, happiness, and vitality.

For some people, motivation comes in stages. Try this:
Engage yourself in the process and commit to a program for twenty-one days. (That's the length of time it takes to break old habits and create new ones.) Just do it, as the ads say. Stick with it until you achieve at least some minor goal—like simply fulfilling your commitment to your program—within that time frame. See how good losing those first two pounds makes you feel. Do you feel the increased sense of self-worth? Even a little bit? Invest that into your emotional bank account and collect interest on it. You'll find it easier and easier to reenlist each time for another twenty-one days. Eventually, the process snowballs and you've got plenty of motivation. Increase your self-image bank account little by little and you'll be astounded at the interest it accrues.

Motivation Secret #2: Identify Immediate Health Rewards

I have a friend who is a runner. She used to have a cigarette habit of a pack and a half a day and for years I bugged her to quit. I told her all the facts about the increased risk of breast cancer in women who smoke. I showed her all the statistics about people dying younger because they smoked. I tore out magazine and newspaper articles with all the horrible facts. Nothing worked. Then one day she was complaining about her time in a 10K race. I looked at her, amazed. "Don't you think you'd have a better time if your lungs were clearer?" I asked her. She quit smoking the next day. Almost immediately, her running improved and her times got shorter. I had harped at her about her health, her chances of getting a terrible disease, and her likelihood of losing years of her life. All I needed to say to her was, "You'll run faster if you quit."

Immediate rewards can be better motivation than almost anything. Fear of the diseases and problems associated with obesity may not help you to stick to your fitness program, since those illnesses may not show up for a long time—in the distant future, if you're lucky. But feeling better and having more energy—*now*—is an "immediate" health reward. You don't have to wait too long to feel better, perform your favorite sport with more ease, or have more energy for friends and family. If huffing and puffing after a short flight of stairs is aggravating to you, then imagine bouncing up them soon with energetic, athletic glee.

Motivation Secret #3: Make Big Little Changes

Many experts recommend making small changes in your diet and fitness routines in order to stick to a program, because people fall off the wagon when plans require drastic changes in lifestyle. I agree that small changes can, in time, add up to big results. I also know from experience, however, that when changes are too small, the results may show up too slowly to keep the average person motivated. Making changes that are too big can be discouraging, but small ones can cause frustration.

Learn the difference between small changes and what I call big little changes. Big little changes will enable you to get early results and stay motivated because it's easier to stick to a program with a little immediate gratification thrown in.

Lucina is a perfect example of someone who learned how to make big little changes. She weighed 288 pounds when she came to me for help. Within two weeks she had lost twenty pounds and she continues to lose weight as she heads confidently toward her goal. Did she go on a stringent diet or undertake an exhaustive program? No.

What Lucina did was make a big little change. I asked her if she was willing to reframe her beliefs about exercise. She was, so we set out to change her mind-set. No longer could she view it, as she always had, as drudgery or something that had to be performed for too hard or too long. Thinking of exercise as fun was a big departure from her former views. That was the "big" part of the big little change she had to make.

The "little" part was easy. She had to learn to relax her attitude about workouts. She thought I was going to make her work out harder in her new program, so you can imagine how surprised she was when I encouraged her to work less hard at the gym and begin to have fun with fitness. Instead of spending a boring hour on the treadmill, she began to sample some new classes at her club. She found that she enjoyed a forty-five-minute funk class so much that it seemed to fly by. On alternate days, when she would formerly have climbed on a Stairmaster for thirty minutes and worked out with free weights for another forty-five minutes, I suggested she cut the free weight workout down to about thirty minutes and then take her dog for a brisk walk around the neighborhood. She loved that!

She told me, "Cory, you taught me a way to think of exercise as a treat and not a punishment, and for the first time in my life—I do! I wake up and look forward to my workout, because it's not just about how I look, or even how I feel—it's about having fun and playing."

When she stopped thinking of herself as some fitness drudge, her life changed. Now there are days when she merely goes for a fifteen-minute meditative walk—and she continues to lose weight!

One big little change that can be quite effective is to keep a workout log. You can use some pages in your journal or get a separate notebook for this. It's very easy, yet incredibly effective. You write down the date and the activity you've performed. Include the length of time (for aerobics or walks) and the number of sets, reps, and amount of weight used (for weight workouts). You'll be able to track—in black and white—what you're doing, when, and how much of it. When you notice that you're working in one area for too long, you can begin to make changes that will create balance. Also, this log can serve as a motivation to keep track of what you're doing, where you're improving, and how well you're sticking to your commitment. Those who keep a workout log stay motivated longer and get better results.

Motivation Secret #4: Discover Play

Successful exercise programs are those in which participants do something they enjoy doing. Think about what you loved to do as a child. Was it skating? Jumping rope? Running on the playground? Just because you're a grown-up now doesn't mean you can no longer have fun playing. Discover what is fun for you, and doing it will be easy! (I'll help you understand more about your Natural Game in chapter 11.)

Motivation Secret #5: Magnify the Positive and Celebrate Small Victories

How many of us rejoice if we lose a half pound? Not many. Because we're focused on the *end*, not the *means*, why would we enjoy any of the steps along the way? We should. Losing a quarter pound means you're getting results and moving in the right direction. Celebrate! Your body has been waiting your whole life for you to love it. Start now. Buy yourself a fitness magazine. Stop at the flower shop and get one small rose and put it in a bud vase in your office or kitchen. Every time you see it, you'll be reminded that you're on the right track.

Remember that each of the small victories leads to the big win. Each step builds momentum. One workout feeds the next. Three minutes of abdominals today will motivate you to do three minutes and fifteen seconds tomorrow.

I once went for a period of ten years without painting, which was very self-destructive, since my painting helps me feel alive. I had a million excuses for stopping. Then my inner critic took the ball and ran with it, telling me that I had no talent anyway. I imagined that I didn't know what I wanted to paint. I told people that I didn't have the right brushes or paints. The disempowering thoughts and excuses went on and on for years, without letup. Finally, the pain of not expressing myself through my painting outweighed the power of the fears and self-doubts. I decided to take one small step for myself and buy some paints and see what happened.

The day I finally went to the paint store to buy new paints was a big day for me. I can still remember the feeling of accomplishment I had from that one small act. The next day I started out with some simple sketches. I was definitely rusty and out of sync, but I celebrated those first simple sketches. I've never appreciated my own talents more! Gradually I did something a little bigger. I painted my furniture. I painted pots. I painted the walls in my house. With the completion of each project I threw myself a mental party. Finally, I started painting on canvas again because I had allowed myself to appreciate my small victories and had not beaten myself up and gotten discouraged. The more small victories I had, the closer I got to the point where I am now. My artwork is very good, I know it is— but it would never have gotten there had I allowed myself to wallow in self-doubt or self-dislike. If I hadn't enjoyed a few small victories along the way it would have been pretty hard to stay on track.

Finally, make it a point to spend time every day talking and sharing (or writing in your journal!) about what's right with your body and your life. You'll be amazed at how soon you have more and more good to talk about. You'll be creating the new Real You.

Motivation Secret #6: Create Ritual

Ritual reinforces commitment. Try to do your journaling at the same time of day—if you can, without obsessing. Make it a healthy new ritual. Block out a certain hour or time of day that works for you and don't let anything infringe upon that small increment of time.

By incorporating these secrets of motivation into your daily routine you'll be on the right track for *life*Balance.

I've battled many of the same demons: lack of motivation, bad eating habits, even divorce.

POSITIVE THINKING ISN'T ENOUGH

You've learned the importance of removing the three-letter words (*not* and *but*) from any communications with your brain. One woman told me after doing so, "Hey, that means that I'll always think positively. Positive thinking must be what makes *life*Balance work." She was partially correct. Positive thinking plays a big role in *life*Balance, but it is only one part of the puzzle. It cannot stand alone as a way to create empowerment or happiness. Take a look at the self-help section in bookstores and you'll see any number of books on the subject. Many of today's most popular writers and thinkers tout it as a valuable tool and I agree with these experts wholeheartedly, but I think it's a small piece of the empowerment puzzle. If, as many have claimed, we need simply think ourselves happy and whole, wouldn't people be getting more out of life? Apparently not, if you look at the eternally optimistic, positive people who have bad luck and find themselves in unhappy relationships, unsatisfying jobs, and unfulfilling circumstances. What is missing when positive thinking gets us nowhere?

Thinking positively is important, but as I will continue to show you throughout this book, only when you link your mind (a positive thought) with your body (physical action) with the inner you (what you really want) will you create *life*Balance and achieve your goals.

I'm always surprised when people come up to me and say, "Gee, you're so outgoing, so confident, so together." They seem to think that I was born with a different emotional or psychological makeup from theirs. Nothing could be further from the truth. I've battled many of the same demons: lack of self-confidence, lack of motivation, bad eating habits, even divorce. The difference between someone like myself, who has won many of these battles, and others who are still fighting them may be in combining all the benefits of positive thinking with the remarkable power of the mind/body connection. Mistakenly, some confuse this inner connection with "willpower" or "positive thinking." Positive thinking and the mind/body connection are two completely different, though inter-related ball games.

WHAT POSITIVE THINKING CAN AND CANNOT DO

Positive thinking is a great habit, as study after study has proven. One study published in the *British Medical Journal* found that patients (64 percent of those studied) given positive consultations and told to expect improvements got better within two weeks compared to those (39 percent) who were given negative consultations. The power of the positive word caused dramatic improvement. But that's not always the case.

The promise of the power of positive thinking was taken too far by my friend Bill, who, like other men of his age dying of cancer, was told to visualize little Pac-Men eating the bad cancer cells in his body. Bill was a very creative person with an above-average ability to visualize anything he desired. He spent hour after hour during the last months of his life trying to visualize his diseased cells being scavenged by hungry little defenders. He believed so strongly in the power of positive thinking that he even refused medications that might have prolonged his life by months, maybe even years. Sadly, he died defending his ability to keep himself alive without any outside help. Positive thinking alone couldn't save him.

I once attended a seminar about the connection between financial health and the power of positive thinking. The seminar leader began by asking, "How many of you have ever had back pain?" Not surprisingly, almost every hand in the room shot up. (Statistics tell us that about 90 percent of us will experience back pain at some time in our lives.) At the big show of hands, the seminar leader jumped up and down excitedly, declaring, "See! That's about money. If you have back pain, it's a money issue. Because you're not using the power of the mind, your bank account and your health are suffering!" She covered her bases by punching two hot buttons at once (too much back pain and too little money) and the audience was hers from that moment on. Heck, according to her, positive thinking could solve their back problems and make them all millionaires. But we all know that all the positive thinking in the world won't add to our bank accounts—directly. It's usually positive thinking in conjunction with other activities that helps us make changes.

LifeBalance EXERCISE: "WHERE DO *YOU* RESIDE?"

There's no drawing or writing involved with this exercise. This is one you just have to think about, so put down your paper and pencil and just use your head on this one.

Here's the question: Where do you reside? Not as in, what's your address?

But as in, where is the soul, the inner you, the observer (or whatever you choose to call it) housed? Where, in your body, do *you* live? Point to the area. Go on, no one is looking, just pick up your hand and point to you.

Did you point to the head? To the stomach? Somewhere else? If you were from India or Southeast Asia, you almost certainly would have pointed to the navel or stomach area, toward what are called the body's "chakras" or power sources. Little children often point to their stomachs. Most Americans would point to their head, since that is where the brain is. Some might point to the heart. I once did this exercise with a group of women and one of them pointed to her stomach. When I asked why, she said, "That's where I can't lose weight. When I look in the mirror, I suck that in to make it look better." For Mary, her entire being is tied up in the excess pounds that have settled around her waistline.

Men point more frequently to their heads than do women, who frequently point to their hearts. Again, there's no right answer to this. It's just interesting to see where you think *you* are. Each of us resides in each and every cell of our bodies and not in one isolated location, but few people ever respond to this question by pointing to the entire body.

The biggest problem with the limiting belief that we are just a brain or just a body, and not a powerful whole, is that it stands in the way of the mind/body connection. A perfect example can be found in those who continue to believe that "mind power" or positive thinking can accomplish anything. The power of positive thinking, they claim, is all we need to reach all our goals. If that were the case, I would *never* have won a single professional bodybuilding title.

YOUR BRAIN HAS A MIND OF ITS OWN

We're backstage at my first Ms. Olympia contest. The excitement as well as the nervousness is palpable. You can cut the tension in the air with a twenty-pound weight. Dozens of perfectly proportioned women, from various countries and of varying ages, races, heights, and weights, are flexing, posing, and putting the final touches of oil on well-defined muscles and painting the last bit of makeup on determined-looking faces.

"Good luck, Rachel, you can do it," a security guard offers in an ill-concealed stage whisper. Rachel McLish does indeed look like a winner—all exotic good looks and icy-cool confidence.

"All the way, Bev, it's all yours," offers an official to Bev Francis, who smiles broadly in return.

The only noncompetitors allowed backstage are contest officials, security guards, and a makeup artist. Although this backstage contingent is small, their interest is not. They're fairly vocal when it comes to expressing their support.

They cheer on first one, then another competitor as she passes within the small confines of the backstage dressing room area. I get a fair share of positive comments from this group, but I am too immersed in my own thoughts to pay much attention to the encouragement.

One of the competitors steps up close to a mirror and stares deeply into it. I can almost hear the inner dialogue that she's engaged in: "You're the best. You can do it. You're the winner." She steps back from the mirror and as she does I notice that the other women are deep in their own thoughts, too. Many sit quietly but intensely, focused internally on some inner self-talk. Like me, most of us have had trainers, family, or friends who have stood by us during the long months leading up to this moment, telling us, "You're the best. You can do it. You're the winner." Now, however, the time has come to focus inwardly and psyche out the opposition with silence. Some of the women are doing what I call the "cover-up psyche-out"—they won't even let the others see them put on their makeup or posing suits. They're covering up every move and body part like something out of "Mission: Impossible." Others, however, like the then–title holder Carla Dunlap and Diana Dennis, remain friendly and openly encouraging to others. Still others, like Rachel, aren't covering up, but aren't friendly either. They're somewhere in between and somewhat aloof, particularly to me, the newcomer. Whatever the outward manifestations or psyche-outs are, however, you can be sure that positive thinking is being sucked into this room by the mental truckload.

Suddenly, a stage manager shouts into the room, "Showtime!" and all of the competitors draw themselves into a prearranged lineup, ready to go onstage. The onstage MC completes his final introductions and all of us take the stage to the cheers and shouts of the enthusiastic crowd. The lights get brighter as each of us steps into position on the stage for the final posedown. Within what seems like only a few seconds finalists are called out and then a hush falls on the crowd as the MC announces the name of the winner: "Cory Everson!"

Shocked, I look into the audience and see the faces of my then-husband Jeff, my mom, my dad, my sisters, and supporters like bodybuilders Rick Wayne and my friend Lynn Conkrite. I am quickly surrounded by photographers and reporters who want to capture my every pose and ask me how I did it, why I did it, and what my plans for the future are.

Even now, years later, I am asked what I was thinking during that fateful first competition for the Ms. Olympia title—the one that would catapult me to the top of women's bodybuilding. Now, removed from the immediacy of competition and the nerves and the insecurity, I can laugh as I remember my mental state. Did I, as one reporter asked, "focus like a laser on the prize"? Or, as a writer for a top fitness magazine asked, did I beat the other remarkably fit competitors through "better concentration and focus"? I cannot tell a lie: Heck *no*! I had the mental focus of a gnat during that first show—and to some degree throughout most of the shows. Want a peek at the "positive thinking" that was really going through my mind? Take a look:

As Bev Francis walked past me, I thought, "I'm too skinny."

When I saw Diana Dennis strike her first practice pose, I told myself, "There's no way I can beat her!"

After current Ms. Olympia Carla Dunlap wished me good luck, I thought, "She's so confident and so classy no one can beat her."

When I actually got a good look at the entire field, I thought, "These women *all* look so much bigger, better, and more like winners than I do!"

In fact, I spent much of my time during that competition figuring out what I would do once I was booted out of women's bodybuilding—which I was sure would happen! It was not my mental focus or the power of positive thinking that won me the Ms. Olympia title. I won through a combination of long preparation and training, family support, and just plain good luck. The Ms. Olympia contest is a tough competition because at any one time during any one year, there are thirty or so competitors on that stage who are all in unbelievable shape. I happened to be the one who, for whatever reason, the universe smiled on and said, "At this particular time, you have the best mix of muscularity, charisma, suppleness, and vitality. You get to win." I can guarantee you there were other competitors with many more positive thoughts than mine that night.

And this is where I depart from the conventional wisdom about what we call "positive thinking." I think it takes something else in addition to that to succeed, or many more of us would be winning in life and succeeding at any goal. We'd all (or many of us would) be Ms. Olympia or we'd all be lean, healthy, rich, and whatever else it is we think we need to be in order to be happy—because most of us can muster up some pretty positive thoughts from time to time.

STUMBLING BLOCKS TO POSITIVE THINKING

In life, only a few get to take home the big trophies, the titles, and the accolades. Why aren't we all succeeding in whatever we choose to do? Plenty of people (maybe you!) with incredible focus or desire *never* get what they want or reach their goals, but still there's this whole industry built upon the belief that if you only get better at thinking right, you'll realize your dreams. Self-help books, tapes, and seminars exist everywhere telling us to merely *think* ourselves thin, rich, sexy, whatever.

But if the technology is foolproof, then why doesn't it work for everyone and how do you explain an insecure, nonpositive thinker, like I was, becoming a champion? It seems that positive thinking is a little like the lottery—it works for some, but not for others.

Let's look at my example again. There I was, full of insecurities and self-doubt, accepting the Ms. Olympia title! I had little or nothing in the way of positive thinking, but I did have one thing: a belief in my ability to train harder and better than anyone else. In the gym, my training partner and I were unstoppable. She pushed me (and I her) to the limits and beyond. We loved and supported each other through four-to-five-hour workouts every day. (I know now I was way overtrained back then, but that's another chapter and another story.) No one could train with more intensity than the two of us. I knew that was where my advantage lay, so I got very good at the process leading up to the competition. I focused not on winning the goal, but on getting really good at the process that led to it. That process took me to the top.

If you've been beating yourself up about not having enough power to change, stop right now. That thinking will only leave you feeling disempowered, guilty, and defeated. If you've labeled yourself "negative" because of past failures, pick a new label. You can chant, "I see myself thinner, richer, sexier" all you want, but unless you've made an MBS connection, tying all that positive thinking together not only with your mind and body, but with the Real You, you still won't fit into your favorite old jeans or experience life as fulfilling and magical. Positive thinking only works when you follow certain guidelines.

I see serious interference with positive thinking coming from two areas. First, whenever positive thinking denies the truth, it cannot work. Here's an example.

Jeannette fixated every day on her desire to be an actress. She idolized Demi Moore and wanted to have a career like the superstar. She imagined herself at movie openings and on exotic movie locations all over the world. She visualized herself dressed in Armani at the Oscars. With every breath she took, she thought positively about this dream of hers to be a Hollywood superstar. The problem was, Jeannette had absolutely no desire to learn to act. She didn't enjoy studying lines or researching a character. What she really loved to do most was to sit quietly doing handiworks, which she then gave to others as Christmas and birthday gifts. Her knitting and sewing were what paid her bills as she began to sell her wares to small boutiques in the Los Angeles area.

Once, Jeannette landed a small part in a low-budget movie. She hated working on the set and exposing herself emotionally in the work. When the director instructed her to open up and be more free with the character she was playing, she froze and couldn't remember her lines. Still, she persisted in her belief that what she wanted more than anything was to be like Demi. To this day, she remains frustrated in her efforts. I believe she will never find happiness as an actress, since that would be a total denial of the truth: that Jeannette hates acting. She can use positive thinking all she wants on this one, it will never happen.

No amount of positive thinking will turn a one-legged man into an Olympic gold medalist in the marathon. He may do well, he may improve his performance with positive thinking, but he won't beat the top two-legged runner. The *truth* is that the world's best runner with two legs will always beat out the one-legged runner.

Likewise, if your mental efforts require that you repress your emotions, they won't work, either. If you're a caring, sensitive, person and your dream is to become the highest-paid lawyer in the business, but the cases in which you're involved require you to throw families out of their low-rent housing so that a huge corporation with a lot of money can expand their holdings, you're going to have a problem living with yourself as the big bucks roll in.

If you deny the truth and repress your emotions, positive thinking will never work. Positive thinking works when it is aligned with truth and feelings (emotions), both of which can be killed off by Negative Emotional Connectors.

Talk about negative thoughts! I thought my sister Charmaine hated me!

seven

THE TIES THAT BLIND: NEGATIVE EMOTIONAL CONNECTORS

Negative Emotional Connectors are thoughts, memories, or ideas related to something in the past that made you feel badly about yourself. They show up in the present when something reminds you of the past incident and reconnects to the bad feeling even though what's happening now is totally unrelated.

It's a rare occasion when you (or any other human being) experience what's happening around you without putting your personal spin on it, whether it's a Negative Emotional Connector or not. You live, listen, and communicate within a maelstrom of experience. Events happen all around you. Words are spoken. Stuff happens. Your mind acts as a filtration system through which all of this must pass. You interpret and translate the data you receive based on the types of mental filters you've built up through past experience, education, and sensory input.

The first set of filters through which you view the world around you is your personal frame of reference. It's "where you're coming from." This first stage of mental filtration shapes your perceptions to fit what is familiar and known to you. You use these filters to interpret information and make it fit your personal definitions so that what's happening around you becomes more understandable. Problems in communication can arise, however, because the complex world around you does not always fit into your own personal frame of reference. Objectivity is a necessary, but often missing, part of good communication. This was demonstrated to me recently in an embarrassing way.

I hadn't had a complete physical in years and had decided to do a complete battery of health tests. I did a stress test for my heart. I had my cholesterol levels checked and other blood work done for a variety of health indicators. Ever the perfectionist, I didn't stop there. I decided to book a major checkup with my gynecologist to see if my hormone levels were good and everything else was in order. I called my doctor's office and his new receptionist answered the phone. I had never met her before and we exchanged pleasantries, then I told her to book me for an exam. She asked me to spell my name for her and I did.

"Oh, Cory Everson, the athlete," she said. "Tell me, are you still cycling regularly?"

"Oh, no," I said, pleasant, but eager to correct her. "I've never cycled. I'm a weight lifter and track athlete."

"I was talking about your menstrual cycle," she explained, politely, as I, on the other end of the phone line, turned about three shades of red. My frame of reference had colored how I had listened to that conversation. Like mine, your listening filters the words and communications you receive.

Your frame of reference and mental filters can work to your advantage. Your education, upbringing, values, and intuition can protect and guide you. In fact, when you choose to ignore these good mental filters—for whatever reason—you can get into trouble. Again, I know this from personal experience.

Years ago, when I was in college, I went to Liechtenstein with the track team. I got off the plane very tired and sore. I was scheduled to run in a race later that day and couldn't imagine how as I hobbled stiffly through the airport. When I checked into the team's hotel, a local gentleman who had been talking to the concierge overheard me complaining to one of my teammates about my sore muscles. He approached me and offered his services as a masseur.

"I will loosen the muscles. You will see," he told me. His English was broken, but we finally made arrangements and a short while later I was in a barnlike building lying on a table. I was more than a little uncomfortable, lying as I was between a horse stall and what looked like a plow. Also, the table was rather makeshift and much harder than those to which I was accustomed in the States.

"Hey," I told myself, as I battled the urge to run back to my room, "it's not like I'm at a spa or anything. This must be how they do it here. Don't be a snob, Cory." The rustic atmosphere, I convinced myself, was charming.

I got even more nervous and embarrassed when the masseur asked me to remove all of my clothes. I complied, not wanting to look like an unsophisticated American—and, after all, he did give me a small sheet to cover my body. The massage was not bad.

That night at dinner after the track meet I told everyone how much better I felt because of the treatment. I described the quaint little barn and the teeny-tiny towel. My coach gave me a strange look and excused himself from the table. He returned minutes later and pulled me aside.

"I checked at the front desk, Cory," he told me. "There is no masseur. There are no spa services here. There's only the landscaping barn and the gardener who manages it."

"Guess I'm lucky he didn't want to hoe my garden," I quickly replied to hide my mortal embarrassment. My desire not to look like a rube or a snob had overruled my intuition.

Sometimes mental filters cause miscommunications that, in retrospect, are funny and harmless—as in the case of my "cycling" or "gardening" stories—but good mental filters are there for a reason and you, like I, should use them. You can rely on them in many situations.

NEGATIVE EMOTIONAL CONNECTORS: BAD MENTAL FILTERS

Another set of mental filters causes miscommunications that are not so benign, however. They cause distortions in your perceptions that can damage and destroy. These filters—which I call Negative Emotional Connectors (NECs)—can become major obstacles that prevent even the most gifted, fortunate, healthy, and lucky women from truly enjoying life. I call them Negative Emotional Connectors because they connect your life and feelings in the present to negative incidents in the past and rob you of empowerment. They undermine positive thinking.

NECs are caused by past incidents that you've experienced or interpreted as embarrassing or painful. NECs are the indelible mark left behind by such incidents. The old incidents live on as debilitating memories and leave lasting impressions that live on like mental land mines. To live a satisfying, powerful life, you have to create your own mental bomb squad and deactivate them. Once they're deactivated, they don't disappear, but become the landmarks of your soul. They were useful in getting you where you are in life today, but they no longer serve you.

Why NECs Are So Potent

Why do these old mental images pack so much power? Before you could talk or communicate with the world, it communicated to you through images. Visuals, in a sense, are your native "language." Images were connected to all that went on around you: the smells, feelings, and emotions present at any given time. Sensory information you receive today can trigger powerful memories stored away years ago. A good friend of mine feels melancholy when she tastes or smells oatmeal. After years of wondering about this emotional reaction to a bowl of complex carbohydrates, she finally realized that oatmeal reminded her of her mother, who had died years before.

When an incident causes pain or embarrassment that is deep and emotion-packed, it becomes lodged in your consciousness as an NEC and acts as a filter to unrelated experiences later on. The formative years are a time when what is *not* said can be as important as what *is* said, because of the mental image accompanying the message. The facial expressions made by significant people in our life can be incredibly potent. These and other indirect communications affect us powerfully. Things like where we are told to wash and where we are told not to touch communicate potent messages to us. Whether or not we are hugged or spanked, included in family discussions or told to shut up, contributes to our images of ourselves and others.

An NEC at Work

As you've already seen, your mind is a filter altering everything you see or hear. Prior to your making conscious judgments about anything, your subconscious has already registered a first impression, which affects how you will react, assess, or process the new information. This first impression (or mental snap judgment) renders you incapable of having a "pure" or truly objective reaction to what people say to you, how you react to them, or how you act in new situations. Each of us identifies with an "I" we have created. The "I" is how you see yourself and the world around you. But the "I" is like a magnet that attaches onto ideas and then makes you believe those ideas are facts and not just thoughts, in a process psychologists call "selfing." This "I" can lock in both positives and negatives with which you identify strongly.

Everything you've stored in your brain has a neurosignature—a combination of emotions and memory shorthand that attaches to all that you see and experience. Since we have all led very different lives and have a wide variety of events and memories, each of us has a unique mental scrapbook of neurosignatures that are called up whenever we process information or thoughts.

For example, most of us are able to sit by a roaring campfire and enjoy toasting marshmallows. Yet, we've all been burned at one time or another and we all know the feeling of pain that accompanies a burn. What enables us to tell jokes and enjoy the companionship of others while seated only a few feet from a roaring blaze? Why doesn't our fight or flight response activate, forcing us to run as fast as possible from the area of the fire? Because we haven't developed Negative Emotional Connectors to the thought of *all* fire. We know from past experience that campfires are fun, not frightening.

NECs are a by-product of selfing and neurosignatures. Unfortunately, once NECs are formed they rush to judgment before you've fully processed all the information available to you in any situation. They're so imbedded in your mind that they become truth or reality for you. You trust them and are unable to see them for what they are: soul toxins.

When an NEC is at work, your nervous system and emotions can overreact to the most simple, common events and treat them like major disasters. Your heart can get overstimulated and your immune system can become weakened. Your hormonal balance can get upset and your reactions can become inappropriate—all because you filtered something that was said or done to you through an NEC and misinterpreted the message or event.

It takes about twenty minutes for an emotional state to affect the immune system. It takes a half hour after an emotional state has ended for the immune system to return to normal. That means that if you allow an NEC to get you down, even for five minutes, you are not only shutting off the possibilities for positive results to take place, but you are negatively affecting your health and well-being for nearly an hour. Can you afford that?

I was little more than eight or nine years old when I acquired one of my most potent NECs, but its effect lasted for years.

I was on the swing set at school with my older sister Charmaine. We were eagerly trying to see who could swing the highest and fastest. Soon our efforts got the attention of some nearby schoolboys who gathered to watch us. Some of the boys stood in front of us and others watched from behind. I remember thinking to myself, "Wow! I must really be doing a great job. Look at everyone watching me!" I was very proud and pushed myself even higher and faster. I looked over at Charmaine to see how she was doing. I was horrified to see that whenever her swing went up, so did her skirt—exposing her naked butt. It was then that it hit me: we had forgotten to wear undies! Charmaine and I were tomboys who rarely wore dresses and both of us had forgotten that girls wear undies under their skirts.

I stopped swinging by diving headfirst into the sand underneath my swing and grabbed Charmaine, pulling her off her swing. I then dragged her toward home. When I told her what had happened, she merely laughed. It didn't matter to her that we had been the source of so much amusement for the boys watching us.

I like to joke that ever since that day I always double-check my underwear before I get on a swing, but the truth is that the embarrassment I suffered that day left a lasting mark that stayed with me for years. Whenever a boy (or later, a man) looked at me for any reason, I was sure that it was because something was wrong with me. I was sure my bra strap was hanging out, I had green stuff in my teeth, or I was dragging toilet paper on my shoe. It was the longest time before I could enjoy a compliment from a male without being paranoid or waiting for the punch line! Once I discovered that NEC, I got the opportunity to hear nice things being spoken to me by a member of the opposite sex and respond in ways that allowed me to feel good about myself.

The first step in deactivating NECs is recognizing that your subconscious mind is a crook that will rob you of motivation if you let it.

Emotional Sabotage

Women often tell me that I can't possibly relate to their problems since I lead such a charmed life. "Look at you," one woman told me. "You're a genetic freak with

no body fat and lots of muscle. You've never been fat a day in your life. How could you possibly know what it feels like to be unpopular or unsuccessful?" she asked. Well, I do know. As I've already shared with you, I had my share of embarrassing moments as a young girl and I truly know what it's like not to fit in. Remember, when I was a kid growing up girls were supposed to be soft and feminine and play with dolls and have tea parties. This was long before every little girl in the country fell in love with Olga Korbut and decided to become a gymnast. It hasn't always been hip and trendy for women to be hard as a rock, particularly not during my childhood years, when girls who participated in sports were considered not "girlie." I've told you how I was nicknamed "Frog Legs," and so wore baggy pants to hide my muscular legs. To further cover up my insecurities about not being feminine enough I started a club with a couple of girlfriends who all swore never to wear makeup, dresses, nylons, or hairdos. We called ourselves the Anti-Femme Society. I was eventually kicked out of the club when I made the cheerleading squad. My love of athletics sabotaged me even with the Anti-Femmes. (I told singer Janet Jackson about this club a few years ago and she wanted to know if she could still join! I guess many people in the public eye know what it's like to have been an outcast at some point in life.)

Unwanted, negative attention to your body can appear in many different situations and forms—often when you least expect or deserve it.

When I was in the sixth grade I stood five feet, six inches tall and weighed 120 pounds. I guess you could say my athletic development started early. By that time I was already involved in a variety of sports, but softball was not one of them. One day my sister Cameo and I went with Mom to McDonald's. We were wearing some rummage sale T-shirts Mom had gotten us because they were cheap (isn't that what rummage sales are for?) and durable. We ordered our twenty-five-cent hamburgers, fries, and chocolate shakes. When the order was ready the counter boy told us the food was "on the house." When we asked him why, he said, "Hey, I'm in Little League too. We guys gotta stick together!" I nearly cried, but didn't, because I didn't want Mom to know how much the remark hurt. Sure, I'd always wanted to run, play, and compete like a boy, but I didn't want to look like one!

Later that same year I learned about yet another form of abuse meted out to those who are different. I was taller, stronger, and faster than almost any of the kids in school, including the boys. In fact, that year I set the record (for boys or girls) in the fifty-yard dash. The day of the race I was excited. I knew I had a good shot at winning and I was proud of my athletic abilities. When I crossed the finish line ahead of the other girls I was ecstatic. My family was there, cheering and celebrating. Many of my school chums were happy for me, too. Surprisingly, quite a few of them were not. In fact, several of the more competitive girls and several of the boys who competed in track were there to put a damper on my accomplishment.

I'll never forget the moment when my classmate Ralph Hartel, who had held the record up till that point, walked up to me and gut-punched me for besting him. I never forgot that; I did, however, get over it—in time.

The emotional impact of the Hartel incident surfaced again years later when I was a teenager and an Olympic track coach approached my parents. He wanted to train me for the Olympics and believed I had a real shot not just at competing, but at winning a medal. My school coaches agreed. They encouraged me to train and try to make the Olympic team. I, however, had a very different opinion of my chances and was sure that everyone was making a big mistake. I didn't feel confident about my abilities and turned a deaf ear on all of the support and encouragement around me. I never accepted that coach's offer to help try to mold me into an Olympian. To this day, I wonder what really frightened me away from the coach's offer. Did I truly doubt my talents or did I secretly fear being ostracized by my fellow classmates? Ralph Hartel was nowhere around but the memory of that blow to my gut (and self-esteem) certainly was. How might I have fared had I taken the coaching offer? I'll never know. The only thing that stood between me and that world-class competition, I am now convinced, was the space between my ears.

Later, when I was preparing for my first bodybuilding show, I almost dropped out. Even though I had my posing routine down cold, I was sure that I would forget it and be laughed off the stage. My inherent shyness, coupled with this irrational fear of being made fun of or laughed at, almost robbed me of my first chance to compete in a sport I would later dominate. Luckily, I realized my fears were irrational and I went to work to unearth the NECs that were disempowering me. My mental circuitry was preventing me from doing my very best. I can now recognize NECs for what they are—emotional saboteurs—and I've developed ways to override them and create a positive mind-set, while still allowing myself full range of emotion. You can't erase old memories, but you can learn how to put them in perspective.

The second step in deactivating NECs is to dig up their roots.

*Life*Balance JOURNAL EXERCISE: "BOY, WAS MY FACE RED!"

Write down five events during childhood which really embarrassed you. They might have happened on the playground, like my swingset episode, or they may have taken place in your neighborhood or schoolroom. Be sure to write down the feelings these events caused you: shame, fear, embarrassment, sadness. Think back to when you were as young as three or four years old. Most people find that their first NEC happened at about that time. Continue to search your memory for subsequent events. Adolescence is also a time ripe with opportunity for the creation of NECs. Try to remember times from childhood to the present when your feelings and self-esteem felt—or were—violated. The memories will range from seemingly harmless to obviously hurtful. Sharon, a seminar participant, remembered the day, at age thirteen, when she was demoted in ballet class because her breasts had developed—seemingly overnight! For years she battled weight problems based around that one NEC. Sharon's NEC is somewhat obvious. Marcella, on the other hand, remembers a day when she was making cookies with her mother. When Marcella dropped some cookie dough on the floor, her mom slapped her hand and scolded her. We've all had things like that happen to us in childhood, right? Well, that memory stands out again and again in Marcella's mind, so I told her to write it down and begin to study it for meaning. Eventually, she put the pieces of the puzzle together and realized that she had built up a belief about herself that she was incompetent—not just at cooking, but at virtually anything she ever tried—all because of that cookie-baking incident. Her self-esteem suffered for nearly thirty years because of the potency of an NEC.

Study your list. It contains some of your NECs. You'll discover more of them as time goes on and you learn to identify them more easily. From time to time take a look at this list and see if any current embarrassment, shame, or feelings of being "less than" might be connected to these early memories. Those seemingly long-ago memories are what may be preventing you from success today. Flush them out into the cold, harsh light of day and expose them for the bad mental filters they are. Only after you've illuminated them can you begin to eradicate them. Bring old memories into the light of day, then ask yourself, "Does this contribute to my health or to my stress? Where did I learn it? Is it logical? Is it true today?" If not, it's an NEC.

The third step in deactivating NECs is to learn to recognize when they're at work.

Peel Away the NEC Layers

The mind is like an onion, with layers and layers of emotions. When you peel away all the layers of memories, thoughts, information, and perceptions, you get to the core—where the Real You resides. When you become more proficient at recognizing and deactivating NECs, you'll begin to have more freedom and empowerment in your life—you'll act in accordance with the Real You and not the powerless infant, child, or adolescent trapped in the NEC.

When I was growing up, I always believed that my older sister Charmaine hated me. When she ignored me or treated me in a curt manner, I was sure it was because I, her baby sister, disgusted her. Often all it took was a look from her to send me into a tailspin of doubt and depression about myself. Sometimes she did things that, although it was typical sibling stuff, made me think she really detested me. (Probably like the stuff I did to Cameo, including holding her down while I let spit drool from my mouth until just before it landed on her face—then sucking it back up. Thanks for forgiving me, Cameo!)

I'll never forget the day Cameo and I had to ride our bikes down Riverwoods Road in our hometown—wearing only wigs and rubber work boots. Charmaine had told us we were being initiated into a club she had just founded. All we had to do was take the naked ride and return to another location where we would find the clubhouse. Of course, there was no club and there was no clubhouse. Even now, when I remember the way I felt as I rode up to the spot where the clubhouse was supposed to be, I get tears in my eyes. I looked up to Charmaine and her opinion meant more to me than anything, so I was always eager to do whatever it would take to make her love me. That I could never get her to be demonstrative toward me was a constant hurt for me as a little girl. It detracted from my self-esteem even after I left home and went out into the world.

Years later we sat down to have a long sisterly talk and she told me that she had not hated me at all. I did not disgust her in the least. In fact, she had been jealous of me throughout our childhood! My straight A's and athletic awards made her green with envy. Her own self-doubt, not a dislike of her baby sister, had been the reason behind many of her actions when we were kids. I had built up negative mental layers of low self-worth when in reality Charmaine's actions had nothing to do with me. She was busy creating her own NECs about me!

Another experience that hurt me deeply happened during my first Ms. Olympia competition—the one I described earlier. I thought that Rachel McLish really disliked me. She was very cold and distant and not friendly at all. I took it very personally—she was, after all, practically my idol—and I thought that her behavior was because she felt I was a loser and didn't belong in any contest with her. (Even though I won it!) Her seeming dislike of me really ate away at my self-esteem and made me feel totally out of place. I was unable to have much fun or enjoyment because an old NEC had been activated. Once again, I felt like I was "different" and didn't belong. That perception flavored my whole experience of that first show and dictated how I felt and acted. Now, when I look back, I realize that she was probably just being territorial and protective of her domain—women's bodybuilding, of which she was the queen at that time. Or maybe competing was easier for her if she distanced herself from the other competitors. Who knows? It's not likely that she harbored any ill feelings toward me, since she didn't know enough about me to form an opinion—negative or otherwise. But my NEC wanted me to believe that I was not good enough.

Turning Off NECs Doesn't Mean Shutting Down Emotions

At the end of one week of working on her NECs, a woman told me, "I don't feel any better, Cory, really I don't." She looked defeated and sad rather than powerful, I have to admit.

"I started to notice times when I felt lousy," she continued, "and looked to see if my feelings were about what was going on right then or if they were tied to some past experience. Then, I tried to shut the feelings down. It was really hard, though, when I heard about a family friend's death, because I wanted to cry—but I didn't let myself. I didn't want to let the bad feelings in," she explained.

I stopped her right there and cautioned her not to use NECs as a reason to become a nonfeeling robot. I explained that finding NECs and their roots is a tool for choosing how to react more powerfully to life, rather than allowing yourself to be run by your subconscious. It's not, I carefully pointed out, a technology to snuff out emotions. Feeling saddened by a friend's death is appropriate. What's not appropriate (or empowering) is getting plugged in or overreacting when someone says something completely harmless that reminds you of a time when you were a helpless infant.

Appropriate Emotions: Positive Emotional Connectors

Feeling emotions is an important part of being human and growing. For example, sadness and joy are healthy emotions and should be expressed. The state of joy is equal to the state of sadness as far as the immune response is concerned. Sadness can be as healthy for humans as great joy. We must allow ourselves to experience the full gamut of human emotions. What you don't want to do is internalize negative feelings about yourself and then incorrectly interpret input around you. Cry if your cat dies, but ignore the insensitive saleslady who tells you large-size women shouldn't wear bright clothing that calls attention to themselves.

It's unhealthy to repress emotions. Better to feel anger, even appropriate rage, and express it than to sit on your feelings and allow them to congeal into depression or illness. Depression is an inability to feel emotions or respond to the environment authentically. Think of depression as a gear in your mental engine which forces the system not just to shut down, but to grind against itself and reverse directions. Your car wouldn't run for very long in that gear and neither can your mind.

The fourth step in deactivating NECs is to rule your mental state, rather than letting it rule you.

Look At Yourself in a New Light

Allison was a very disciplined athlete for her entire life—until that fateful day when she had the accident that broke her neck.

"I hated myself so much of the time after the wreck," she admits. "It's been very hard."

Allison went into counseling and learned that she had one huge option available to her which would make all the difference in the world for her emotional survival. That option was how she now chose to view the accident. She could choose to look at it as a permanent obstacle or she could begin to see it as a unique, though challenging, opportunity. She realized that the universe often moves us in new directions for good reasons, which are not always immediately apparent. Allison began to earnestly seek the meaning behind what had happened to her. Since she was no longer able to pursue her favorite sports, she looked for different ways to occupy her mind and her time. She became a voracious reader. She began to draw and soon discovered she had a real gift for drawing. Today, she finds it difficult to imagine her former life—devoid as it was of the artistic expression that currently brings her tremendous joy.

> The grass isn't greener on the other side of the hill—the people over there are just doing a better job of watering theirs!

There's a fitness instructor at a famous health spa who got shot by an ex-boyfriend and lost the use of one of her arms. Instead of bemoaning the physical loss, she went right back to work and learned how to teach great classes with the one arm. She discovered that she could still motivate and educate and her enthusiasm wasn't diminished at all! She continues to teach the same aerobics classes she did before the incident.

The fifth step in deactivating NECs is to practice Mental Trash Compacting.

Discovering NECs and recognizing when they're running your life are important steps toward empowerment and *life*Balance. But wouldn't it be great if they showed up less and less frequently? And wouldn't it be great if, when they did show up, they had lost some of their potency? They can with Mental Trash Compacting. This is such an important step that it gets the next chapter all to itself.

TAKE CONTROL WITH MENTAL TRASH COMPACTING

Wouldn't it be great if you could take all your negative past experiences, unhappy memories, and disappointments, throw them into a big blender, grind them up, and render them powerless? With Mental Trash Compacting you can do just that! Mental Trash Compacting is a set of techniques for disconnecting NECs so that you can spend more time and energy being productive and positive. It's a series of mental exercises that disconnect NECs from your emotional supply line so that they no longer provide a direct link from your past to the present. Mental Trash Compacting allows you to get back in the driver's seat of life and take control—maybe for the first time ever!

"Control yourself," we say to ourselves and others. "I felt so out of control," we say when we fail to take charge of our own life for whatever reason. "She's a control freak" is how we describe someone who takes command and gets things done in her own time and in her own way. Control can be a way to steer ourselves in either good or bad directions.

The need to be in control is a big one for most of us. Having control can improve the quality of life; not having any can make life stagnant and scary. Statistics tell us that planes are safer than cars, yet far more people fear flying than fear driving. That's because when you fly you have to put your faith in the abilities of the pilot, but when you're behind the wheel of a car, you're personally in control. When you believe you're in control, if you're like most people, you feel safer. When you feel powerless and out of control you stay trapped in the same old driver's seat when you'd be better off flying to new heights. NECs can stop you from soaring

Don't let NECs score a knockout! Fight back with Mental Trash Compacting.

toward your potential. With Mental Trash Compacting you're no longer run by emotions from the past and you can allow your life to take flight and soar!

THE POWER OF CONTROL

A friend of mine was in the hospital not long ago recuperating from abdominal surgery. She was in a great deal of pain after having a noncancerous fibroid tumor removed. She was given powerful pain medication to help her get through the first couple of days after surgery. At first, the doctors administered the drug at regular intervals of about fifteen minutes apart. The pain was so intense that my friend was finding each fifteen-minute stretch interminable as she was anxiously awaited each dose.

After about twelve hours of administering the painkiller to her, the doctors gave my friend a control button, which allowed her to control her own dosage. She was allowed to push the button up to once every ten minutes to release medication into her system. Once she was given the control button, my friend found that she was able to lengthen the interval—to only about once every twenty minutes or so—and not be in excruciating pain. The doctors explained to her that self-regulation of medication worked because the sense of control provides patients a better ability to deal with pain. The more in control the patient feels, the less pain he or she experiences!

There is a negative side to control. When people beat themselves up about mistakes or failures in the past, and blame themselves for losing control or misusing it, then control becomes just one more way for them to beat themselves up.

"It could have been done perfectly, but I screwed up. I was in control and I failed" is what perfectionists (usually control freaks) seem to say. Perfectionists' "total control" beliefs are disempowering. Learn to distinguish between empowering control beliefs like, "I can change" or "I can improve" and negative control beliefs like, "I have to control everyone and everything around me or I'll never get what I want" or "I have to be in total control."

Control freaks are really the opposite of what they appear to be. They suffer from feelings of helplessness—not personal power—and are fearful and insecure rather than confident. Empowering control beliefs, not total control beliefs, teach us that some factors are outside of our control. If something isn't working out the way you wanted it to or thought it should, you have to know when to accept it for what it is. Other things are within our control. Empowerment comes when we learn to work on those things we can change and accept those we can't. We learn when to *push* and when to *pull*—and when to do neither.

THINKING EQUALS FEELING

Increasingly, the psychological and physical sciences are communicating with each other as they develop the new mind/body science. What has spurred them on in their studies is the discovery that neuropeptides, cells formerly believed to inhabit only the brain, are found throughout the entire body, which means that your mind can be found in every cell of your body, not just in the space between your ears!

The mind/body connection begins at the cellular level. Your cells have receptors that act as mini satellite dishes, receiving messages and instructions like "Eat food!" "You're thirsty, drink water!" and the like. These messages, involving all sorts of body activities, happen constantly in a dynamic and ever-changing fashion.

Emotions are also an important link between the body and the mind. Blushing is a perfect example of your emotions playing a role in physical reactions in the body: you probably know what it's like to be so embarrassed (a feeling originating in the mind) that your face gets flushed and red (a bodily reaction). When you begin to practice Mental Trash Compacting you begin to rid your mind of the emotional connections that affect your emotions and your health.

If your mind is full of negative thoughts and feelings (NECs in particular!), do you think you can send out quality programming to the cellular satellite receptors all over your body? If you think of the mind as the TV studio from which you send out your "shows," wouldn't you, as "program director," prefer to schedule award-winning shows than B movies? One of the first things you might consider, as the executive in charge of programs, is to get rid of the old programs that are no longer timely. Mental Trash Compacting enables you to do so. The old emotional baggage isn't eradicated, because your memories can never be fully erased, even though many people waste good time and effort trying to do so. You can't eradicate the past, as though it didn't happen and as though you can simply forget unhappy experiences. What you can do, with some of the exercises I'll explain here, is learn ways to create a powerful here and now—and leave the past where it belongs: in the past! Mental Trash Compacting renders the past powerless over the present. It's good mental housecleaning.

Before you can practice Mental Trash Compacting, you must identify NECs and bring them into the cold, hard, light of day, as you learned in the previous chapter. Next, it becomes time to crush the mental crud with the exercises described later in this chapter, and finally, you'll replace NECs with powerful new mental imagery. (We'll learn more about this process, called Power Connectors, in the next chapter.) Mental Trash Compacting requires that you recognize NECs, release the emotional charge they carry, and renovate your thinking.

CLEAN OUT YOUR MENTAL CLOSET

I was working on a sculpture once which wasn't going well. I didn't know what was wrong, just that I wasn't enjoying the work or getting the result I wanted. Finally, at the end of my rope, I dismantled the whole piece and started over from scratch.

It was emotionally painful at first—I had to let go of weeks of work and energy. I had to face frustrating, uninspired days. Finally it worked, however, and I sculpted a beautiful piece I call *The Skier.* By recognizing that I was at a creative stalemate and releasing my attachment to how I thought the piece should be, I was able to generate a work that was not only different from, but better than my original vision.

The job of specialists who offer their services as wardrobe consultants is to take a look in your closet and see which items of clothing work for you and which don't. They try to make what you already own work in a stylish, fashionable way, but they don't hesitate to throw out what doesn't. They create a whole "new" wardrobe by reorganizing what you already have, getting rid of what doesn't work for you anymore, and adding a few completely new fashion staples here and there to complete an entirely different "look" for you. That's exactly what you have to do for your mental closet: keep what works, lose what doesn't, and then add in some valuable new material to create a difference.

Before we move on to the Mental Trash Compacting exercises, I want to make an important distinction about emotions. When people hear about this process, they often confuse it with stuffing down or shutting out emotions. That's *not* what Mental Trash Compacting is about. Your emotions can be valuable and you must honor them.

Anger and Other Emotions: Keep What Works, Throw Out What Doesn't

There are few things as cute as a mother dog with her litter. That sweet image changes dramatically if you try to approach the mother while she's feeding her puppies. The minute you come near, her demeanor changes instantly and she begins to growl and threaten you off. This behavior comes instinctually when she senses a threat to her pups in their vulnerable, infant stage.

The mother dog's apparently angry behavior is appropriate—without it, the pups might not survive. If anyone trained her to stop her feelings of protectiveness they would be doing both her and the pups a disservice. Yet many of us consider such a display of emotion nasty, inappropriate, and destructive: something to be avoided or repressed. Many even have the crazy notion that healthy, well-adjusted individuals should ignore or stuff their emotions. However, pent-up emotions have a way of surfacing—as depression, illness, or self-destructive behavior.

Emotions can be helpful indicators of how you're dealing with what's going on in your life and should be experienced fully if you are to become a whole individual. With *life*Balance, you can create an environment in which the full range of emotions (in particular, love, happiness, joy, and serenity) can be expressed. You can acknowledge and accept anger, sadness, and fear. Mental Trash Compacting allows you to experience authentic emotions (about what's going on now) distinct from antique emotions (about what happened in the past).

Don't Be a Robot

Your mind determines what you're going to do, say, and feel each and every day. Unless you make a conscious effort otherwise, your buttons will get pushed and your NECs will take over without your even knowing it, putting their spin on your life. You lose your power over whatever positive thoughts you had or whatever plans you might have made, and you become a robot being run by the past.

Your brain is a very literal contraption. It cannot distinguish between what's happening on the outside (external reality) and what's going on internally. I read once that a profit record had been set back in the 1960s during screenings of the movie *Lawrence of Arabia.* The long, hot desert scenes had driven theater-goers to the concession stands to buy a record amount of cool, refreshing beverages. How many of us have cried during a sad movie? These reactions are examples of how your body responds physically to images, thoughts, and emotions. You need to capitalize on the body's ability to respond to mental thoughts and train it to do so in a positive way, but you cannot if NECs exist.

LifeBalance PARTNER EXERCISE: "WHEN YOU THINK, YOU CREATE"

(This will only work if you are able to lift your partner at least an inch off the floor.) Have your partner stand with her feet hip-width apart and her arms hanging slightly out at the sides. Now, slip your arms under your partner's armpits and lift her off the ground. Notice the effort it takes.

Next, have your partner begin to visualize herself as extremely heavy and solid. She should imagine that she has long, heavy legs that reach deep into the ground and a muscular, leaden body that weighs so much it is beyond human comprehension. Now, try to lift your partner again. Let your partner try to lift you both ways.

Most people report that their partner's visualization actually made them harder to lift. That tells us much about the power of our thoughts to affect the body. While the heavier "feeling" may not register on a scale of any kind, it certainly does register in your mind and your experience of yourself. And, it extends to others' perceptions of you as well.

LifeBalance PARTNER EXERCISE: "FEEL THE ENERGY"

Stand about a foot or so apart. Both of you hold your arms in front of you, slightly bent, with your right palms face down and your left palms face up. Your left hand is below your partner's right hand and your right above her left.

Relax your body. Close your eyes and get centered with your breath. See if you can feel the energy radiating from your partner. One of you should call out hand commands like "Side to side" or "Up and down" and both should follow the direction given, moving your hands slightly side to side or up and down.

Notice the feelings you have in each hand. Is one more sensitive than the other? Does one hand sense the partner's hand more strongly than the other does?

Most people will sense feelings more in one hand than in the other. The left hand corresponds to the right side of the brain and the right hand with the left side of the brain. Those who feel the most energy in their left hand are usually right-brain people: intuitive, receptive, artistic. Those who feel most in the right hand are usually left-brain people: verbal and mathematical.

Now, stand with your arms slightly bent in front of you, palms facing your partner's palms with your fingers toward the ceiling. Slowly begin to step apart. Think of energy beams joining your palms to those of your partner. Keep the connection between the imaginary beams, but continue to step farther apart until you can no longer feel the energy. Most people will report that they felt heat in their palms during this exercise. Yet, as they stepped farther apart, it's unlikely that they could have continued to feel *body* heat. This sensation of heat, I think, is proof of energy that exists outside our realm of thinking. Science has proven that we have energy fields all around us and that we, like everything else in the world, are made of energy. Powerful energies exist which have yet to be categorized and we should strive to be in harmony with these powers, our life, our world, and others. To do so, we need balance and clarity—and little of either is available to those who don't consciously deal with NECs.

Get Rid of the Garbage

NECs aren't the only mental and emotional obstacles we have to battle. According to a recent article, a Harvard University researcher estimated that the typical employee in this country works 163 hours more per year than he did twenty years ago. This researcher figured that the average working mom spends seventy-six to eighty-nine hours per week handling her job, her household duties, and her mothering chores. If you factor in the amount of time we all spend with responsibilities like those listed, as well as that spent on self-judgments, old scripts, and memories from the past (as well as plans for the future), it's no wonder many of us are walking around in a state of burnout and emotional overload. Many of us have become, as mental health professionals refer to us, "overfunctioning." We've sold ourselves a bill of goods about having to do it all, be it all, have it all. Our brains, as well as our to-do lists, are filled to overflowing with a laundry list of things that "have to be done" every day. We allow a lot of mental trash other than NECs to build up, because we're busy putting out fires or we simply haven't been taught any alternatives. When you haven't done enough mental housecleaning, you may turn to using drugs, buying or doing more, trying to change other people, beating yourself up, and other distractions.

An overburdened mind can no longer see the beautiful scope of life. It truly cannot see the forest for the trees. You can take exciting journeys once you clean out your mind and provide mental space for the new you.

MENTAL TRASH COMPACTING EXERCISES

Ready to set up a new mental household? These first two exercises will start you on your way.

LifeBalance EXERCISE: "PUT A SOCK ON IT!"

Put your negative beliefs about yourself, your life, your future, on paper. Write them down and put the piece(s) of paper in a sock. For an entire day, carry the paper-packed sock around with you on your wrist. Let it hang there, in the way, at work, home, or wherever. No matter how much it gets in the way, work around it. Deal with it. At the end of the day take off the sock, remove the pieces of paper—and burn them!

LifeBalance EXERCISE: "TAKE A MEETING!"

Take a meeting with your body. Sit down and imagine that millions of cells within you all have human features. They are like little cell-people. Explain to them why you don't take proper care of them. For example, the liver needs to know why you're drinking things that make it sick. Tell it why. Give it the reasons. The lungs need to know why they can't get enough air. Tell them why you smoke, or don't exercise, or whatever. The stomach cells need to know why they need little ladders to avoid the fat that floats all around them. Tell them straight out why you continue to inundate them with fat. The muscles and tendons need to know why they get so little use each month (or why they get overused through compulsive exercise!). Come clean and confess. (Like they say, it's good for the soul.)

Next, negotiate with these cell-people team members. Tell them what you plan to do differently. Let them know that you understand that unless things change they'll prepare for a strike!

What Goes in the Compactor First

Enabling stories are the first items to go into your Mental Trash Compactor. After all, why keep them around when all they do is allow you to stay stuck? If you're not sure what an enabling story is, here are a few examples of how they usually begin:

"I'll start my program when I feel better. . . ."

"I had a bad childhood; I have to be excused if I'm not perfect. . . ."

"You don't understand, I've had a rough life. . . ."

Enabling stories begin with an explanation of some sort, but in reality they are nothing more than crutches. Some people rely on them for years—even a lifetime—to prevent them from getting on with life. Rid your mental inventory of anything resembling an enabling story.

Mental Trash Compacting Technique #1: Into the Compactor!

Imagine a little red devil lives in your brain. This nasty little guy is your worst enemy because he likes to remind you of all the negative things that have happened or the past mistakes you've made or the whatevers that keep you from succeeding. He just loves to come up with excuses for you to abandon your workout program or diet. He usually lies in wait until just the right moment and then he sneaks up on you when you've finally gotten into the gym or are thinking about taking a long walk. You've heard his voice a million times. You sometimes mistake it for the voice of reason or moderation.

"It's too chilly to go walking outside right now—wait until it gets a little warmer," he's told you early in the morning. "Didn't you just eat? Better wait a few hours for your food to digest," he cautions you as you begin to fill your gym bag with workout clothes. He masquerades as a good friend who cares for and looks out for you, but don't let him fool you.

The next time he shows up, here's how I suggest you deal with him. Take a walk around the block and talk to him. Ask him why he's trying to sabotage you. Tell him he's a lazy little guy and you won't listen to his input anymore. He doesn't want you to succeed because he's unhappy and he wants you to be unhappy too. As you walk (or ride the bike or run on the treadmill) try to reason with him. Then, when he refuses to shut up—and he probably will refuse—imagine that he looks like a horrid, lazy, miserable little guy. Next imagine walking up to him, towering over him, and see yourself as you toss him into a Mental Trash Compacting machine. Your compactor can look like anything you want. Mine is like a big gargoyle with a huge mouth and sharp, gnarly teeth. Create a mental picture of your own Mental Trash Compactor and use it whenever you need it. You may have to dump the little guy, and others like him, into the compactor on a daily basis. Don't be afraid to use your Mental Trash Compactor. It won't wear out, but it will eventually weed out the little red devils of disempowerment in your mind. With time you'll find that you may even begin to laugh at the negative, demotivating thoughts and excuses that show up to slow you down.

Kim is a perfect example of a woman who learned the value of Mental Trash Compacting as a form of empowering control. When a health crisis forced her to quit her job, she was thrown for a loop. Depressed, unable to continue in her job, and in fairly constant pain, she saw her problems as insurmountable. Day after day she stayed at home, miserable and discouraged. She convinced herself she was alone with the problem and she cut herself off from her husband and her friends.

Finally, her husband realized what she was doing. He could no longer bear to see her in such distress and told her, "No, this is not just your problem. Our marriage is at stake. This is our problem. We'll deal with this together." He pushed through her emotional resistance to being in partnership with him and, almost immediately, she got better. Nothing had changed except Kim's mind. Her husband and friends had always been there; she just couldn't allow them in. Once she'd thrown out (with her loving husband's help) the mental garbage about having to go it alone, she created the mental space to accept the love and support that had always been there for her.

Mental Trash Compacting Technique #2: Sandwiching

It's often impossible to stop the inner critic from going on and on about just about anything. If you've used the first technique and are still having problems with negative thoughts, then try this: Sandwich each bad thought with two good ones. For example, if you missed a workout for whatever reason and the little devil in your head keeps telling you something like, "You can't do anything right, you've blown it now!" mentally place that thought between two good ones like, "I worked out yesterday [or a week ago]" and "I'll train even smarter tomorrow." If you're beating yourself up because you stuck to a healthy eating plan for two meals and then ate too much fat at the third meal, place the self-criticism between two good thoughts like "I did really well for two meals today" and "It's better to eat right for two of three meals than for none at all." Position one negative between two layers of good, and eventually you'll compress, if not compact, the negativity.

Mental Trash Compacting Technique #3: Appreciate the Small Victories

If you're having a difficult time throwing the negative thoughts into your Mental Trash Compactor, don't give up. When sandwiching a negative between two positives is difficult, it's usually because a perfectionist or a pessimist in you is having a hard time even thinking a positive thought. When that is the case, this third technique can be helpful for creating positive layers with which you can surround a negative.

Begin to think that, as the old saying goes, your glass is half full instead of half empty. That will give you the positive layers for mental sandwiching. Let's say you've cheated on your diet and eaten a piece of cake at dinner. The piece you ate, however, was smaller than any you formerly would have cheated with. That's a positive! Use it. Eating a small slice of cake when you really wanted a big piece is a victory. Congratulate yourself.

A short, brisk walk is better than none at all, particularly if you were considering skipping the walk completely. Doing a quick, fifteen-minute weight workout is better than none at all. I showed you how to reward the small victories previously. Now use them as positives to overwhelm the negatives.

Mental Trash Compacting Technique #4: Make the Not-So-Great Great

A very good friend of mine, the great fitness star Gin Miller, said something that I'll never forget. She said, "If you have a big butt, then say, 'I'm gonna have the best big butt I can.'" I love that attitude! It's such a great way of looking at things and a useful way to crush negativity and mental trash.

Once I realized that my froggy legs weren't going anywhere, I decided to make them the best froggy legs ever!

For those with genetics that no amount of training or dieting will change, this is a particularly useful Mental Trash Compacting technique. Take me, for example. Once I realized that my genetics weren't going to change, I determined to make my froggy legs the best froggy legs they could possibly be. I did, and I've got a shelf loaded with trophies to prove it!

When a physical trait causes you pain or embarrassment, compact the mental garbage by finding the good that is underneath the surface. Instead of obsessing about your bountiful butt think about how frustrating it would be to try to build curves into a flat behind. Rather than complain to yourself about a flat chest think about how much sportier it looks in a jogbra or halter top and how much less sagging you'll experience due to time and gravity.

If you've encountered a lot of spiritual and emotional roadblocks during childhood or later in your life, don't build a library of enabling stories about your background. Think about how much stronger your experiences have made you and how much better equipped you are to deal with many of life's inevitable issues. You're probably stronger and more eager to look for the good in life than you would have been had you led a storybook life.

One big difference between successful and unsuccessful people is that the successful ones recognize opportunity and then take action. Taking action with Mental Trash Compacting is a huge step in the right direction. When you've mentally cleaned house and created healthy space, you've got room for Power Connectors.

nine

POWER CONNECTORS

As you've seen, NECs create a disempowering mental environment. When they're present and operating full speed ahead, your mind becomes a bad neighborhood for you to hang out in. You can lose sight of anything positive and often don't even realize how many negative words or feelings you're creating (and believing!) about yourself. Power Connectors, on the other hand, are positive thoughts and feelings about yourself, which ground you firmly in the present and connect you to the powerful real you, not only here and now but into the future.

DETONATE DOWNTIME WITH DISAPPEARING CRUTCHES

When you wake up in the morning do you look in the mirror and say, "Oh, baby, you are beautiful!"? Probably not. Many women beat themselves up constantly with negative thoughts like, "I have fat thighs," or, "My nose is too crooked." They start the abuse machine the minute they wake up and catch sight of themselves in the mirror. I once watched a stunning woman laughing happily at a party. Then she caught sight of herself in a hallway mirror. Her whole mood changed as she stopped to look at herself in the mirror. She stopped laughing. Later, I asked her what had happened.

"I hate my nose," she told me. "When I laugh it appears even bigger and I look really grotesque." This woman was a tall blonde with a beautiful, athletic body. When most people looked at her all they saw were long legs and flashing green eyes. She, on the other hand, couldn't get past her aquiline nose, which was actually quite distinctive and attractive. She was unable to enjoy her many

Until I learned to use Power Connectors, my life was out of control.
I had low self-esteem and was a slave to my own life. Now, I like who I am.

great physical attributes because her nose didn't fit her idea of what was pretty.

I knew another woman who was healthy and vibrant on the outside—radiating good health and vitality. On the inside, it was quite a different matter. She had low self-esteem, felt insecure, and believed herself incapable of ever enjoying life. She felt completely enslaved by the circumstances of her busy life and depended totally on those around her—her manager, her agent, her husband, her family— for validation and feelings of self-worth. When she was alone—which wasn't all that often, since she always surrounded herself with these people—she realized just how out of control her life was.

When I travel the world I meet many insecure women like the lonely one described above. These women, whether they're in Russia, California, or Japan, have the same self-doubts. Many times it is self-perpetuated. Others have been pushed into the pit of low self-worth by mental or physical abuse from significant others. Whatever the cause, many of these women have given up on caring for their bodies and have little hope of ever achieving self-esteem. I can relate to their insecurities because I've felt them myself. In fact, I'm the woman in the example above. Luckily, I learned how to mold myself into a happier, more self-loving person. But it didn't happen overnight. With time and work, I've learned to like what I see in the mirror in the morning. You can, too.

Wouldn't it be fun to wake up every day and see a goddess in the mirror? It's possible! Your belief system creates your reality: if you believe you're OK, you will be, and if you believe you're not OK, then you won't be. You create "OK" or "not OK" in your life with every waking thought. What you're thinking as you drive your car, do the laundry, take out the trash, or shop for groceries is creating who you are today and who you'll be tomorrow. You're thinking powerful thoughts all the time, but what percentage of them are positive and what percentage negative?

Once you've disconnected NECs and provided space with Mental Trash Compacting, you're ready to build a bridge to your powerful new future with Power Connectors.

POWER CONNECTORS

A Power Connector is a thought or phrase that can motivate, encourage, inspire, and empower you. It can be an affirmation, a memory or reminder of your own personal capability (a time when you achieved something through your own power), or it can be a statement that counters or nullifies something negative someone has told you about yourself. Or that you have said about yourself!

When you use Power Connectors you don't deny the realities of your life or turn into a Pollyanna. Power Connectors replace NECs to act as a better mental filter and bolster your feelings of self-acceptance and self-esteem. With Power Connectors, rather than focusing on what you don't like about yourself, you begin to focus on the things you do like and create new, empowering ideas about yourself.

Power Connectors enable you to take control over your well-being, your immune system, your energy level, your ability to feel optimistic and enthusiastic about life, and your self-image. They give you a hands-on role in the creation of who it is you're going to be tomorrow, the next day, and the next. You can begin to create your life just like an artist creating life on a canvas.

Power Connectors cause a shift in consciousness that allows you to enjoy your body and no longer be in an adversarial relationship with it. I discovered this early on in my bodybuilding career. When I first started training, my mind was scattered. I had heard from other bodybuilders that it helped to visualize the muscle being worked in the mind's eye. Before and during training, I developed the habit of closing my eyes and imagining how I wanted a particular body part to look. I would mentally go over every detail—how my legs would look, what shape my abs would take, and the curve of my delts and biceps. Once I learned to perform this mental imagery, my results increased dramatically.

This type of visualization, which can actually reprogram your neurocircuitry, can work in the rest of your life, too. When you focus in, day by day, and create a positive mental picture of yourself, you can override the negative in your subconscious.

HOW TO HARVEST PRODUCTIVE TIME

Life has become so fast-paced that it's nearly impossible to find private time to take care of ourselves, but there's a way to harvest time during the day which would otherwise be wasted and nonproductive. From this point on, there's no such thing as useless downtime in your life! With Power Connectors you'll be able to turn all the little "wasted" moments in the day into a fertile breeding ground for the mind/body connection and *life*Balance.

Here are some examples of when you can steal time away for Power Connectors:

- Waiting on hold on the telephone.
- Standing in line . . . anywhere.
- Waiting for the computer to boot up.
- At the car wash.
- In any waiting room.

With Power Connectors you'll never again wait zombie-like in a line, moving narcoleptically until it's your turn. You'll savor the time you're forced to wait during the day because you'll be using those minutes, seconds, or hours to empower yourself in a number of ways. You'll be feeding yourself powerful "mind food," which will nurture you physically and emotionally. If you feed your subconscious "junk food" (negative thoughts and ideas), it will perform poorly, which will make you feel emotionally weak and puny. On the other hand, the subconscious that is fed good, healthy thoughts will grow strong and powerful, empowering you to reach your goals and achieve satisfaction in many areas of your life.

Sound too simple to be true? Not according to the experts. This relatively quick remodeling of the mind is the basis of cognitive restructuring (or cognitive therapy—psychology's newest trend), which enables people to reprogram their minds by creating newer, more positive thought patterns, not by spending years and years on the couch or through painful retelling of the past. By overlaying their old history with new and empowering information, patients can change the circuitry in the brain from negative to positive and enable their mind to use new information and new experiences to build a more positive, motivated outlook. Power Connectors are based on a similar approach.

The power of your mind and its connection to your body is illustrated in the following exercises.

*Life*Balance EXERCISE: "THE POWER OF THE MIND"

Draw a circle, eight to ten inches in diameter, on a page in your journal or on a separate piece of paper. Dissect the circle with a line drawn horizontally through the center. Draw another line going vertically through the center. Your circle should look like a pie with four big pieces.

Then, find a pendant on a chain in your jewelry box. Or hang a heavy metal or gemstone ring from a string about a foot long. Rest your arm on your elbow, holding the top of the string between your thumb and forefinger. Hold the pendant or ring about two inches above the center point of the circle, where the two lines meet. Hold the string very still and stare at the ring or pendant.

Now, imagine that the ring or pendant is going up and down along the vertical line. Keep thinking about this for a minute or so. Next, imagine that the ring is following along the horizontal line. Now, imagine that it is following the circular outline of the circle. Finally, imagine it following the vertical line for a while, then changing direction and following the horizontal line. Do this now, before reading further.

If you're like me, the first time you see the pendant swing in tandem with your thoughts, you start dreaming about touring the country as a master illusionist like David Copperfield or the Amazing Kreskin. The first time I tried this test I was ready to charge people admission to watch me perform feats of mental magic.

Did your ring or pendant, like mine, seem to follow your every imagined whim? Every person to whom I've ever shown this little trick has seen at least a little movement of the pendant in concert with their thoughts. For some, the movement is quite dramatic.

What does this little trick prove? Are we all mentalists capable of taking a magic act on the road? No, but we do all have the ability to use our mind to affect our bodies. Your muscles will follow the whims of your mind. Your muscles *think*. In fact, you think with your whole body. Be careful what you think about because your thoughts do create your reality.

LifeBalance EXERCISE: "THE QUESTION GAME"

This exercise is like a human Ouija game. It's a lot of fun. Hold the pendant over the middle of the circle again. Think of a question that can be answered with a yes or no answer. If the string moves vertically (up and down), the answer to the question is yes. If the string moves back and forth horizontally, the answer is no. This can be a fun way to explore your real feelings—without all the mind chatter. The pendant game is like a hotline to your real emotions. Use this exercise to answer questions—just be sure to temper the answers with reality. If you ask "Should I go to Tahiti?" be sure that your budget is in shape for such a trip. Yes, you may really want to go to Tahiti, but you may not be able to afford to do so at the present time.

USE AFFIRMATIONS TO BUILD POWER CONNECTORS

Affirmations and visualizations are terrific Power Connectors. This can be as easy as 1-2-3 with a method I've used for years.

Step 1: Make yourself a set of self-help flash cards by writing down favorite thoughts or goals on index cards.

Step 2: Carry the cards with you at all times. Stash them in your purse, jacket, car, or desk drawer.

Step 3: Whenever you have a spare moment—in line somewhere or during a break at work or waiting during kids' soccer practice—get out your flash cards and read through them randomly. Focus on a particular favorite or just shuffle quickly through them all for a quick review.

If you find it difficult to come up with your own Power Connecting affirmations, use some from the Power List (on page 242) to get you started. An affirmation that I, and others, have found particularly effective as a starting point is: "I am safe in the world." Another personal favorite is: "I release anger and let go of pain." Or try "I turn my past disappointments into my personal power today" for a little magic.

If you want to come up with your own Power Connectors, I encourage you to do so. Have fun and enjoy yourself as you come up with the little messages for your flash cards. Use your imagination. Get in touch with old, nearly forgotten dreams and goals. The affirmations don't all have to be deep, meaningful, and serious. Some can be humorous. In fact, Power Connectors based on humor are twice as powerful as NECs based in fear. For example, if you have an old NEC based on a childhood incident in which a family friend, teacher, or relative remarked on your weight—and you never forgot it—write a Power Connector on a flash card with the message you wish you could have delivered to that person. You don't have to be polite or subtle here. Have fun. Tell that person from the past something that makes you laugh. Humor can be healing and when you use it to create a Power Connector, it is doubly so.

Affirmations, positive memories, and humor can be used to create terrific, empowering Power Connectors, but you may also use other emotions or feelings to create them. Power Connectors don't have to be nice and they can be used as a powerful way to vent anger or rage. For women who lack self-empowerment, using Power Connectors to safely vent anger can help create inner strength. The Power Connector then becomes a great Mental Trash Compactor, too. I wrote a Power Connector directed at a guy who really plugged me in when he yelled something at me on the street one day.

"Hey, girlie, are those all your muscles?" he shouted from his perch on a construction site. His outburst pushed a button and reminded me of Ralph Hartel, the schoolboy bully from my past. Rather than let the old NEC come back from the past to dictate my response, I ignored the guy and later jotted down a Power Connector that I carried with me for weeks. It read, "Hey, you cigar-breathed, pot-bellied, big-mouthed schmuck with jeans hanging halfway down your bare, cracked butt, at least I've got some muscles—which is more than I can say for you!"

When you write your flash-card messages, try to be mindful and in the moment. If you really believe that you're going to be fat forever, overcompensating by writing "I can stick to my plan forever and never cheat" won't work for you. There's no reality in the affirmation for you. You'll set yourself up for disappointment if/when you stray or fall off the wagon, and you'll have a hard time getting motivated again. The all-or-nothing attitude doesn't leave much room for error. If you doubt—right now—your ability to ever lose weight or reach your goals, take small steps, even with your affirmations and flash cards. Make your Power Connector say, "Today I can stick to my plan"—and guess what? Today you probably can! You'll set yourself up for the win and with time your reality will grow to include bigger goals.

Power Connectors can be used to improve any area of your life, including not just your body image but relationships, too. In fact, Power Connectors can be downright sexy if you want them to be. Use your imagination and get as X-rated as necessary!

The flash cards and the Power List I've provided at the end of the book can be very useful. There is nothing more effective, however, than full-blown personalized Power Connectors with goals attached. Once you learn how to create very specific thoughts, goals, and dreams, you'll be amazed at how soon they begin to show up in your life—for real!

POWER CONNECTORS, STEP BY STEP

For many, the thought of creating specific Power Connectors is daunting. It's relatively easy, though, once you know the steps you have to take and in which order. Step-by-step, let's see exactly how all this Power Connector stuff works.

Let's say this is your belief: "I have a big butt." When you look in the mirror, that's what you see. That's what you think because, face it, you've created a whole story about yourself built upon NECs: "It's my genetics, it's the way I'm built. Slim hips will never be mine unless I starve myself or undergo liposuction." There's a lot of emotional junk in your trunk, so what do you do?

The first thing you have to do is *stop* the self-defeating thoughts. Telling yourself over and over that you have a big butt will not help you feel great about yourself, nor will it change anything. Change the way you speak to yourself. But, desperate to cling to your old way of thinking, you rationalize, "I have my mom's build. I'll always be fat." No, you don't have your mother's body but I'll bet you do have her belief system. How many times did you hear your mother say, "I have a big butt"? Heck, it's not even your own inner critic you're often listening to, but your mom's!

Put down this book and go to the nearest mirror. Stand in front of it and tell yourself, "You are beautiful." Then come back to the book.

What did your mind say? It might have said, "Yeah, but . . ." and then given you all the reasons why you're not beautiful.

More importantly, how did you react to the inner thoughts? Did you agree with them? If so, you gave the inner critic permission to continue the chatter!

Did you disagree? If so, an argument probably ensued. "No, you're not beautiful!" the critic might have said. "Yes, I am!" you may have defended yourself. And on and on.

Well, there's only one effective way to stop the chatter. Say, "Thank you for sharing," and move on to a new thought. Or, notice the chatter and stop it by saying, "Hello, you're telling me a lot of stuff." That's it.

The next step is to *replace* the negative thought with another, better one. You may be thinking, "But how can I think of something positive about a big butt?"

Well, it may be hard at first, but it can be done. You might even use a Power Connector that has nothing to do with the negative thought. The important thing is to replace the negative with a positive.

When your mind starts beating you up, just stop it with a "Thank you." Then, think of *one* positive thing. For example, you might tell yourself, "I make a great angel food cake." It may sound silly, but that one little thought will mask the chatter, even if only for a moment. Gradually, you'll have more and more Power Connectors in your mental arsenal with which you can ambush the chatter militia.

To change your body or your life you have to change your mind first. When you look in the mirror you have to focus on what you like about yourself, physically or otherwise. The first and second steps enable you to do that. Then you can move to the third step—*change!*

Remember, whatever you focus on, you give power to. All that time spent obsessing about what you dislike about your body only creates more to dislike. All those hours agonizing over what's "bad" in your life only creates more "bad."

POWER-CONNECT TO YOUR DREAMS

Here's how I created my own most Power(ful) Connector. As I mentioned briefly earlier in the book, I suffered a life-threatening blood clot. This was definitely the biggest stinking problem I've ever had to face. Imagine, if you can, waking up to a leg swollen to twice its normal size. On top of that, it happened to me one week before a major competition. Doctors told me this clot was the worst they'd ever seen. In fact, I think I made history with that rumble phlebitis. That clot knocked me for a loop.

Instead of wondering how I would survive the upcoming competition, I started to wonder if I would survive—period! The only question after "Will I live through this?" was "Can we save the leg?" since there was a good chance it would have to be amputated.

When it became clear that I would live, the doctors told me we could save the leg, but that I would always have to worry about preventing another clot like that from happening again. There was also the little problem of me learning to walk again.

After six weeks of intensive physical therapy, lots of tears, and plenty of frustration, I could walk feebly. Later, I walked well enough to begin to entertain thoughts about competing in the future. My doctor discouraged me from that line of thinking, however, and told me that I would never be able to walk normally.

My rehab continued. I progressed slowly but surely. I can still remember my first full walk. It lasted for about thirty seconds or two inches, whichever came first. I had a friend visiting and we walked down that hospital hallway a full two inches and that was that. Those were plenty for me, however, since I had been told that ever walking at all would be nearly impossible. I used those measly two inches as Power Connectors, though, and they propelled me on. Gradually, I would walk a few more inches and eventually a few feet. I swam a few strokes. Each accomplishment became a Power Connector to the next. My first Power Connector was, "I walked two inches when they told me I wouldn't walk at all." Then it became, "I walked the length of the hall today when before I could only walk a few inches." I regained my ability to walk and I regained control over my life. Step by step and inch by inch I became powerful. I might have looked like a little invalid hobbling those first few steps, but internally I was a power generator beyond compare.

I entered a gym again twelve weeks after the blood clot. I couldn't do any leg work, so I focused on what I could do: upper body training. A few months later I entered my first bodybuilding contest. It would make an even better story if I could tell you that my Power Connectors took me immediately to the top and that I won the show. The truth, however, is that I didn't. In fact, I looked pretty horrible up on that stage, but my Power Connectors didn't fail me. I felt on top of the world after that show. Just being in that contest, standing on that stage, being in a little bit of shape, was a huge victory for me. I had my health back and I had my leg! I had my family. I was grateful as all get-out! I didn't expect to win. I was happy to be alive and healthy.

Instead of allowing the blood clot to stop me in my tracks with thoughts like "I'm doomed" or "I'm worthless," I coached myself through this scary life detour with Power Connectors that enabled me to believe in myself again. I didn't know what kind of inner strength I really had till then.

Now, I use that little reminder to create even bigger Power Connectors. Whenever I feel down or lack confidence, I go to my mental files and find the Power Connector labeled "Blood Clot." It tells me that I am powerful and capable. It reminds me that I have the ability to make things happen in the worst of cases, so imagine what I can do when things are a little less dramatic. A couple of years after the blood clot I competed in a contest with a broken foot. Hey, I told myself, if I can train with a blood clot I can do anything with a little stress fracture!

Later, in 1985, I had shoulder surgery about six months before my first Ms. Olympia competition. Yes, I could have given up and used that funky shoulder as an excuse not to compete. But I didn't. I refused to be derailed by a little thing like a shoulder problem. I rearranged my workouts and worked around the shoulder. I did more leg work. I put all that extra energy into shaping my legs and lower body. When I was allowed to do some shoulder workouts, I did. That year, I walked onstage with the best pair of legs of any competitor. I also won the contest. I took what could have been a total negative and darn good cop-out and turned it into a total positive. Instead of sitting around and complaining, "They'll think I don't have any shoulders" or "It's not fair," I got tough, used my Power Connector, trained hard, and became known for my legs and improved symmetry. My Power Connectors never fail to keep me going.

LifeBalance PARTNER EXERCISE: "TRUTH TEST"

Your partner holds her arm out to the side. She becomes "the speaker." Then, she states her name ("My name is [her name]") as you, "the mover," try to push her arm down. Notice the amount of effort needed to move her arm.

Next, she says, "My name is Steve." Once again, you try to push her arm down. Notice the amount of energy you have to exert to move her arm.

Now you become the speaker as she becomes the mover. Repeat the exercise. Notice how much energy it takes for you to resist her as she tries to push your arm down each time.

Feel the difference in energy? You probably found that when you spoke your real name, you were much stronger, and when you spoke the phony one, you were much weaker. I've performed this test on hundreds of women and there's usually a big strength difference when the body is in an "authentic" state.

Your body is stronger and more powerful in all ways when it is dealing with truth. The truth about you is that you are magnificent and powerful. Stop any negative mental chatter that denies that truth!

LifeBalance PARTNER EXERCISE: "NEGATIVE VERSUS POSITIVE"

Hold out your arm. Think of a body part you don't like. Stare at it (if you can) and get mentally tough. Inwardly, tell the offending body part what you think of it. Give it a real dressing-down. Be mean. Be cruel.

Then, signal your partner with a nod to push your arm down. Notice how difficult or easy it is to resist your partner's effort.

Now, with the arm still out, inwardly tell the same body part how great it is. Compliment it to no end. Stroke it. Make nice.

Now, signal your partner once again to start pushing. Notice the difference? See how strong you are? Negative thoughts affect you negatively and positive thoughts affect you positively. Every time you beat yourself up about your body, remember this exercise and know that self-criticism will not have a positive effect on you mentally, physically, or emotionally.

LifeBalance PARTNER EXERCISE: "LOVE WHAT YOU HATE"

Talk to your partner about the thing(s) in your life that are bothering you, without focusing on the negative. For example, if you dislike your small breasts, focus on the positive attributes of smaller breasts. They can be pert, perky, cute, youthful, healthy, bouncy, even athletic. They look good in tank tops. They can be elegant in evening wear. Think of the good points. If you're unhappy with your job, don't discuss what's wrong with it, but pick something positive. Your office is very sunny. You enjoy one of your coworkers. Talk about work in positive, glowing terms for at least sixty seconds.

Next, your partner should tell you about what's bugging her in the same positive terms.

When both of you have finished, talk about how it felt to do this exercise. Many people find it "hard" or "silly" or report that, "It felt like I was lying." Your job is to become comfortable with this kind of positive self-talk. Use this exercise on a regular basis to develop positive self-talk habits.

When it's difficult to come up with positives, remember that there are so many wonderful aspects to each and every human being and some good can be found in most situations. Power Connectors help you stay in touch with that.

LifeBalance EXERCISE: "CREATING POWER CONNECTORS"

I like to take time to create Power Connectors at least twice a week, if not more. In the beginning, it's a good idea to practice for a few minutes each and every day until you become fairly skilled. It's relaxing, it's fun, it's creative. Research shows that your brain can take in more information when it's in a relaxed state, so I like to dim the lights and put on a little soft music to help set the creative mood. You might like to add candles, incense, or whatever helps you. Once the "stage" is set, lie down with your arms at your sides, palms facing up. Inhale and exhale slowly to a count of ten (five counts in, five counts out). Do this several times until you feel relaxation beginning to enter your body through every pore.

Starting at the feet, slowly tighten and then release each body part. Begin with the toes, the ankles, the calves. Move up to the knees and thighs, the hips, and the lower abs. Gradually work your way up through the chest, back, and shoulders. Finally, think about tightening the muscles of the face, including the eyes, nose, and mouth. Scrunch up the face and hold it for a beat, then relax. Finally, tighten the entire body from head to toes and hold for a two-count. Relax. Lie still and breathe quietly.

Now picture yourself when you did something of which you are proud. Remember every detail of the event or moment. Imagine the way the room smelled. Visualize the colors there. Remember how it felt. The mental picture you just created is your first Power Connector.

As you get better at re-creating these positive moments from the past you'll begin to get adept at visualizing things that have yet to happen. You can then set exciting goals for yourself and actually see them happening in your mind's eye. Fill in every detail so that your neurotransmitters can begin to make the goal happen in intricate, exact detail, then jot down the outline of this mental picture on an index card to jog your memory during the day. Your mind will recall the fully detailed picture from the quick reference on the card.

A makeup artist friend of mine was tired of the self-defeating thoughts she created about herself whenever she failed to get a job she had tried for. Instead of dwelling on the defeats, she began to create a rich visual imagery of her desire to one day have her own line of products. She began to design—in her mind's eye—a world in which she was the best makeup artist. She imagined the theater in which the awards ceremony would take place. She went shopping and found a dress that she would love to wear to store openings. (She even tried the gown on, so she knew exactly how she would look in it!) She visualized how each counter would look. On an index card, she wrote "Best Makeup Artist" and every time she read those words the whole scene was called up in her mind, complete with sights, sounds, smells, and colors. Today, she has her own makeup line sold in stores all over the country.

Wendy's Story

Wendy works in a wedding cake store. When I first met her, she was depressed most of the time. She had given up on her girlhood hopes and dreams that life would turn out great or even OK. Optimistic as a little girl, Wendy became disappointed with life and finally gave up on herself. Her depression took on a life of its own and she became stuck in negative patterns that sent her into deeper and deeper spirals of depression during which she further punished herself by overeating.

At 230 pounds, she felt that she had finally bottomed out. She asked me, "How do you do it? You're so positive all the time. You just keep going and going and winning at everything that you do. I'm such a failure."

I told Wendy about Power Connectors and together we set out to discover some positive past memory we could use to begin to create a base of emotional well-being for her. "I can't think of anything good about me," she cried. "I've been overweight and unhappy for so many years that I can't even remember when I had any control over my life," she said.

I asked her what other people praised her for or what her parents or others had ever said to her that was positive as she was growing up.

"Nothing," she replied sadly. "My parents criticized me constantly for one thing or another." She sat silently for a moment and then added, "I mean, I did keep this poinsettia plant alive for years and years. People always remarked about that. No big deal."

"How did you keep it alive for so long?" I asked her. "I can barely keep one going through the Christmas season!"

Her face lit up as she talked about her luck with the plant. "Oh, it was easy, really," she said. "When it started to wilt or look sickly, I'd find a new place for it in the room and I'd move it there until it got better. I always knew, somehow, when to water it, too. Everyone just kept waiting for it to die, but it lasted for almost three years—until the cat knocked it over."

"How did you know when to water it and where to move it?" I asked her.

"I just did," she said. I encouraged her to explore the memory further. "It was like I just knew, automatically. I didn't have to really think about it or anything."

"Kind of like intuition?" I asked her.

"Yeah, like that," she said hesitantly.

"So, you're intuitive!" I said.

We played with that idea for a while. She realized that much of her success in making the wedding cakes for her customers came from this same ability to "know" how and where to place the decorations and what color scheme to use on the frosting. People would often say to her, "How did you know my favorite flowers were gardenias?" or "I love blue—it's my favorite color. How pretty."

From a childhood memory of a poinsettia plant, Wendy was able to piece together the idea of herself as intuitive—a great attribute! This Power Connector became very important for her as she began to rebuild further ideas and images in her mind. I encouraged her to use the Power Connector "I'm intuitive" to replace the old "I'm fat" or "I'm a failure" NECs. She began to trust and cherish her intuition.

Wendy called me one day months later. "Guess what, Cory?" she asked. "I was driving to work when it hit me: I felt positive! Normally, I'd fight my way through traffic, cursing at the other drivers, hating my life, hating my job. Today, for the first time, I felt really terrific. Traffic didn't bother me. I looked forward to getting to work." She sounded so full of optimism and joy. It was clear that she had reclaimed the optimism of childhood and cast off the depression that had haunted her for so many years. When she told me she had also lost ten pounds, I knew she was well on her way to wellness!

With Power Connectors your mind works like a twelve-CD changer with a missing CD. It notices the empty spot where the NEC used to be and searches for the missing "disk." Use a Power Connector to immediately fill the missing space before your multitrack mind can latch onto another NEC and replay it over and over.

LifeBalance EXERCISE: "USE YOUR EYES"

Remember the best birthday you ever celebrated. Think about it. Imagine it. Now, think about another fun event, party, or holiday and notice what happens with your eyes as you remember this happy day. Your eyes probably look up and to the left, as most people's do, when retrieving this type of information from the memory banks.

This is a habit you can use to enhance your visualization and Power Connections. Your eyes can be used almost like file clerks to access important images for you. By looking up and to the left (look at a spot about three inches above the outer corner of your left eye) you can lock an image of yourself into your mental computer file. Take in a deep breath as you visualize and you'll add even more power to the new "memory."

During the day, imagine the body you want or the confidence you'd like to have. Look up and left before you daydream or visualize this exciting you. These daily visualization sessions can become the building blocks to personal success. (These are different from meditation, which will be discussed in a later chapter.)

CAN PEOPLE EVER REALLY CHANGE?

Your inner critic is probably having a field day right now. "Who's she kidding, girl? People don't change. We all know that," the little devil chides you. Maybe she's right. After all, can a leopard change its spots?

If we all have our own unique neurosignatures and NECs, does that mean we are doomed to stay locked into our old, disempowering ways? No. Your mind is constantly under construction. Each new little tidbit or nuance is being processed by your mind in every moment. Your mind is constantly busy creating new thought patterns, memories, and connections; these alter your neurosignature slightly and add to the vast mental library from which you create your ideas, hopes, and expectations. When people "can't change" it's because they are unwilling to do the work necessary to make change happen. They may want change and they may need to change, but they get lazy.

Yes, there are certain inbred survival mechanisms that cannot and should not be altered or ignored. These rules governing survival and well-being are like important computer programs that must be stored on the hard drive. Goals, dreams, and visions can be stored on a floppy disk—ready to be input at any time and added to the programs on the hard drive, without overriding them. Most of us have become lazy computer programmers, relying on our "hard drives" alone when we need to become creative and input some creative and empowering "floppies." Debbie's a great example of a woman who learned to reprogram herself for change.

Debbie's Story

Debbie is a wonderful woman, but she didn't always know that. She spent many years of her life being very unhappy about nearly everything in it. She was overweight. She was controlled both physically and mentally by an abusive husband. She had absolutely no self-confidence, no sense of self-worth, no job, and no control over her life. She hated her existence but did nothing to change it. She was so afraid to pick a direction that she stood in the middle of the road and continually got knocked down by traffic going in both directions!

One day Debbie made a decision for herself. She wanted change and took my advice about creating lasting change in her life by starting slowly. First, and most importantly, she changed her mind about herself and stopped thinking of herself as someone who never exercised to thinking of herself as someone who did. She began to exercise at home. Her controlling husband would never let her join a gym—where she might meet nice men or begin to get in shape and lose the fat she had accumulated—so she took the bull by the horns and began to work out in the living room. She started to watch my fitness show. She followed the advice I dispensed on television and started to eat low-fat foods, to do certain exercises, and to take vitamins and supplements, all of which would help her get the results she wanted. She even began to take quick walks in the neighborhood when her husband was at work. She stuck to this program for weeks and slowly began to see change in her body and her attitude.

Debbie began to like the person she saw in the mirror in the morning. She experienced power over something in her life for the first time in many years. To prevent her domineering hubby from sabotaging her efforts she hid her body from him in the same baggy clothes she had always worn. He was so oblivious and out of touch that at night when she took off the baggy stuff (lights off, of course!), he didn't even notice the change.

Once she realized that she had control over one part of her life Debbie discovered she could control (change) other areas, too. It dawned on her that she didn't have to take the abuse her husband doled out regularly. She had options!

Guess what little Deb did? She packed up her stuff and left. She was gone in an instant. She grabbed her purse, her sweats, her protein shake, her dog and got the heck out of Dodge. She left everything behind except her newfound self-esteem and her inner strength.

Debbie now leads a motivated, grateful, giving, and happy life. She's become an aerobics instructor and has a new home, a loving husband, three great kids, and a career as a motivational speaker to abused women.

Debbie's story is a great one because it shows the power not of money, fame, or beauty, but the power of personal pride and empowerment. If Debbie can turn her life around in so many ways, so can you! Use Debbie's story as a foolproof Power Connector. Think of her when you're feeling out of control or victimized. Later, you'll create your own Power Connectors out of the victories, small and large, you begin to enjoy. Learn to be your own best friend and to love yourself, because that's what it takes to be happy—not fitting into a size two or losing weight or getting the right guy.

WHAT TO DO WHEN YOU JUST CAN'T DO IT

Some people have spent so many years beating themselves up that it's nearly impossible for them to think about themselves in positive terms, no matter what. For them, I suggest taking a small step by simply beginning to notice the chatter. That's an important beginning—to be conscious that the chatter exists and is ongoing.

Once you can acknowledge the chatter, it's time to take more small steps to tame it. You have to be careful at this point not to attempt too much at once. If your chatter tells you, "I hate this body," you can't go directly to a Power Connector like, "I love my body." (The body knows a lie when it hears one. This is why "positive thinking" that denies our own truths can never work.)

So, where do you go from "I hate . . . "? You start at "It's now OK to like my body [or life or job or whatever]." Many will find that mentally they want to add a "but" to this statement. "It's now OK to like my body, but it's really hard to do so," or whatever. Remember to *remove the* but*'s* (especially if you're trying to remove some of your butt!). Your mind is never as brilliant as when it finds ways to make your thoughts happen. Our job is to give it the right assignment.

People who have spent most of their entire life beating themselves up need to give their mind homework in small, incremental doses. It's like the old joke: How do you eat an elephant? (One bite at a time!)

You can't learn the alphabet in one class. You may want to go from A to Z, but you can't. Remember the first time you tried a sit-up? You may not have been able to do it. Personal trainers working with clients who are just starting out have them do assisted stomach crunches until they develop the muscles to do a full one. Your mental muscles need you to be a smart personal trainer. Start out at square one and progress from there. Slowly, as you make adjustments in the mental assignments, you'll begin to get results and truly like parts of your body!

Start by saying "It's OK to like my body [or myself]" and stop there until you feel comfortable with that. If even that is too difficult for you to "believe," start by stating only your willingness to like yourself. "I'm now willing for it to be OK for me to like my body [or myself]." Still too hard to imagine? Then try, "I'm now willing to be willing to like my body (or myself)." Reach as far back as you have to on the "willing" scale until your system says, "*yes!* I can do that!" I've known women who had to start at, "I'm now willing to be willing to be willing to like my body" and who went on to achieve great results!

Write your willingness statement on an index card and read it during the day until it becomes real for you. Train your mind like you train a dog. When you give the "Sit" command to a dog the first time it's unlikely she'll obey. When a dog hears a command but ignores it, you tell the dog "No" and give her the command again. Eventually she obeys. The mind will, too!

LifeBalance JOURNAL EXERCISE

Divide a page in your journal into two columns. In one column, write down ten wonderful things about yourself. In the other column, write down ten things you don't like about yourself.

Did you have a hard time filling up either column? My guess is that you had no problem writing about what you don't like and a more difficult time finding good things to say about yourself.

Now take a look at both columns. Are most of the items cosmetic or related to your body? You'll probably find that the notes in the "Like" column are more internal ("I'm considerate"; "I have a good sense of humor"). The notes in the "Don't Like" column usually relate to the body or exterior, cosmetic features. Here's a typical sample:

LIKE	DON'T LIKE
I'm spontaneous.	I'm fat.
I'm funny.	I'm lazy.
I'm considerate.	I hate my hair.
I'm a quick learner.	I'm short.
I'm creative.	My knees are knobby.

As one woman in a seminar told me, "I could write the negative stuff all day long. It's like being on autopilot. The thoughts just flow. The positive stuff was hard to come up with."

Think about the items in the "Like" column. Take a look at each of them, one by one, and just think about them for a few seconds each. How does it feel when you think about these qualities? Probably pretty good. When you think about the "Don't Like" items it undoubtedly feels pretty bad, although comfortingly familiar. Most of us walk around thinking about the "Don't Likes" about 90 percent of the time. Is it any wonder we don't function optimally, given that we don't feel great about ourselves for the better part of most days? Wouldn't it be nice to walk around feeling like you do when you're thinking about your "Like" column?

Power Connectors provide that feeling. They're the voice that says "Phooey" to the bad thoughts. When you wake up feeling negative, say, "That's *not* OK." Then make up a Power Connector. If you're unable to do that, say to yourself,

"Something wonderful is going to happen to me today." (It always does!) It's your choice!

As a human, you like to be right and your mind works very hard on your behalf to help you accomplish that. You always get to be right: *What do you want to be right about?*

The mental part of life is an art. With Power Connectors you get to become an artist creating a beautiful landscape for your life.

ten

DISCOVER YOUR INNER ATHLETE WITH THE FOUR FITNESS MODES AND THE 50% EXERCISE SOLUTION

Your mental and physical health are inseparable. George Sheehan, the running doctor, once said, "The waste of a mind is a terrible thing; the waste of a soul is worse. But it all begins with the waste of a body." I love that quote.

Not surprisingly, a study in *Psychology Today* found that regular exercisers are better off in more than just the physical sense than those who don't work out. People who train tend to be more imaginative and they have more self-sufficiency and emotional stability. Other health statistics back up the magazine's findings. Research has shown that when you exercise for just ten minutes you raise your body's level of a hormone called epinephrine, which is a form of adrenaline. We all know what it feels like to get an adrenaline rush: without any effort on your part, the body experiences a blast of energy that supersedes any former feelings of lethargy or tiredness. You feel powerful and positive, all due to this natural chemical called adrenaline. It's no wonder that daredevils and participants in extreme sports like car racing, skydiving, and bungee jumping get addicted to the chemical high (adrenaline) they get when they participate in their sport. I look at exercise as a cheap form of therapy. Think about it—you can visit your "shrink" by taking a walk.

WORKOUTS DON'T HAVE TO BE GRUELING

Relaxing, balancing, and inner awareness (what *life*Balance is all about!) have all been used to improve athletic performance. Once you begin to improve your *life*Balance, you'll find that workouts seem only half as difficult as they once did. Your attitude and your ability to focus improves, as does performance. (Why do you think golfers practice visualization to improve their swing?) Choosing the right *life*Balance workout will not only improve your game and enable you to have more fun at sports and fitness activities, but you'll enter into a circle of benefit in which the rest of your life is affected positively, too.

DISCOVER YOUR NATURAL GAME

Whether you were the star of the school team or the bookworm who never played a childhood sport, finding *life*Balance requires that you discover your Natural Game(s). Each of us has at least a few of these, since there is an inner athlete residing within each of us—and she's dying to get out and play!

"You're dreaming, Cory," Laura told me when I suggested this. "No way I'm an athlete. I've been fat my whole life and I'm not good at anything that has to do with sports. Leave that to the jocks, not me!"

I began to explore with Laura some of her fears about athletics which were causing her reluctance to try them. I knew that she, like all of us, had a Natural Game or two she could truly and wholeheartedly enjoy, if not excel at. I began by having her walk on a treadmill at a gym. Laura hated that. She didn't like the club atmosphere, preferring to be alone when she sweats. She was embarrassed to wear gym clothes in front of both men and women club members and was too uncomfortable to enjoy herself at all. The treadmill and the gym were definitely not for her.

We started taking long, easy walks outdoors and she immediately liked those. She loved the fact that they afforded her privacy and she enjoyed the one-on-one camaraderie of having a walking partner. Soon she became addicted to the walks and when I couldn't accompany her, she took to listening to some audio walking workout tapes I gave her. Laura, unlike women who need the crowded, high-energy atmosphere of a gym to help get them motivated, was a much more private athlete. Each of her Natural Games, like walking, would almost certainly be private ones, I deduced.

I followed a hunch and suggested she take a golf lesson from a pro at a local course. Bingo! She called me after the first lesson. "You won't believe this," she began.

"Oh, I'll bet maybe I will," I countered, hearing the optimism and enthusiasm in her voice.

"Well," she explained, "I was pretty good at this golf stuff. By the end of the lesson I was hitting the ball nearly two hundred yards!" We had another opening. Laura now had two Natural Games: walking and golf. Later, she discovered belly dancing and started to enjoy that with a group of women who met twice a week to practice. Her inner athlete was free (at last!) to play and Laura began to develop *life*Balance. Today Laura weighs ten pounds less than she did when she first started her neighborhood walks and she's excited about her fitness future. She "plays" almost every day!

Each of Us Is an Athlete

Why do we think of athletes only as those who play on a pro team, participate in sports for a living (like personal trainers), or go to physical extremes? I think we're all athletes waiting to happen, it's just that some of us have discovered our Natural Games and others have yet to do so. As in Laura's case, Natural Games aren't always found in the gym, which isn't surprising given that the original Olympics included things like dance, poem recitals, and musical performances.

Finding your inner athlete and discovering your Natural Game(s) isn't as difficult as it may sound. The discovery process will unfold naturally once you begin the search, since you, as a human being, are genetically programmed to be a jock! Way back when, long before there were gyms or fitness videos, men and women engaged in play. Early (wo)man learned to play before she devised a culture or rules or structure. Even before humans showed up on the scene, animals engaged in play. The need for play is something that is in our genes, just like eye color or bone structure. It's firmly embedded in each of you, yet you don't always allow yourself to do it. You may engage in some form of it to reach goals that are strictly physical, like "lose weight," or "fit into that flashy gold bikini," but your goals will work much better once you choose them for the right reasons. Once you begin to experiment with different exercise classes, sports, and fitness activities and search until you find the one that "fits" for you, you'll discover your Natural Game(s). Then, you can allow your inner athlete the luxury of play and begin to experience an ease as you work toward your goals.

THE THEORY BEHIND THE *LIFE*BALANCE WORKOUT

To find your own personal balance, you have to think of working out as an important part of your total health picture and not just as a way to help you squeeze into a new pair of jeans. Don't work out to be perfect—work out in order to be whole. Use your workouts to help you find the Real You—the inner source of power that is invulnerable to loss, suffering, decay, or disease—the part that shines through no matter what. When you work out for the wrong reasons you may be magnifying your personal problems rather than doing good for yourself. By exercising for the right reasons, you can use your workouts to add balance to your life.

LifeBalance JOURNAL EXERCISE: SETTING GOALS

Get out your journal and write the date at the top of a fresh new page. Next, put a heading: MY GOALS. This is going to be your mission statement. List ten purposes for getting into better shape. Be very clear and specific, and remember that you're trying to achieve *life*Balance. For example, instead of "I will work out to feel better," write, "I want to be in better shape so that when I pick up my niece and run with her at the park, I am not winded." Instead of "To be thin," write, "I want to be in better shape so that my body fat is 20 percent and my lean muscle mass increases, raising my metabolism." Get very clear about what it is you want and be very specific.

From time to time go back to this page in your journal and think about what it will take for you to reach these goals. Take responsibility for finding a program that will help you reach them. Don't wait, create. Choice—not chance—is what creates your future in fitness and the rest of life. Set up your game plan now without waiting for situations or people to change. Action results in reaction. If you don't make the right moves you don't prove and you won't improve. This is your chance to begin the creation of the new you.

Take advantage of it. Think it through. Write it down.

I'm sure you all know someone who went to college and majored in courses that made their parents happy—but not themselves. They became a doctor or lawyer to please Mom and Dad and now they have a degree in hand and a career to match—but they aren't really satisfied. Their life doesn't work optimally for them, since they went into a profession to make someone else happy.

Exercise can be like that, too. If you pick a workout because it's all the rage or because it's popular and it's what you think you should do, you probably won't be able to stick with it and you won't get results. We all have sports and activities that suit us uniquely. It's your job to discover the games your inner athlete loves to play. Finding the perfect workout(s) for you—your Natural Games—can be easier when you discover which of the four fitness modes is yours.

THE FOUR FITNESS MODES

Mode One

Mode One people are often labeled Type A in other areas of life. These are obsessive-compulsive perfectionists who exercise too much, too strenuously, and, too often, all wrong. They have an expectation of perfection in life which they frantically try to achieve. This thinking is so stressful that it can counteract almost any of their good intentions. When Mode Ones don't achieve perfection—which, of course, no one can—they feel guilty and beat themselves up by trying even harder. Their guilt and feelings of inadequacy force them to work out each day to the point of exhaustion and to an extreme that leaves them too tired to enjoy the rest of their day and activities. They neglect other areas of life so that they can keep their exercise schedule intact. They are very goal-oriented and highly motivated, but often do not enjoy the exercise process at all. They keep going, however, because they have an inner imbalance that drives them incessantly, allowing them no respite.

Mode Ones are frequently "loner" exercisers who engage in long-distance running or swimming. They are incapable of changing their workout schedule, regardless of what emergencies arise, what is needed from them at work or at home, or for any other reasons. Usually, Mode Ones have friends who are also Mode Ones. They associate with one another because of their similar emotional needs and for support in the way they prioritize their workouts.

Mode Ones often lose sight of the fact that each workout isn't the last they'll ever have. They train as though each workout is the big one. They don't realize that it's great to have focus and concentration (as well as dedication) but that it's also important to remember that what you do today adds up with what you'll do tomorrow and the next day. The latest research tells us that small, incremental "episodes" can be just as beneficial as one long workout. If you did three sit-ups this morning, then walked during your lunch hour for ten minutes, and then rode a bicycle for a half hour—it all adds up to getting in better shape.

Mode Ones aren't happy unless they're nearly dead at the end of each and every workout. Their guilt at being less than perfect leaves them little choice. When their energy level is low or they're sick and they miss a workout, their anxiety level goes through the roof. If they ever allow themselves to just do nothing— to relax or recuperate—they experience waves of guilt mixed with anxiety, a feeling that is temporarily alleviated only by the next fatiguing workout.

I know the Mode One type very well because I've been there and done, done, done that. When I was deep into fitness competition and did not live up to my own perfectionist expectations and standards I was incredibly uncomfortable and edgy most of the time. After all, wasn't I Cory Everson, the six-time Ms. Olympia winner, the leader, the motivator? Didn't I owe it to myself and everyone else to be the perfect representative of fitness? This guilt became psychological suicide because it inhibited my actions and did little for my self-respect and confidence. Eventually, it caused me to completely burn out on exercise and I went for two years without doing any at all. So much for balance!

Mode One guilt can become as destructive to the mind and soul as cancer can be to the body. It takes a huge toll on one's health as well as one's relationships. (Just ask me!) It sneaks up on you, hits you behind the head, and knocks you to the ground before you even realize what's happening. If you allow the guilty feelings to become more destructive, they gather momentum like an avalanche that starts out slowly but quickly builds to crisis proportions, destroying everything in its path.

Mode Ones' feelings of anger, failure, and frustration put them out of control and leave them negative and unproductive—drained, numb, and incapable of stopping the negative emotional avalanche.

Suzanne is an example of an extreme Mode One who allowed her obsessions to nearly ruin her life. She was impossible to be around when she missed a workout. She complained constantly and was a pathetic partner to her husband. When she missed a training session one day she would make up for it the next by working out like a maniac. She'd run miles and miles and eat like a bird. She'd squeeze in weight training instead of time with her husband, who sorely missed her. She'd lose a few pounds through overexercising and anorexia, then briefly feel good about herself for a day or two.

I call the weight loss she experienced negative weight loss, since it did her more harm than good. She dealt with her guilt by obsessing and engaging in eating disorders. This torture program always turned on her within a few days, when she'd begin the guilt part of her cycle again and become even more miserable. To this day, Suzanne punishes herself and everyone around her with this extreme behavior.

This type of response to life's pressures has become a huge problem in today's society and I think that's why we're seeing such a rise in eating disorders among both young and older women. Years ago, a girl on my college gymnastics team actually admitted herself into a clinic because she was so frightened by her own eating disorder. She acknowledged she had a problem, even though it scared her to death. It all began when our college coach told her that she needed to drop a few pounds to improve her gymnastics and she went overboard. Her already low self-esteem and a history of family problems didn't help either. When Kari ate more than her self-imposed daily allotment—an egg white and a grape or two—or when she didn't run that extra mile during her running workout, she felt horrible guilt. She dealt with this emotional upset by exploding into inhuman extremes of exercise or starvation. Later she began to binge and purge.

Even after she admitted herself into the hospital she would disconnect the nourishing IVs at night and run the fire escape stairwell for hours. She'd sneak food into her room and then feel so guilty about it that she'd do a midnight stair workout to try to alleviate the horrible feelings.

Kari, like many others, was way out of balance, but trying desperately to remain in control. She, like so many women today who suffer from eating disorders, tried to cleanse herself of negative feelings through unhealthy, extreme measures. She eventually found help with counseling and she was able to forgive herself for being less than perfect. She wasn't a perfect person (who is?). She wasn't a perfect gymnast (even Nadia Comaneci stumbled sometimes!). She accepted that. She became OK with not having a perfect body—which is impossible anyway!

Mode Two

Most people don't go to the extremes of women like Kari. Some, in fact, go in the opposite direction and don't do anything at all. They may still have similar feelings of low self-esteem and guilt, but they lie back and give up, justifying their lack of activity by saying, "I was never meant to be lean and fit." They accept their genetics almost like an award, telling themselves, "I was born this way and why fight it? Think I'll have another box of Twinkies." They lose sight of the fact that they don't have to be overweight just because their grandparents were overweight or because they're going through emotional distress.

Have you ever tried to start riding a bike on a slight incline? Do you remember how difficult it is to get your bike going uphill? That same hill is easier if you're already in motion when you hit it, but when you try to start up it from a dead stop, inertia works against you and it can be very difficult to start pedaling. Fitness inertia is what Mode Twos have to deal with all the time. It's no wonder that they can't seem to get started. They don't have the advantage of any momentum to help them get going! They have a difficult time taking that first step out the door since inertia dictates that "an object at rest tends to stay at rest and an object in motion tends to stay in motion."

These people seem very unmotivated and are often called couch potatoes, but in fact they're no different from anyone else except that they've lost touch with their inner ath-

I've been a Mode One for much of my life, but especially in college.

lete and have yet to discover the Natural Game(s) that will make fitness fun for them. They're standing downhill, looking uphill, and wondering where the energy will come from to get them going.

I went through a Mode Two period after many years as a Mode One. My Mode Two era lasted not two days or two weeks or even two months—it was a full two years! It was after my sixth Ms. Olympia and I was so burnt out that I couldn't bear the thought of training for one minute more. I did nothing . . . zip . . . diddly-squat . . . for the next twenty-four months. It was a terrifying time for me because I had spent my entire life working out. I had been a Mode One for as long as I could remember and I thought I would always wake up raring to go and ready to train to exhaustion. I was more comfortable with the overachieving workout ethic than with the one that hit after that last Ms. O contest.

Deep into this Mode Two period I was sure that I would never find the motivation to begin again. I procrastinated. I came up with stupid excuses not to work out. Even monetary concerns couldn't budge me, as I turned down guest posing appearances—my bread and butter in those days—because I was afraid I wasn't going to look good enough. Each day brought with it a new excuse not to start training again. The longer I went without a workout the easier it was to go without another one and so on and so on until working out was truly a thing of the past.

When Mode Twos tell me all the crazy excuses they have for not working out, I can honestly say, "You can't kid a kidder. I've used that excuse, and more, to get out of training!" I know all the excuses intimately.

I wasn't able to break the Mode Two pattern until I finally put myself on the hook to so many people that it would have been beyond embarrassing not to start working out again. I told everyone I met that I was going to start training again. I enlisted my sister Cameo to be my training partner. I begged her to be tough on me. I told the checkout girl at the grocery store my plans and I told Diane, my dog groomer, that I was back on the program. I told the guy at the post office who always sold me stamps. Now I was responsible not only to myself, but to a host of others. I had to become mentally committed, physically responsible, and energy-oriented or a lot of people would think I was full of hot air.

Mode Twos aren't always unmotivated in other areas of life and can be quite driven at business and career. In fact, some of our country's biggest movers and shakers are Mode Twos. They're great at moving and shaking everything but their booties! They simply can't find the motivation for fitness and usually are the first to acknowledge that they neglect their health. My friend Dr. Williams is a perfect example of this type.

"Cory, my practice is terrific. I'm busy from first thing in the morning till last thing at night and I love what I do. My clientele is great. But let's face it, what can I do about workouts? I have no time to train," he complained to me once. "I'm tired by the end of the day and have low energy most of the rest of the time."

I told Dr. Williams, "Look at it this way; the way you feel—the lack of energy, the tired body—could be hurting you and your practice. It could be affecting your family without your even knowing it. Your loved ones need you healthy and happy and energetic, not beat up and run-down. You owe good health not only to yourself, but to your loved ones."

I told the same thing to Sarah, a single woman with no living family members who had recently experienced the demise of a romantic relationship. She said, "So what if I'm out of shape? I don't have any family to think about or owe anything to." I reminded her that her beloved rescue mutt, Buck, a lively spotted spaniel, would much rather go for a brisk evening walk than lie at her feet watching her eat potato chips all night long while watching TV! She owed him that!

Mode Twos like Dr. Williams and Sarah need to remember that if you neglect your health, no matter how talented, smart, or clever you are, you'll suffer in the long run. You cannot ignore the body. It cries out for exercise and it complains to you in the form of back pain, headaches, migraines, and low energy.

When Dr. Williams told me, "I start work at six A.M. and by the end of the day the last thing I have energy for is exercise," I told him, "Not exercising is exactly why you don't have energy!"

The Mode Two woman may complain about her lack of energy, bad muscle tone, and fatty diet, yet do little to change her unhealthy lifestyle. She may talk about beginning a fitness program "someday" but almost never does. She may be a perfectionist, but her self-criticism brings her to a dead stop before she can begin any fitness plan, turning her into a workout slacker. Mode Twos may be very well motivated in other areas of life and may do well at business or homemaking. In fact, they are often executives at their companies and capable as heck at getting a lot done at work. Some Mode Twos pride themselves on the fact that they never set foot in a gym or spend even two seconds working out. They carry their excess weight around like a croix de guerre, their own personal badge of honor. "I'm too competent and smart to worry about a silly thing like exercise," they seem to say. In reality, since they're not ignorant and are often among the brightest and most competent, the extra weight and poor cardiovascular health bother these otherwise successful women. Ironically, the Mode Two is often good friends with Mode Ones, who constantly badger her about her fitness habits.

Mode Three

Mode Three women are commonly referred to as yo-yo types. They vacillate between being a Mode One and a Mode Two. They may become workout fanatics for a period of time and then drop out completely until a new fad captures their fancy. The exercise phase of a Mode Three may last for as short a time as a month or go on for a year or more. Then, the Mode Three may remain inactive for up to six months before she jumps on the next fitness bandwagon. When she's in her exercise phase, she may attend the gym daily and train for hours at a time. Unfortunately, she loses interest just as quickly as she gets excited and gradually drops out of the excitement phase until the buzz about a new workout or a motivating mood swing gets her back into the gym.

I was a Mode Three in my painting habits—before I learned better ways. My experience with painting, I think, illustrates what goes on in the fitness Mode Three mind. If you're an artist or you know one, you (as well as I) know how long an ultimate masterpiece takes, yet whenever I started to paint a new piece of art I was very impatient. I wanted to finish quickly so that I could view the completed work as soon as possible. I used to rush some areas on the canvas and paint them as totally finished detail sections rather than work on the entire painting. I just wasted a lot of time when I did that because later I had to repaint those detailed areas. They didn't work with the entire painting, when more of it was completed. I was too enthusiastic for the artistic benefit of the final outcome and I was too impatient to do the work correctly at the start. It cost me precious time.

I had to develop the patience to view the entire canvas as a whole. First, the color and texture gets laid down in layers to create depth. These layers gradually build up stroke by stroke until the very last touches of color and definition are added. Then the accents complete the picture. There's a long time during the process, however, when the final outcome is unclear. You have to trust the process of the layers. The very last thing that is added is the sparkle and twinkle in the eye (in a portrait) or the light glancing off the clouds in the sky (in a landscape).

Like me ignoring the correct sequence for my painting, Mode Threes often fail to see the systematic approach required for health and fitness. Finding *life*Balance is the result of the sum of all the brush strokes that ultimately create the long-awaited masterpiece. Mode Threes jump into the latest fitness craze with more enthusiasm than any other type, but they lack the ability to see the big picture and to have patience about the result. When they don't begin to see their dream picture right away, they get discouraged or bored and lose interest, often for long periods of time. Instead of being constructive, they are destructive, never acquiring the ability to maintain balance. Instead of jumping into the latest fad with all the energy in the world and then abandoning the program, they would be better off laying down a fitness foundation and adding layers detail by detail, day by day. It takes less time to get the masterpiece right the first time than it does to constantly start over and rework it.

When Mode Threes jump off the fitness wagon it becomes really difficult for them to get back on. Once they stop working out, they lose not only interest, but energy, since energy is fed by momentum. Because exercise doesn't take energy from you—it gives you energy back—you will be ten times more productive if you exercise than if you don't. Once a Mode Three falls off the wagon she can become very disheartened, since she knows not only how good it feels to be fit, but how hard it is to get going again once at a standstill.

Mode Threes who have fallen out of the exercise habit need to look at the hiatus as a stoplight that can stay red forever or can be turned to green with one small step. If you wait for all the stoplights to be green, you'll never get downtown, will you? If you've taken time off for a baby or an injury or just because you got lazy, you can begin again by taking that first step and watching momentum grow.

Mode Four

Patience is the single most important element for any of the fitness modes. When I was training for the Ms. Olympia titles there were many, many, many times I just wanted to give up and quit. I got incredibly frustrated and told myself, "Give it up. You're working so hard and your body's not responding immediately." I'd be frustrated and on the verge of quitting or retiring because I told myself that I wasn't good enough or I didn't deserve to win or I didn't have the genetics or whatever. Nevertheless, I just stuck with the workout and good nutrition day in and day out.

Mode Four is typified by those who have learned to cultivate patience. They know how to succeed without the stress and to gain without the pain. They have achieved balance in their lives and fitness programs. These are the lucky few who have found a way to incorporate healthy eating habits, effective exercise, and empowering mind/body techniques.

I've gotten pretty good at maintaining a Mode Four lifestyle, even though I've gone for many years as a Mode One and even a few as a Mode Two. But Mode Four is becoming easier and easier for me as I see the difference it makes in my life. I went through a period many years ago in Chicago when I was functioning in Mode Four without even knowing it. I was a full-time interior designer with a demanding job. I had very little time for training. Rather than make myself nuts with guilt, or agonizing over my rare training sessions, I made a few simple adjustments to my daily schedule. I got up thirty minutes earlier than usual so that I could do some aerobics at home before I went to work to sit on my booty all day. Twice a week I cruised to the gym at lunchtime and got in twenty or thirty minutes of weight work. I'd eat a healthy lunch—prepared at home—after my workout and still make it back to work in time without having to kill myself. On some days I'd park my car a half mile from the office and walk to work. I wasn't on some crazy diet during that period, either. All I did was prepare healthy, delicious food at home and avoid the vending machines when I got hungry. No big deal, but it enabled me to stay pretty darn fit without all the obsession. I was in pretty good *life*Balance back then when you consider that I got a raise at work, had more energy during the day, and even won my first national bodybuilding championship that year!

If you are lucky enough to be among the minority of people who are in Mode Four, congratulations! If not, don't despair. Knowing your mode will help you determine the time of day you should exercise and the type of workouts that will work for you. Your goal is not to try to become something you're not—but to acknowledge where you're at and begin to learn techniques that will move you closer toward Mode Four.

One of the biggest reasons Mode Fours get great results and still have plenty of time in each and every day is because they make use of an important *life*Balance principle: what I call the 50% Exercise Solution.

THE 50% EXERCISE SOLUTION

When I was doing the Ms. Olympia contests I was so overtrained it was ridiculous! I didn't have to work that hard and neither do you. The 50% Exercise Solution enables you to train less and stay leaner and stronger than before. It's not complicated and doesn't require special gadgets or equipment. It's guaranteed to make working out more fun and more effective than ever before. Plus, the 50% Solution is so easy to use that you don't have to be a brain surgeon or a nuclear physicist in order to figure it out. Unlike many other plans you may have tried, which are generic and designed to be used by everyone from a 200-pound man to a 130-pound woman, this solution is based on your individual fitness personality type, combined with common sense and logic. It's a general framework that can be tailored to your individual schedule, utilizing your own likes, dislikes, and needs.

The three chief components of the 50% Exercise Solution are:

Time of day of workout
Amount of exertion
Type of activity (based on your fitness mode)

Never again will you think of exercise as time taken away from your day. For each active hour you invest, you gain one and a half hours of extended life!

Time of Day of Workout

When you work out is a critical part of any exercise equation. Finding the right time of day for you can make all the difference in reaching your goals. Experiment and find the time of day to work out that works best for you. Each time of day has its own unique advantages.

Morning

Mentally, this can be a great time of day for fitness. Mode Ones generally prefer to train first thing in the morning. That way, they can have their workout out of the way without disrupting their busy schedules. They get the guilt out of the way (temporarily) and it can't distract them during the rest of the day. The sense of accomplishment that comes from exercising first thing in the morning can be very motivating for most people, but especially for the Mode One.

For Mode Twos or Threes this is also a great time of day to fit in a workout. By working out first thing they eliminate obligations or distractions on their to-do list and have the rest of the day to accomplish much. They eliminate the excuses that usually show up later in the day. Taking a small step toward motivation first thing in the morning sends them on their way to higher motivation and bigger steps on following days.

Midday

Many people report experiencing an energy lag after lunch. How many times have you felt tons of energy early in the day, only to have it dissipate shortly after noon? By about 2:30 or so it can feel like nap time. Contrary to popular belief, this dip in energy levels is not always due to eating or altered blood sugar levels. Often, this post-lunch energy dip has to do with our natural daily body rhythms.

The good thing about midday workouts is that they can make the after-lunch lag less exaggerated, since norepinephrine and epinephrine are increased by exercising at midday. When I was working in interior design in Chicago my midday workouts rejuvenated me mentally and physically—and didn't take a lot of time, either! Try training in the middle of the day and see what happens to your energy level for the rest of the afternoon. But don't neglect lunch! Eat some light, healthy foods for energy, relax or stretch gently for about fifteen minutes, then exercise and see how much get up and go you get!

Night

While most people think of this time of day as the worst for workouts, there are physical reasons why that is not always the case. For the body, this can be the best time of day to do physical activity. The airways of the lungs are more open, the muscles are stronger due to a higher body temperature, and flexibility is increased. If you've managed to save any energy reserves for an early evening workout, go for it. This is not the perfect time, however, if the day's hassles have left you feeling enervated. Mode Ones are usually too impatient or compulsive to wait until the evening hours to work out, but Mode Twos may find that this time suits them very well.

Gluconeogenesis: Morning's Secret Weapon

I'm now going to let you in on a big part of the 50% Solution which, used alone—without changing any other element of your program—could transform your fitness results. Gluconeogenesis is a big word with huge significance for those who want to lose body fat. Even if you're the most confirmed night owl, finding time for exercise in the morning will allow you to capitalize on your body's gluconeogenesis. If you can make this one change—exercising first thing in the morning rather than later in the day—I promise you'll be amazed by the results.

Starting out with aerobics first thing in the day allows you to:

· Optimize aerobic activity while burning fat
· Create a condition in which the body will continue to burn fat even after cessation of exercise

The Genesis of Gluconeogenesis

In the beginning (of the day, that is) the human body is in a state of fat oxidation, not having absorbed anything for at least an eight-hour period of time. Serum Free Fatty Acid (FFA) levels are at their highest and this is the optimal time to burn fat during exercise. Food consumption immediately *after* morning exercise will result in an insulin-mediated suppression of FFAs, while increasing blood glucose. This causes our fat-burning furnace to favor carbohydrate burning. What the heck does all that mean? Well, remember that blueberry bagel you had for breakfast? It's less likely that your body will store it as blubber in your thighs if you've already utilized morning's window of fat-burning opportunity through gluconeogenesis.

There is some research that shows two additional ways to widen the fat-burning window by accelerating FFA levels: (1) by taking a combination of readily available supplements including Citrin (-HCA) with L-carnitine and chromium picolinate and (2) by drinking one or two cups of coffee forty-five minutes before exercise. We'll talk about the Citrin supplement combo later in this book. As for the pre-exercise coffee, I know plenty of bodybuilders who swear by it as a pre-exercise aid. I'm not advocating caffeine addiction, but I suggest that if you're a coffee drinker and you're practicing moderation (balance!) you might drink one cup of coffee (of the one or two per day you consume) before you work out. Try this for a while and see how it works for you.

These are easy suggestions (50% Solution, remember?); they don't require that you totally change your life or make dramatic revisions in the way you do things now. They are simple, doable habits you can try at any time.

You've figured out the time of day which will work best for your fitness mode type and busy schedule. Now let's take a look at how hard you need to work out—and why you need to work out at all.

Amount of Exertion

Why Work Out at All?

As one woman said to me, "Once I'm so centered and balanced and full of *life*Balance, why should I work out at all? Maybe I don't need to do anything else at this point." Wrong! Finding *life*Balance doesn't mean that you spend the rest of your life meditating on a beach somewhere or burning incense in a dark, saffron-lined room. People with *life*Balance are full of energy and excitement. They just don't spend as much time worrying about their workouts and they do spend more time enjoying them!

The Benefits of Exercise

There are healthy, nonobsessive reasons to work out. By doing so, you empower your body with health and reward it for all the hard work it does for you. Your body carries you around from day to day with vigor and vitality. It serves you as you perform your daily activities. Empowering *life*Balance fitness habits help ward off disease and disability.

Regular exercise has been shown to:

· Aid in preventing obesity
· Reduce the risk of heart disease and some forms of cancer
· Help the body mobilize stored fat for energy
· Enhance physical endurance
· Tone muscles in legs, thighs, and abdomen (for better strength and performance)

A Mindful State

Many of us need to rethink the way we view exercise. American workout obsessions seem to be failing us in many ways. If you take a look at the health habits in other countries, many fall short of ours, but there are other cultures, particularly in the Far East, from whom we might learn a few things. The Chinese, for example, believe that the body must be moved every day to stay healthy. Too bad we don't believe that in this country. I think more of us would be able to manage our fitness based on that style of thinking. Much of the pressure about fitness would be removed. There would be many more healthy, long-lived people.

For too many of us, physical fitness means what I call superficial calisthenics. That's when you force yourself into a gym and move around in order to break a sweat, burn calories and fat, and get your heart rate up; you're focusing strictly on the physical. That's not all bad, because at least an effort is being made. You're neglecting, however, a most important element when you forget to include the mind in your daily workouts. How many times have you walked into a gym where dozens of men and women are lined up like fitness automatons, reading magazines or watching the news on televisions as they huff and puff away on stair-climbing machines or treadmills? People are desperately trying to go mindless so that the torture will be over sooner. Often, busy men and women believe that they're getting more done by reading a business report or watching the daily news while they hop around on an aerobics machine. In reality they're getting less done because they have split the mind and the body. They're not totally focused on what they're doing with either their bodies or their minds. Yes, the time seems to go faster, but the results are less than they could be.

By incorporating a meditative, mindful state when you work out, you create a mind/body balance that is very powerful. Physical movement combined with a mindful state creates wonders. Early in my bodybuilding career I realized that. When I worked out without really focusing or while worrying about the day's problems, my results suffered. When I focused on the body part on which I was working, I got better results, faster. Also, when I gabbed with my training partner or allowed my mind to obsess on the day's problems or other matters, I didn't get that great post-workout endorphin buzz that is so satisfying! I might as well have gone for a hot fudge sundae!

When you work out, don't do so just for movement's sake. Don't think about worrisome distractions. Focus on the mind/body connection and feel the *life*Balance begin.

Type of Activity

Choose an activity (Natural Game) that fits your mode and engages your inner athlete. It doesn't have to be a difficult process, as I've already shown. Let's add another element to the 50% Exercise Solution: the type of activity.

There are two factors involved here. One is the importance of aerobic (fat-burning and cardiovascular) training and the other is the necessity for resistance training. *Life*Balance requires that we fulfill "obligations" in both areas. Let's take a look at our aerobic needs first.

The Exorcist: Aerobic Activity

Aerobic exercise, even a gentle walk, can ease anxiety and muscle tension (two of the common results of stress) for at least two hours and, according to some research, for much, much longer. It can alleviate mild depression. It strengthens the cardiovascular system, boosts levels of the "good" (HDL) cholesterol, bolsters the immune system, and lowers blood pressure.

The types of exercise that increase the fat-burning ability of your body are called aerobic because they increase your body's use of oxygen. Walking, cycling, and gentle jogging are all good examples of aerobic exercise. However, you can substitute any sustained exercise that uses the major muscles of the body. The key is to do the activity for a minimum of thirty minutes at least three times a week. Remember, the 50% Solution is, above all else, about training smarter, not harder.

Let's take a look at how exercise helps us burn fat:

· The amount of fat we burn tends to be roughly proportional to our serum FFA levels, so it follows that increased FFA levels tend to promote more fat-burning.

· Intense exercise (70 percent of VO2 max) coupled with a low-calorie diet may accelerate muscle loss and reduce the body's metabolic rate. Roughly translated, this means that if you don't eat enough and then force your body through a tough aerobic workout you won't burn fat, but you will lose muscle tone!

· Better fat-burning occurs with moderately intense exercise, such as walking, performed for forty minutes. In addition, by doing resistance training, you'll preserve lean mass (muscle) and get even more benefits.

· Though fat-burning peaks at the end of exercise and then declines, FFA levels often continue to rise for an hour or so following exercise. Thus, the post-exercise period represents an excellent opportunity to continue to burn fat.

The 50% Solution teaches that getting an aerobic workout doesn't always take place in a gym, spa, or other fitness "designated" area. Making time for aerobics doesn't require a degree in time management or an MBA. You've got more time than you know in which to find your way to fitness. According to the Centers for Disease Control and Prevention, here are some examples of moderate exercise that can keep you healthy:

Wash and wax a car for 45–60 minutes.
Clean your floors and windows for 45–60 minutes.
Play volleyball for 45 minutes.
Work in the garden for 30–45 minutes.
Bicycle five miles in 30 minutes.
Fast social dance for 30 minutes.
Push the baby in the stroller for one and a half miles in 30 minutes.
Rake leaves for 30 minutes.
Walk two miles in 30 minutes.
Perform water aerobics for 30 minutes.
Swim laps in the pool for 20 minutes.
Jump rope for 15 minutes.
Run one and a half miles in 15 minutes.
Walk up and down stairs for 15 minutes.

Resistance Training

We all need to get in an aerobic workout (you pick what works for you!) at least three times a week for the best health benefits. Do your aerobic work more frequently if you need to lose weight and/or if you have the time and find it enjoyable—which you will if you pick the right workout for you!

In addition to this much-needed aerobic training, *life*Balance requires resistance training. Most people immediately think of weight lifting when I get to this part of the program. "Here's the part where it gets hard, right? This is where you tell me I have to pump about fifteen hundred pounds of iron for three hours a day, right?" They're partially right, but also very wrong. Weight lifting needn't make anyone a slave to a gym.

Weights

Getting fit is like a self-fulfilling prophecy: you know that what you're doing is good for you . . . so you feel better . . . so you tend to stay motivated. . . . so you have a better self-image. There is no doubt anymore about the psychological advantages of regular exercise. It's great for self-esteem and helps alleviate, if not eradicate, depression, stress, and anxiety. As people enter middle age or older, most will do so with less muscle, making formerly easy activities like gardening, carrying shopping bags, and even walking the dog seem more tiring than before. Sedentary people begin to sense this muscle loss and energy shift in their *life*Balance as early as their thirties. That's why weight lifting is so important. Also, having more muscle and strength makes doing any aerobic or other activity easier and more enjoyable. Fat tissue burns many fewer calories (if any!) compared to muscle tissue. Muscular, toned individuals can eat more without putting on weight, so using weights to build more muscle is a great way to become a better fat-burner. Plus, weight lifting shifts the metabolism into high gear for hours after the workout! Estimates for this metabolism boost range from seven to fifteen hours, depending on the intensity of the workout. Don't neglect your weight training as you learn to create *life*Balance. Make sure that you lift weights two or three times a week.

How Much Weight Lifting Is Enough?

My workout program is so moderate these days you probably wouldn't believe it. During my athletic career I did some damage to my back during track and field events and all the time I spend on planes these days exacerbates the problem. Like most of us, I have to maintain and correct what I've done in the past. I've been working with terrific physical therapists who have put me on a stretching and toning program. For aerobics, I walk every day when I'm in town and I try to walk whenever I'm on the road. But my weight-lifting routine is honed to a science. I strive to do a twenty-minute weight circuit workout two or three days a week. Some weeks I fail miserably, but I always have those two or three times a week as a goal in the back of my mind. Also, when I work with weights now I work them fairly slowly because the slower you train, the more muscle fibers you activate.

It's a long road to get in shape, make no mistake, but it's easy as pie to stay there once you've arrived. Once there, it's a breeze. It's like the pot of gold at the end of the rainbow!

Not Just Pumping Iron

Resistance training covers a much broader spectrum than simply pumping iron. By limiting our understanding of all that resistance training can be, we limit our options and thus find it more difficult to achieve balance. If resistance training, which is recommended by health experts, medical authorities, personal trainers, and *me* (!) meant just weight lifting, most of us would be in a real pickle! Many times it's difficult to get to a gym with weights. It can be costly buying equipment for the home, and hey, let's face it, sometimes you just don't feel like lifting weights. These are valid excuses for missing weight workouts, but they don't mean you have to skip resistance training completely. Creating *life*Balance means removing the excuses and overcoming the objections—easily. You can remove some of the excuses when you broaden your understanding of resistance training.

Resistance training means just what it says: training with resistance. If you get down on the floor right now and do a push-up (or try to) you'll immediately feel resistance at work as you try to lift your body up and then lower it slowly down. That's resistance training. It can be found in a variety of sports and workouts that can be done at home, without special equipment, at your convenience.

Finding the type of resistance training you can incorporate into your program means experimenting a bit, having some fun, and trying new things. I'll always lift weights and I suggest you do, too. But for those times when it's difficult, or for those who just don't like weight lifting, learn alternative resistance training methods.

Let's look at some basic guidelines for picking the right type of resistance and aerobic training for each of the first three fitness modes. (Mode Four already represents a successful fitness routine!)

Basic Moderation Tips for a Healthier Mode One

Mode One types need to change their motivation and create moderation. Mode Ones have to revamp the way they work out, revise the motivation behind their goals from outer-directed to inner-directed, and learn physical activities that facilitate this. I suggest that Mode Ones reread chapter 5 on motivation. In particular, though, if you are a Mode One, read again the "Old Cory" Commandments. Sound like you? I think they might. Now take another look at the *new* Cory Commandments and see if you can begin to incorporate some of them into your life, while removing the old ones. Also, the following tips can be very helpful for Mode Ones, since they help to refocus the incredible (sometimes insane!) energy level they possess.

- Select exercises or activities you enjoy. Don't punish yourself with workouts. They can be fun, if you let them! You don't have to end up in the Intensive Care Unit at the local hospital to know that you've worked hard enough.
- Vary your routine. Don't plow through the same old grueling workout day after day, or even hour after hour. Alternate walking with an aerobic exercise videotape or riding a bike. Some days your workout will be lighter than others. That's OK. Allow your body time to rest, recuperate, and relax!
- Change your environment. Americans, especially Mode Ones, like their

workouts in high-tech, artificial, controlled environments. I'm always amazed when I stop by a gym on a beautiful day and see the many people who have chosen to run or walk on a treadmill indoors, under the bright fluorescent lights, when outside a beautiful day awaits them! Working out in areas of natural beauty is a great way to get in touch with the Real You. If you're a Mode One, take a regular break from your routine and learn to enjoy a different type of workout without feeling guilty. Kayak in the ocean. Ski down a beautiful mountain. In your own neighborhood, find a walking or running route that takes you past some lovely flowers or a cluster of tall trees.

· Exercise with a non–Mode One friend. Rigidity encourages more rigidity. Let yourself enjoy a workout with a friend who isn't quite as extreme as you are. Socializing is good for you and you might find—every once in a while—that you enjoy a workout that doesn't push your body to the max.

· Lighten up. Yes, it's important to do something every day, but don't kill yourself to do so. Don't always do the same thing two days in a row. If you're pressed for time, don't cancel time with friends and family in order to get your workout. Just take a mindful walk for fifteen minutes or get down on the floor and do some sit-ups.

· Relax and enjoy. Smile or say hi to four people on the way to your workout—or during it! Compliment a friend. Positive interaction with other people lifts your spirits and changes your outlook. Mode Ones tend to look at their workout as a time when any interaction detracts from their efforts. Focus is important. Obsession is not.

Tiny Changes for a Better Motivated Mode Two

Mode Twos achieve moderation starting from the opposite end of the scale from Mode Ones. A Mode Two needs to focus on ways to find motivation that lasts for her. If you're a Mode Two, reread chapter 5 on motivation. Then, since you have to learn to walk before you can run, begin to find motivation by making small changes. See if any of the tiny changes I've listed here can be of help to you.

Tiny, incremental lifestyle changes can really help in staying motivated. Even the teeniest, tiniest changes, when added together, can add up to big benefits. Think about it: if you do one little thing each and every day, at the end of one year, you will reap huge rewards!

The little lifestyle changes listed below can help kickstart an exercise program for anyone, but are especially good for Mode Twos. Try one of them this week. Think of it as an experiment. Write about it in your journal.

- Plan social activities that revolve more around movement and less around food. Have a rollerblading date, a doubles tennis match, or a hiking lunch with a backpack loaded with fresh chicken sandwiches, veggies, and fruit.
- Rescue a pup from the pound. Take up the active hobby of walking your dog every day. Your "fur person" will love you and you'll have a training partner who is always ready to go!
- Put your workout clothes by the foot of the bed at night, so they're there first thing in the morning staring at you!
- If you're bored with your workout, take up a new sport or activity. Don't get into a rut and don't overtrain. Do just enough each day so that you're looking forward to the next day's activities, rather than dreading them because you're so beat up. When I was competing I often found myself "leaving it all at the gym"—meaning working out so hard that I had nothing left for later in the day for other parts of life.
- Always use stairs rather than escalators. Park your car away from work so you have to walk a bit to get to the office. If you are in a parking structure, park at the top and take the stairs down and back up again after work.
- Buy yourself a cute new pair of tights, a leotard, or a sweatshirt. Pump more enthusiasm and variety into your workout life!
- Pick the right time. Make time for exercise when you feel strongest and most energetic. If early morning workouts don't work for you, don't feel guilty. I know many professional bodybuilders who like to work out at midnight! Also, don't plan workouts that are impossible to make. If you have to carpool the kids to school at eight A.M., planning an early morning workout might be setting yourself up for failure. Pick a time that works for your schedule.
- Stay fully engaged. Don't spend your workout hour or half hour or fifteen minutes worrying about the office, the family, or housework. Take advantage of this great opportunity to make contact with the Real You.

Suggestions for a More Consistent Mode Three

The Mode Three is often capable of finding *life*Balance more easily than a Mode One or Mode Two, since she knows the in's and out's of both fitness extremes. She teeters back and forth between motivation and moderation and knows what it feels like to have both. The key for this fitness type is learning to regulate the swings between exercise extremes.

To bridge the gap between periods of total inactivity and flurries of activity, if you're a Mode Three you should focus on consistency. While in the throes of an exercise flurry, focus on the suggestions listed for Mode Ones and consciously taper off the periodic exercise obsession with moderation, so you don't start to burn out and switch over to Mode Two. By preventing the burnout from setting in, a Mode Three can prevent a standstill in her exercise program.

If you are a Mode Three who has fallen into an energy stall, read the section above on creating motivation for Mode Twos. By getting motivated and then maintaining the motivation with moderation, a Mode Three can break out of the vicious cycle of inactivity versus overexuberance she may be struggling with.

*LIFE*BALANCE FITNESS AND YOUR NATURAL GAME

Everybody's responses to fitness choices are as unique as their feelings about everything else in life. The fitness activities they choose to do depend on how they are wired emotionally. Are you wired for sensation or stability? For example, when you go to the amusement park, do you like the roller coaster or the merry-go-round? Is a mountain retreat your idea of the perfect vacation, or does a skydiving weekend turn you on? Find fitness activities that make workouts fun and you'll de-stress, be healthier, and stick with the plan. When you can say, "Today I *get* to do . . . " instead of, "Today I've *got* to do . . ." you'll know you've found the right ones for you.

The scores included here are intended as a way for you to determine which activities will help you best achieve *life*Balance, given your specific fitness mode. I suggest your weekly *life*Balance exercise score total at least twenty-five points. The scores given are for the amount of time listed with each activity. It's important that your total of twenty-five points include at least three *different* activities each week. For example: if you went running on Monday, you'd score nine points. Then, on Wednesday, you might try golfing nine holes (five points) or playing tennis (four points). By Thursday you'd have about fifteen points. That means you'd have four days in which to take a yoga class, try Pilates, or use the treadmill at the gym. You'd have participated in some great mind/body activities and completed your cardio-conditioning at the same time. You'll be amazed at how good such a balanced program will make you feel, particularly if you're used to struggling through the same old workout grind day after day.

I've also included here suggestions for new, noncompetitive ways to look at

Find fitness activities that make workouts fun.

each of the sports. These suggestions can help you stop seeing the games (activities) as "body versus body" and may enable you to enjoy them more. When you play your fitness games this way, you silence the inner critic before she even gets a chance to critique you by putting in her two cents' worth.

RUNNING
(*life*Balance score: nine or 10 for one half hour at a moderate pace)

Imagine yourself running down a long and winding road. The wind is warm as it blows across your face and body. You are moving at top speed, planning to slow down as soon as you get winded. After what seems like a very long time you check your stopwatch and realize with a start that you have just finished a mile in less than eight minutes—something you have never done before. You continue on, feeling a strength and energy that you have never felt before. It's as if you're a huge rolling cloud, gaining—not losing—momentum as you go. Your body begins to feel weightless, as though you're just bones and skin and little else. Your mind is clear of all thought or care. It's as though you have become one with the wind. When you finish, you sit quietly by the side of the road until your mind and body return to a normal state.

You've just visualized the reason so many people have turned to running as a way not only to change their bodies, but to alter their consciousness. The regular rhythm and repetition of putting one foot after the other after the other tends to lull the mind into an altered state.

Athletes who have set world records or performed exceptionally well often talk about the ease with which they accomplished their best efforts. They talk about time seeming to come to a stop, as everything seems to happen in slow motion. They observe their performance almost as though they're spectators and they talk about the lack of effort and concentration required when optimum performance is happening. People who have reached these athletic pinnacles have tapped into another dimension that exists outside of the mind or the body.

Having a home treadmill is a great way for those who enjoy running to guarantee themselves workouts in even the worst weather. Because only 20 percent of running injuries are due to structural factors in the body, while more are due to environmental factors like running on hard surfaces, treadmills are a relatively "low impact" and safe alternative to outdoor jogging. Once a pricey item only for the very rich, treadmills are now purchased by many people of all income brackets. They account for nearly half the sales in the billion-dollar retail exercise equipment market.

GOLF
(*life*Balance score: 5 for nine holes)

Golf is great for a variety of reasons. There's the fresh air and the camaraderie of golfing with friends. There's the quiet. Your body is engaged while the beautiful environment expands your consciousness and quiets your mind. If you focus on the beauty and the stillness rather than the scorecard, you'll find incredible benefit in this sport.

SKIING

(*life*Balance score: 5 for a half day of downhill skiing; 7 for a half day of cross-country skiing)

This sport is gravity-based and balanced. There's a flow that has to happen—whether you're zooming downhill or gliding cross-country—that encourages the mind to relax and calm. Plus, as a friend of mine puts it, "skiing is the one thing that makes me focus totally on the moment. When you're cruising down a steep hill, it's impossible to be anywhere but present in the moment. There's a tremendous relaxation that skiing provides that is hard to find in other sports."

TENNIS

(*life*Balance score: 4 for one set of singles or two sets of doubles)

Tennis was one of the first sports to openly embrace the mind/body concept. In 1974 W. Timothy Gallwey wrote the best-selling book, *The Inner Game of Tennis* (he coauthored a similar book on skiing three years later) and for the first time, many people were exposed to the close relationship between thoughts (the mind) and sports performance (the body).

Unfortunately, tennis can be a very competitive sport. I know of a couple who almost got divorced over the game. She played better than he and the relationship suffered until a talented therapist helped the two work out the marital kinks. Believe it or not, tennis can be a wonderful, noncompetitive game. Focus not on annihilating your partner, but on getting into a flow. Think of the ball as an energy that flows from you to your partner, and the harder you hit it, the more difficult it is to return, and the more energy you draw forth from your partner. You help your partner improve her energy in certain areas and she does the same for you. Tennis then becomes a game of mutual enrichment and empowerment. Plus, it burns fat calories!

PILATES®

(*life*Balance score: 8 for forty-five minutes)

This seventy-year-old overnight success (it's pronounced "puh-LAH-teez") began in 1926 at Joseph Pilates's studio in Manhattan. Then, dancers, socialites, athletes, and celebrities arrived in large numbers for the therapeutic, restorative benefits developed by the legendary physical trainer. Pilates had been a frail child but became a boxer in later life. He served as a nurse in World War I and developed the prototype for what would become his famous Pilates Reformer by attaching springs to hospital beds for use by non-ambulatory patients.

The Pilates® Method combines Eastern and Western philosophies in a way that is useful for total body conditioning, flexibility, and strength. Physical therapists, chiropractors, and orthopedists use it as rehabilitative exercise and physical therapy to speed recovery of soft tissue injuries.

The Pilates® Method is a series of more than five hundred movements that are low-impact and controlled, and that engage the mind as well as the body. There are five major pieces of Pilates apparatus and the movements are best performed under the supervision of trained instructors. Only teachers who complete the rigorous training program approved by The Pilates Studio®, including two weeks of seminar training and six hundred apprenticeship hours, may call themselves Pilates instructors. (Romana Kryzanowska, master teacher, was taught by Joseph Pilates and is still teaching the method in New York City.) The emphasis in Pilates is on breathing and body alignment, particularly in the areas of the abdomen, buttocks, and lower back. (These three areas are called the "powerhouse" in Pilates-speak.)

The Pilates® Method can be found at more than seventy locations in the United States and internationally in fifteen locations. There is a rigorous teacher certification program required of Pilates instructors to assure that instruction is consistent and uniform from location to location and to guarantee adherence to the principles of Joseph Pilates. Other methods have sprung up which copy many of the principles involved in The Pilates® Method—but they may vary radically from strict Pilates technique. You can do Pilates at home by purchasing The Pilates® Performer, a commercial version of the Reformer used in Pilates studios. (Check appendix for Pilates information.)

YOGA

(*life*Balance score: 10 for sixty to seventy-five minutes)

The word *yoga* comes from the Sanskrit word meaning "yoke." It began as a spiritual discipline in the Far East and was taught in many different forms and styles, most of them more about the mind than the body. In typical American fashion, we extracted the most physical styles of yoga—in particular hatha yoga—and turned yoga into a fitness workout. The beauty of yoga, however, is that it's a foolproof mind/body science that works in spite of any practitioners' superficial intentions. The benefits will come to you just by virtue of showing up, breathing, and getting into the postures. It's like mind/body magic!

Practicing yoga joins, or yokes, the individual to the universe, enabling those who practice it to unite with something bigger than themselves. It's a great way to learn to experience yourself nonjudgmentally and noncompetitively. There's no place for competition in a yoga class. When you practice the yoga poses, do so without comparing yourself to others in class. Go for sensation within your own body. Try to go deeper into the poses with time and don't compare where you may be today with any other day. Each day is a different day in yoga practice, just as it is in life. The body is in a different place from day to day and responds uniquely depending on a number of variables. That's OK. There will be days when you'll go deeply into a pose and others when the body will feel less limber. Allow the body to have these variances. Breathe, relax, and feel.

If you follow those few simple rules, yoga will do so much more for you than just keep you limber and strong. As one fairly new yoga student told me, "Cory, it's really amazing. Yes, I feel more agile than ever before and my thighs are firmer than when I was doing tons of step classes, but the best part is that my feelings about my body have changed completely without any effort on my part. I'm much less judgmental about myself now." Many women have reported similar attitude changes. For some, this nonjudgmental acceptance and enjoyment of self has transferred over to other areas of life.

It's not only in finance that the rich get richer. If you already do yoga or meditate, you're way ahead in the search for *life*Balance.

POWER PACING, SPINNING, TOTAL BODY BIKING

(*life*Balance score: 9 for forty-five minutes)

This hot new fitness trend is powerful for many reasons. It's one of the best ways to burn fat, break a good sweat, and get an endorphin high. It's also a fabulous way to make a strong internal connection and get in touch with yourself.

It's called by different names depending on the brand of the stationary bike used at your health club. The basic premise is always the same, however: to simulate the relaxation and rigors of a real road ride without leaving home or gym. Pacing, or spinning, offers riders a chance to go totally inward while working out with a group. A pacing or spinning bike is different from the average stationary bicycle in that its gearing more accurately mimics that of a road bike. The class is set up so that the instructor faces the class on her or his bike and students follow directions about how fast to go or how hard the pedal resistance should be. There is music for motivation.

Studios featuring this sport are springing up all over the country. Try it, you'll like it!

AIKIDO

(*life*Balance score: 10 for forty-five minutes)

At first, much aikido class time is spent simply learning to quiet the mind. Meditation and centering the body are important first lessons. Then, the student learns to sense the approach of others and to blend with energy flows. Finally, some physical activity takes place. Morihei Uyeshiba reached enlightenment through his dedication to the martial arts, so it's no surprise that the art he created is contemplative as well as active. Users learn to utilize "ki" (life energy) to create powerful yet relaxed energy. They learn to send their ki down deep into the earth to become "stronger and heavier" than their opponents. There are many variations—all involving one arm reaching upward, one arm downward. There is balance. There is no combativeness. A basic concept of aikido is that there is already a flow of energy and activity happening all around us—we merely have to learn how to join it. Most of this sport is taught as simple, flowing movement.

LifeBalance PARTNER EXERCISE: AIKIDO POWER

Have your partner stand with her arm extended in front of her. She should use every bit of her physical strength to resist as you try to bend her arm at the elbow. Once you've tried that, have her hold the arm out with no strength behind it. Try again to bend it at the elbow. Switch places as you hold your arm out and your partner tries to bend your arm.

In the first instance, you both were very unyielding and forceful—using sheer strength and will. In the second instance you both were limp and weak. Both are extremes.

Now, try the exercise again. This time, when each of you hold out your arms, do so with the hand open and the fingers apart. Center your breathing and relax the body. Think of the arm as a bright beam of pure energy extending through the walls and out into the universe. Concentrate on becoming one with the beam of light.

Hopefully, you both discovered the power in this type of being. That is the core of aikido.

TAI CHI CHUAN
(*life*Balance score: 7 for one-half hour; 10 for one hour)

The words mean "grand ultimate fist" and the emphasis is on internal strengthening of the organs, intestines, and blood. In this practice, the outer body stays relaxed and soft as the internal organs get stronger and stronger. Tai chi chuan's advocates claim it improves concentration, balance, and coordination. Improved flexibility, circulation, and health are other by-products. Students of tai chi develop awareness and chi (inner power). Tai chi can also be used for self-defense.

CHI KUNG
(*life*Balance Score: 7 for one-half hour; 10 for one hour)

This is designed to nourish and channel the life force (chi) through breath and postures. There are classes in this discipline as well as very good instructional videotapes.

LifeBalance Can Be Found in Unexpected Places!

Finding fitness balance in your life can often happen in the most unexpected ways. There is no *one* way. There is only *your* way. Experiment to find the style that works for you and discover your Natural Game.

You may discover your fitness favorite in an unexpected place. Here are two examples that may surprise you:

HOUSEWORK OR GARDENING

There are women who consider doing housework a relaxing luxury! If that's the case, more power to them! In fact, they may be onto something. Check out these facts about what I call "functional fitness":

Tub scrubbing burns 441 calories per hour. Mopping floors burns 252 calories per hour. Window cleaning expends 234 calories per hour. Forty-five minutes of vigorous work on your lawn or in your garden burns as many calories as thirty minutes spent in an aerobics class. It can also lower blood pressure and cholesterol. I started composting recently and let me tell you that turning compost can be as rigorous as lifting weights. When I rake leaves I try to think of the rowing machine at the gym. People who still use old-fashioned, un-motorized lawn mowers get terrific workouts—not unlike a boxer with a punching bag.

SQUARE DANCING

It's fun, it's aerobic, it has the same healthy benefits as walking briskly, and it combines the intellectual stimulation of chess with the fun of music. While many people think of it as corny or too homespun, there are about a million square dancers in ten thousand clubs across the United States, Canada, and forty other countries.

Few things are just as plain fun as the search for your Natural Game. You'll make mistakes along the way and go off on crazy tangents, but that's half the fun. Stay with the search and you'll be amazed to discover that, sure enough, you *are* an athlete!

BODYWORK AS A *LIFE*BALANCE FITNESS TOOL

"[W]hen the body gets working appropriately, the force of gravity can flow through. Then, spontaneously, the body heals itself." —Ida P. Rolf, Ph.D.

For those who are just discovering their Natural Game, as well as for those who have enjoyed participating in one for years, there are ways to experience

145

even higher levels of well-being. Years of bodybuilding, running, participating in sports, and just surviving the rigors of everyday life and stress can cause physical damage to the body. The damage isn't limited to the body, however. When you get immobilized physically due to injury, overuse, or stress, you often lock in negative emotional states as well and the NECs can actually cause physical damage to the body.

If you're looking to make a strong MBS connection, you may want to look into some form of bodywork as a way to free up important pathways in the body, which can in turn free up your emotions.

Many of us already know when it's time to release irritated or congested areas of the body. I always know when it's time for physical reorganizing when my neck and shoulders get painfully tight. Others may experience this blockage as lower back pain or even migraine headaches. Often, however, we've been bound up physically for so long that we're out of touch with the pain signals our body is sending us. We've learned how to block out the pain messages so that we can get through the day.

Being *out* of alignment with gravity absorbs energy. Being *in* alignment with gravity means there's more energy available for the body to utilize constructively. When you're in alignment, you can move through life with less effort and authentically experience more while expressing yourself more fully. Plus, all your good exercise and nutrition habits will be supercharged! Here are some great bodywork and other techniques for facilitating the mind/body/soul connection.

Biofeedback

A study published in 1995 in *Medicine, Exercise, Nutrition, and Health* concluded that heart rate biofeedback performed daily for ten minutes resulted in significant long- and short-term stress reduction. Did the participants in this study need some expensive, high-tech machine to perform in this study? No. All they were armed with were Polar Heart Rate Monitors given them by Dr. James Rippe and his research team at the center for Clinical and Lifestyle Research at Tufts University School of Medicine. The study, called "The Effects of Heart Rate Biofeedback on Psychophysiological Responses in Anxious 40–59-Year-Old Women" offers exciting hope for those who wish to manage stress in their hectic lives. Since the mind/body journey is about living in the "here and now," this type of feedback is a great way to focus on your natural biological rhythms and ground yourself firmly in the present. Much of the biofeedback field involves responses such as brain waves, skin temperature, or blood pressure. Measuring and regulating these require very technical machines and equipment, as well as supervision by a doctor.

Rippe's simple method, however, requires only three things, two of which most of us already have: stress and a heartbeat! The only missing element is a heart rate monitor, and those are available at most sporting goods stores in a price range that suits most budgets. The reason you can't just take your own pulse is that the visual feedback provided by the monitor is a key component in the biofeedback process.

Says Rippe, "Using the heart rate monitor to focus participants in the 'here and now' proved to be the intervention that elicited the accumulative, long-term anxiety and stress reducing effect."

I like this type of biofeedback because it works from the first time you try it and, as I've already pointed out, immediate results are always a great motivator for people. Also, the benefits of biofeedback are cumulative and long-term. It's a safe, flexible, and convenient way to tap into state-of-the-art technology without all kinds of professional fees or equipment.

Massage

The fascia is a three-dimensional system of elastic and weblike tissue that gives our bodies the shape they have. It not only surrounds the muscles, but it runs through them, as well as through bones, organs, and even blood vessels. In the healthy state, it's slippery and very pliable. Our tissues slide easily when we move. When the fascia hardens, as it does with time, tension is put on the joints and muscles and we become imbalanced and more immobile. Massage can help prevent this imbalance, as well as that caused by other stress and imbalance in the body.

Massage is seen very differently in this country than in Eastern ones. We tend to attach some sexual connotation to it, rather than see it as a healthy adjunct to health care of the body and mind. In other cultures, it's seen as a process for caring for someone rather than just a way to work out cramps, nerve spasms, and pulled muscles.

In China, massage commands much respect as a healing practice. Practitioners must undergo years of schooling and training before they are allowed to work on people. But then, the Chinese view many healing practices much differently from Americans. Their traditionalist doctors learn some forty different types of pulses, what they mean, and how to tell them apart. They study over one hundred different appearances of the tongue. Their doctors spend the first ten minutes or so of each office visit simply sitting with the patient and assessing that person's physical as well as emotional state.

We tend to polarize between two extremes in our views of massage: sexual or purely mechanical. Massage is seen either as a way to instigate sex or as a physical remedy for the body, like rotating the tires is to a car. Bodyworkers who are intuitive, compassionate, and caring can truly be healers. Much research has been done regarding touch therapy and its proven benefits for healing.

Rolfing

In the 1930s Ida Rolf, a biochemist and physiologist, began developing the bodywork she called "Structural Integration." Her followers would eventually call it simply "Rolfing." Years later, in the psychedelic sixties, Ida Rolf's technique would be lumped in with primal screaming, Birkenstock sandals, and tie-dyed dresses as part of the survival kit of truly groovy flower children. Its reputation changed, however, once the sixties gave way to the seventies and many who tried it found it too invasive, even painful, to endure for the requisite ten sessions it takes to be officially "Rolfed." Reports from those who had it done back then compared it to everything from nirvana (rare) to torture (the rule).

But Rolfing is once again gaining favor as more and more people search for a way to make the mind/body/soul connection, and it has been refined from its former, more painful, incarnation. Rolfing practitioners now use a kinder, gentler method, so its notorious reputation as brutal is no longer valid. Also, its adherents undergo stricter, more standardized training and know more about anatomy, kinesiology, physiology, and psychology than ever before. Dan Kuchars of the Rolf Institute in Boulder, Colorado, has said, "Rolfing today is a natural growth and maturation of a process that was started years ago. We know more about the body and the mind and how they work. We use more finesse." Rolfers no longer proudly ignore their clients' pain.

Today, the list of "celebrity Rolfees" includes track star Edwin Moses and pro baseball player Craig Swan, who actually became a Rolfer when he ended his pitching career! ("It's ironic that now I'm a Rolfer working on the same thing that ended my career," he says.)

Levar Burton, star of "Star Trek: The Next Generation," "Reading Rainbow," and the TV miniseries "Roots," spoke on the "Oprah Winfrey Show" about how Rolfing changed him physically. "I always felt great after each session. . . . I was really solid and I finally felt totally at home in my body."

Mentally it changed him also. "Who I am today is the sum total of all my experience. . . . Sometimes the Rolfer would be working and a belief I held about myself would come up. So during the session, I would examine that belief to see if it was true. Despite the success I had attained, I had walked around for more than twenty years of my life feeling like I wasn't enough. You know that feeling: 'Everyone else is better—I have to do more to be accepted, get better grades, perform better than they did.' That belief wasn't serving me at all. But it was brought to my attention through Rolfing so I could deal with it in a conscious way. Then, I could say to myself, 'That's no longer true. That's a lie.'"

Here's how Rolfing works: The body's fascia, or connective tissue, wraps and surrounds the muscles, tendons, organs, and bones and plays a key role in our movement and skeletal support. The fascia supports and locks into place our skeletal structure. For many of us, this can be the bad news, because negative emotional experiences, as well as physical stress on the body, can "lock" us into awkward body misalignment, which is not only physically unhealthy, but can be emotionally and psychologically damaging. We've all known or seen people who have horrible posture and who have slumped for so many years that they are literally locked into a hunched-over position. These people have become prisoners of their own bodies. But the damage is not only physical to these unfortunate "slouchers." Bad emotional habits have likely also been locked in by the position of their body.

Susan, for example, had arthritis in her right hip since her early teens. When the Rolfer began to work on her hips, she cried out. The practitioner told her, "Listen to your crying. Hear what it's saying." She suddenly remembered moments back in her early childhood. Her father had been a strict disciplinarian, often administering harsh punishments and spankings. "He spanked very hard," she remembers. "I always tried to pull away." Long after the spankings, she would subconsciously "pull away" her hips. She can only speculate now, but she believes that this habit is what caused her arthritis, because there is no other good reason. She feels fairly certain that she has finally figured out the answer to a question that has puzzled both her and her physicians over the years.

Your body is a scrapbook of the way you've lived your life. Rolfing is a way of editing the scrapbook and putting it in better order!

The next chapter is devoted to three powerful workouts that will round out your *life*Balance fitness program: a twenty-minute circuit training workout (for effective resistance training); an aerobic activity (a walking program that will help you effectively and easily take care of the aerobic factor in your workout program); and a beginning yoga routine (for making terrific inroads into the mind/body connection).

> "Some individuals may perceive their losing fight with gravity as a sharp pain in the back, others as the unflattering contour of their body, others as a constant fatigue, yet others as an unrelenting, threatening environment. Those over 40 may call it old age. And yet all of these signals may be pointing to a single problem, so prominent in their own structure, as well as others, that it has been ignored: they are off balance. They are at war with gravity."
>
> —Ida P. Rolf, Ph.D.

twelve
*LIFE*BALANCE WORKOUTS

Once you've determined which fitness mode you fall into and your inner athlete has discovered the Natural Game she likes to play, you're well on your way to *life*Balance. The following three workouts will round out your *life*Balance fitness program. I've included one workout from each of three varieties of exercise—resistance, aerobic, and mind/body—to give you a good solid foundation. Be sure to check with your healthcare professional when you are starting a new exercise program.

Before you try any of these workouts take a moment to try the following centering exercise. All of the *life*Balance workouts require that you work from a strong center and this exercise can show you why that is so important.

LifeBalance EXERCISE: CENTER YOURSELF

Sit in a chair. Now, stand as you normally would.

Did you notice that you probably started the movement with your head or upper body? Now, try again. This time, focus on the center of your body and think of it as the area initiating the move. The rest of the body just goes along for the ride upward as your strong center provides the power.

Didn't that feel easier? Isn't being centered an easier way to move and be in the world? Use the *life*Balance workouts to help you build a stronger center.

*LIFE*BALANCE RESISTANCE TRAINING

Twenty-Minute Circuit Workout

Dieting alone is not as effective as exercise for losing body fat. If you diet without exercising, you lose mainly water and also some muscle. You may get thin, but you will also get flabby. Your body fights back when you're not eating enough food and it does so in a really nasty, ironic way: by lowering your metabolic rate! There you are starving yourself to be thin and your body responds by shutting down the fat-burning mechanism and eating up lean muscle mass. You suffer first from the food imbalance and then from the metabolic imbalance. To help the body find its natural balance as it loses fat, you have to exercise to help maintain the muscle.

This workout is a brand new way of doing weight training. Use the visualizations described here to assist your physical efforts and supercharge your mind/body connection. You can also do Mental Trash Compacting as you strengthen your muscles. I'll explain some mental techniques to try with each movement. Along with the visualizations, be sure to use proper weightlifting protocols. Use moderate, not heavy weight for each movement. (The weights listed are those I use. Yours may vary.) If you haven't used these machines before, ask the trainer at the gym to help you with selecting the appropriate resistance as well as with the proper form. Perform each rep slowly. Use your mind as well as your body and see how great you'll feel!

Stretch first! As you ease into some stretches and begin to warm up the body, get your mind ready as well. Think about what it is you wish to accomplish with your resistance training. Visualize loose areas of the body becoming more toned and taut. Don't think about getting more thin, but of getting more hard. Imagine that your body is a big puddle of water that is solidifying and turning into a big block of solid ice.

Legs

These are my favorite part. They're big muscle groups and burn more calories, utilize more muscles, burn fat, and help achieve the cardio effect, so I work these big muscles first and smaller ones last.

LEG EXTENSION (80 lbs.)
15 reps

At the bottom of the move, with legs tucked under the leg extension bar or rollers, take a minute to imagine that your leg muscles are asleep. When you give them the command, they awaken and rise. Think also about your self-esteem. It, too, may be sleeping. Time to wake it up!

As your leg muscles awaken, they rise —lifting to the top of the move. Yourself esteem also begins to "swell"—lifting you to new, more positive feelings about yourself. At the top, hold for a moment to lock in the feelings in your leg muscles. Imagine the power of full self-esteem—of being on top of the world. With each rep, visualize your leg muscles getting harder and harder and your self-esteem growing stronger and stronger.

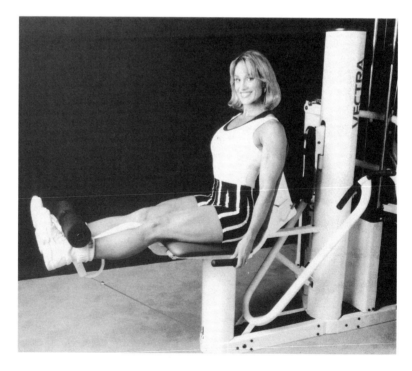

LEG PRESS (80–100 lbs.) 20 reps

Make sure that the knees track over the feet to prevent knee injury!

After getting into position on the leg press machine, take a moment to recall your most potent NEC. Feel the destructive emotional weight of this negative memory.

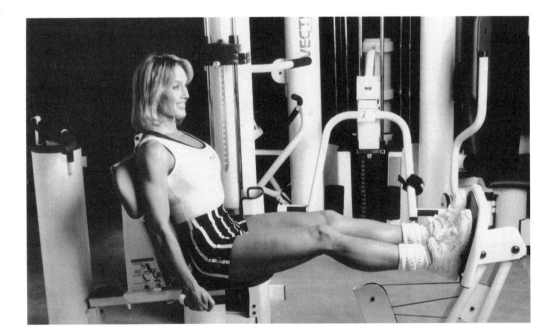

As you push the weight away from your body, imagine that you're pushing the NEC away—forever! Mentally Trash Compact the NEC into kingdom come as you build stronger, harder legs!

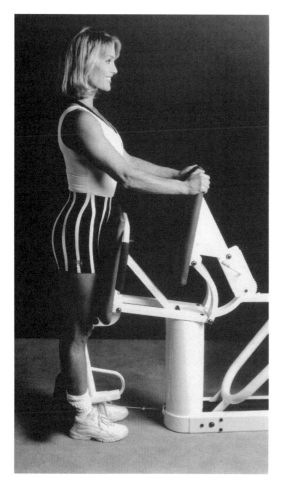

LEG CURL (30–40 lbs.) 15–20 reps

Stand tall and think about your favorite Power Connector. Feel good about yourself. Feel good about your strong legs.

Curl your leg up toward your butt. Mentally embrace the Power Connector—and yourself. Feel the power in the muscles behind your legs and imagine them harder and more toned than ever before. They will be soon!

Upper Body

LAT PULL-DOWN (60 lbs.) 15 reps

Make this a big, powerful movement. At the top of the move, with arms wide on the bar, imagine that you're grabbing all of your scattered intentions, dreams, and goals.

As you pull the bar down, imagine pulling all the good thoughts and ideas closer to you, where you can hold on to them. Bring them in and hold on tight. With each rep, embrace the positive even more. Make it a part of you.

SEATED SHOULDER PRESS (20 lbs.) 15 reps

Think about the barriers that have kept you back in the past: lack of energy, lack of motivation, lack of self-esteem. As you hold on to the weights or handles, think about getting a grip on old barriers.

Push the old negative stuff away. With each rep, push further and further past old barriers. Nothing can stop you now!

SEATED CHEST FLY (15 lbs.) 15 reps

With the arms open, take a breath and visualize all the muscles in your body, not just your chest muscles.

When you squeeze the arms together, think about your entire body, but especially your pectoral area. Imagine that the muscles are getting harder and harder as your body gets tighter and healthier than ever. Push the arms together and think about pushing health and vitality into your body. If you're used to thinking of yourself in a negative way, begin to unravel that way of thinking. Start now to think about yourself in a positive way. You may not be at your goal weight yet, but you can be healthy at any weight. Push the vitality into your body with each rep.

STOMACH CRUNCH (start with 10 lbs. on a machine and work up) 20 reps

Do some lying down and then some on a crunch machine, if available. Stomach work is great for Mental Trash Compacting! As you crunch and contract those ab muscles, grind old NECs into oblivion. Take out your aggression here rather than in road rage or on family or friends. Get rid of stress as you get that washboard look.

Repeat entire circuit twice without rest.

On alternate workout days do biceps and triceps instead of shoulder presses. (Legs and back are always part of this twice-a-week workout.)

BICEPS (25 lbs. for cable or barbell; 10 lbs. with a dumbbell) 15 reps

You can do biceps curls with a cable, standing, as shown here, or with a bar or cable, seated, or with a dumbbell. Take your pick, but be sure to use the time for—you guessed it!—Mental Trash Compacting.

TRICEPS (15 lbs.) 15 reps

Triceps exercises performed overhead can be a great way to visualize your self-esteem as it gets bigger and better. As you pull the weight or cable to the top of the move, think about your inner self as soaring skyward. As your triceps muscles grow, think about your inner strength doing the same.

Remember that you are striving for *life*Balance, even as you kick butt pumping iron. When working with weights remember:

- *Stay both strong and flexible.* Most women need to work on strengthening the front of the body and stretching the back of the body. Working with weights is great for strength and to prevent osteoporosis; however, don't sacrifice your back to your resistance training. Tight hamstrings can cause harmful torquing in the lower back. Calves and thighs need to be flexible to protect the back also. All those leg extensions to tighten the area above the knees won't mean a thing if you've got tight hamstrings causing stress on the spine!
- *Find your center.* This means literally and figuratively. Keep a strong midsection to help protect hips and back from injury and to keep you strong during most athletic activities, especially weight training. Mentally, find your center and you'll make everything you do much easier.

*LIFE*BALANCE AEROBIC WORKOUT

30-Day life*Balance Walk-Fit Program*

I'm a big fan of walking. I do it almost every day. It enables me to spend time with my dogs. It gives me time to "meditate on the move" and find quiet in the middle of a busy day. Occasionally, when my schedule is especially busy, it's the only time I get to spend with my sister Cameo or other friends. Plus, it's a great way to burn fat and tone the legs and butt.

Walking is a great way to relieve stress. If I didn't walk I'd be a nutcase. Walking gives you a temporary reprieve from anxiety-producing people like your boss or kooky family members. Mad at your boss? Go take a hike at lunch! Give your mind a chance to relax, recharge, and get creative. I come up with my best ideas when I walk: that's when I think of new art projects; that's when I created my best Ms. Olympia posing routines. When you come back from a walk, if you're like me, you'll find you're more capable of dealing with your problems and are more relaxed about those you can't control.

Being outside with nature every day helps keep

> Walking has been the number one most frequent fitness activity for the past eight years. According to 1995 American Sports Data, there are thirty-six million U.S. walkers—seventeen million of them "dedicated" walkers who walk at least two times per week. Sixty-four percent of walkers are female, and baby boomers make up the majority of walkers with 13.3 million boomers walking. It's now considered an excellent aerobic activity for anyone. Beyond the health factors, walking offers a chance to explore the world around you. Walking as an exercise can not only change your look, but it can change your outlook as well.

people healthy, regardless of what activity they're engaged in. Walking is a great way to get this outdoor benefit, weather permitting. But even when the weather is bad you can get moving. Taking a purposeful walk in an indoor mall (save window shopping for later!) can be a great way to get in your daily walk.

Walking does not require tremendous athletic ability or expensive equipment. All you need are your feet and a comfortable pair of walking shoes. Because it's self-paced, you can easily walk with family members or friends or spend time alone as part of a break from your daily routine. You can even join a walking club. Chances are that your own town or neighborhood already has an organized club or program. Not only can these clubs be fun and sociable, but walking with others can also keep your motivation high.

Regardless of when or how you walk, the goal is to make the exercise a regular part of your day. That's the real key to maintaining consistency!

Proper Preparation

Before you begin your walk:

- Select a good pair of shoes. A good walking shoe should bend at a forty-five-degree angle when you "push off" and have a rounded crash pad to absorb the heel strike. Unlike running shoes, walking shoes feature less cushioning to contribute to greater flexibility.
- Make sure you warm up and cool down for at least five minutes before and after you walk. (See below.)
- To achieve the maximum benefit from your walk, start with your shoulders back but relaxed and swing your arms in opposite directions. Your stride should be the deliberate, "I'm going somewhere" type of walk.

Stretching

Before you begin your program, remember to properly prepare your body for the routine. Proper stretching is important to maintain good muscle tone and to decrease your chances for injury. It's a good idea to stretch both before and after exercising to ensure your heart and muscles work more efficiently.

Warm-up

Always warm up your muscles first. The warm-up period is simply a few minutes devoted to slow exercise that allows your heart rate to increase gradually. The warm-up period also allows your blood vessels to open slowly to accommodate the increased flow of blood needed by the muscles during exercise. Most walkers almost automatically start at a slower pace and increase to a faster, more energetic pace as they walk.

Cool-down

The cool-down period after exercising has the opposite effect. It allows the heart to slow down gradually, putting less strain on it. Also, when you exercise, lactic acid is formed in your body by the glucose in your system. Lactic acid can remain in your muscles, causing cramping and fatigue, especially in the leg muscles after walking or running. By slowly walking after the exercise period, you can help flush the lactic acid out of the muscles and help prevent soreness the next day.

Setting the Pace: Heart Rate Training

Much of the research associated with aerobic exercise has centered around the effects of walking. Virtually all of it shows that rapid walking can produce cardiovascular benefits in most people. It's interesting to note that nearly every cardiovascular rehabilitation program in the country bases its exercise program on walking and it's an exercise endorsed by the American Heart Association.

The key to proper exercise is to gradually increase the heart rate and raise the body temperature until you reach your "target heart rate." A person's target heart rate is calculated as a percentage of his or her maximum heart rate. It's one indicator that the heart is pumping hard enough to gain benefit from the workout. Studies show that the ideal range for cardiovascular conditioning is between 50 percent and 60 percent of your maximum heart rate.

To determine your target heart rate zone, subtract your age from 220 and multiply the remainder by .50 to determine the low end and by .60 to determine the high end of the range. When participating in your exercise program, you should be able to reach and maintain your target heart rate for at least twenty minutes for maximum aerobic benefit.

Take your pulse during your exercise to determine your heart rate. Use your second and third fingers (index and middle fingers) to locate the radial artery in your wrist. First feel for the wristbone at the base of your thumb, then move your fingertips down your wrist until you find your pulse. Count your pulse beats for fifteen seconds and multiply by four to determine the beats per minute. (An easier way is to use a heart rate monitor like those mentioned in the section on biofeedback in the last chapter. The Circuit Series Heartrate Monitors are available at leading sporting goods stores or fitness and running specialty stores and cost from about $99 to about $199.) The number should fall in the range of your "target heart rate" as calculated below.

Here's an example, calculating the target heart rate for a twenty-eight-year-old person:

1. Subtract your age from 220.

$$220 - 28 = 192$$

2. Multiply the remainder by .50 (low end of range).

$$192 \times .50 = 96$$

3. Multiply the remainder by .60 (high end of range).

$$192 \times .60 = 115$$

Target heart rate would be between 96 and 115 beats per minute.

(*Note:* The only way to know your exact maximum heart rate is to be stress-tested at maximum exertion by a physician or health professional. The above formula is only an average, and 30 percent to 40 percent of the population may not fit this average.)

A simple rule of thumb: You should be walking fast enough to increase your breathing but not so rapidly that you can't carry on a short conversation. If you feel winded or out of breath, slow your pace. On any given day, if your walk seems to be a strain, fall back to the preceding day's schedule until it seems too easy. Listen to your body; it will tell you if you're setting the proper pace.

Below is the schedule for the Thirty-Day *life*Balance Walk-Fit Program. It's adapted from a program designed by John Gustin, a research scientist responsible for the discovery of the "Uncoupling Effect," the latest advancement in fat loss. This walking program offers a balanced approach to muscle strengthening without the risk of injury common to other forms of exercise. This program is designed for the person just beginning an aerobic exercise program. It starts you at ground zero and continues from there. Those who are already involved in aerobic activities might gain some helpful pointers here.

Here's to happy walking!

The Thirty-Day lifeBalance Walk-Fit Program

Day 1: Begin with an easy fifteen-minute walk.

Days 2–6: Walk one minute longer on each consecutive day. By day six, you should be up to twenty minutes.

Day 7: Rest.

Days 8–14: Continue to add one minute of walking each day to your walking time until you're up to twenty-six minutes per walk. You may notice some discomfort in your calves, shins, or feet. If so, drop back to your previous time for two or three days. Try to walk at least three times per week, preferably more.

Days 15–21: Again, add one minute for each day of walking, trying to work up to thirty-two minutes. If you lag behind, don't worry. Remember, this is *your* exercise routine. You're doing this for yourself, not for anyone else. What's important is to create a routine that you can look forward to and learn to enjoy.

Days 22–28: If possible, continue your thirty-two-minute walk each day.

Day 29: Celebrate your newfound fitness! Take the day off!

Day 30: You made it! You're a true *walker!* Keep up this schedule and you can look forward to better health, improved fat loss, and a happier outlook on life. Stay with the program to gain all the benefits and use your newfound fitness to maintain a happier, healthier lifestyle! You deserve it!

(*Caution:* As with any physical activity, consult your personal physician before starting. If you begin to feel dizzy or short of breath, stop immediately.)

Improving Your Chances for Success

Listed below are some simple rules that can improve your chances for success with the Walk-Fit (or any other) Program. Keep them in mind and you'll significantly increase your ability to lose weight safely, keep it off permanently, and find *life*Balance. Success is there for all of those who want it, plan for it, and take action to achieve it.

- *Commit to following the entire program.* For best results, I recommend that you follow the *life*Balance Walk-Fit Program for the entire thirty-day period. Don't be discouraged if you cheat. Nobody's perfect. The important thing is to maintain your commitment to a healthy lifestyle. You'll succeed if you see weight control as a process that involves real change that happens over time.

- *Don't measure your progress with a scale.* This is a program designed to help you achieve fat loss and toning through mind/body balance. Therefore, the scale is not really an accurate gauge of your success because it focuses your efforts on a number and not a healthy process. Plus, the scale gives you the total weight of your entire body (fat, muscle, body fluids, bones, and tissue). Because you'll be losing fat and gaining lean muscle, your overall weight may not fluctuate as much as it would on a conventional weight loss diet. A more useful indicator for your progress is how you feel and how your clothes fit.

- *Set realistic goals for yourself.* You should expect to lose at a safe and healthy pace in order to achieve permanent results. Don't expect miracles from this or any other program. Realize that your weight will fluctuate throughout the process as you lose fat and add lean muscle. Focus on how your clothes fit, how you look, and what kind of reduction you see in your stress levels as well as reductions in your waist, hips, thighs, etc. After thirty days, if you are overweight and have not formerly exercised, you should see, for example, a one- to two-inch reduction in your waist size. As your body changes, you'll begin to develop your slimmer, leaner physique. Make this, not actual weight loss, your goal.

The walking program is designed both to help you lose fat and to be the cornerstone of your *life*Balance fitness program. Begin it today.

Balance the walking program with other workouts. You'll still need to do some resistance training and the *life*Balance Twenty-Minute Circuit Workout is great for that. The *life*Balance Yoga Flow is great for reaching inside and nurturing the Real You as it tones, stretches, and shapes your body.

THE *LIFE*BALANCE YOGA FLOW

If you're not ready to go to a beginning yoga class in your area, or if you prefer to work out at home (alone or with your training buddy), I suggest you try the following work out to get acquainted with this wonderful practice. For the first few times, work with your partner as you both try the poses shown here. As one of you assumes the pose, the other can help with alignment or proper positioning. Take turns as each gets into the pose and stays for ten long, slow breaths. Do the workout in the sequence suggested, since a good yoga flow provides a great yoga workout.

MOUNTAIN POSE

What it does: Believe it or not, this first pose is an advanced one. I know that it looks as though nothing more is happening than I'm standing very erect. That's true. However, it's also a very fundamental and essential yoga pose. It's great for posture, focus, and building strong legs.

Especially good for: This pose is incredibly beneficial to Mode Ones. In this pose they, like a mountain, can just be still. They can learn to tune out their frantic schedules and the demands of the day and simply be. If you're caught up in the "bad body image" game, it can show you how you "stand" in the world and how you hold yourself. When you assume this pose, you, like a mighty mountain, gain strength, conviction, and patience.

How to do it: Stand with your chest lifting up and out. Pull your shoulders up, back, and down as you totally relax. Hold this pose for at least three complete breaths (one inhale and one exhale is one breath). Let the belly round and fill with each inhale and then allow it to collapse with the exhale. The hips and thighs are firm. Keep the back in a straight line from the top of the spine all the way down to the buttocks. No sway-backs or slouching! Your weight should be evenly distributed on all the edges of the feet: inner, outer, heels, and soles. If you find yourself swaying slightly or tipping this way or that, don't worry. Your body is simply finding its natural balance. As you get quieter inside, the body will begin to get still. Make constant adjustments until you find your balance, just like you do in creating *life*Balance. Don't rush. Breathe. Relax. Quiet your mind. Say hello to your inner self.

HALF MOON POSE

What it does: Enlivens the back and rib cage. Creates balance as it improves respiration and strengthens the heart.

Especially good for: Mode Twos and those with eating disorders. This pose enables even the most anxiety-ridden to find relief and calm at any time during the day. It helps those who tend to vacillate between periods of high energy and periods of total lethargy to balance out their energy level.

How to do it: Start in Mountain Pose, then breathe in and raise your arms in a wide circle over your head. Clasp the hands high over your head. Think about pulling the biceps and triceps toward the back of the room, behind your ears. Don't allow your head to crane forward or pull backward. The head stays in place as the arms straighten as much as possible.

Next, inhale deeply. Exhale and lean to the side as far as you comfortably can. Push the hips slightly forward and keep them square to the front of the room. Eventually the lower arm will be parallel to the floor. Feel the stretch in the bending side, ribs, and hip. Hold to this side for 3–5 full breaths. Return to the center.

Repeat to the other side.

FORWARD BEND

What it does: The Forward Bend is a real boost to the digestive and circulatory systems. The heart and lungs get tremendous benefit from this pose also. It's a great strengthening and stretching pose for the legs and back. This pose can help reduce body fat around the middle.

Especially good for: Mode Ones will benefit from the release of tension in the neck and upper back. Mode Twos will feel especially energized by this pose. One of the great benefits of inversion (head toward the floor) is generation of energy. Anyone who needs a quick pick-me-up in mood or energy level should use this pose during the day.

How to do it: Arms over head, stretch up, out, and forward, and slowly bend forward from the waist. Keep the back as straight as possible as you reach toward the floor. If you have any lower back discomfort or problems, keep the knees slightly bent. Go only as far as you comfortably can. For some, this will mean going only until the hands can rest on the knees. For others, this means touching the floor with the palms. Go only as far as your body can without discomfort. Allow the body to go limp and relax. Let the head hang and the neck stretch.

When you reach your full stretch, hold and breathe for three complete breaths. If you are working with straight legs, keep the kneecaps lifted by tightening the quadriceps muscles. This will protect the knees and allow the hamstrings to stretch further. To release this pose after the third complete breath, bend the knees and slowly roll up, vertebra by vertebra. You may repeat if you like for up to five full Forward Bends.

BACKWARD BEND

What it does: Excellent move for posture and balance. When performed properly, it's also an upper back and rib cage stretch. This type of backbend, like others, is serious therapy for the spine.

Especially good for: All Modes.

How to do it: Arms over head, stretch up and back as you slowly bend from the waist. Think about separating the vertebrae as you look toward the back of the room. Release the hands and arms back as you lift and stretch the upper back and torso. The head and eyes are the last to follow. Hold for five complete breaths. To release this pose, slowly return to standing.

AWKWARD POSE

What it does: Strengthens the leg muscles and tones the midsection. This pose also firms the upper arms and creates definition in the shoulder muscles. It's a great way to relieve tension in the upper back.

Especially good for: This is an excellent pose for Mode Twos and Threes. It generates energy and improves strength, making exercise of any other kind much easier.

How to do it: Stand with feet about shoulder-width apart. Raise the arms over the head, keeping them shoulder-width apart also. Palms should face each other as you look up and slowly sink down as though settling into a chair. Keep the thighs tight and the midsection lifted. Think about lifting the sternum toward the sky.

TREE POSE

What it does: This is great for strengthening the legs while creating poise and concentration. It's also a good way to improve your posture.

Especially good for: All Modes.

How to do it: As you perform this pose, it will help to balance if you stare at a spot on the wall in front of you. Raise your right leg and position it high on the left leg—without losing your balance. Point the toes on the lifted foot down and relax that leg. Hold for three complete breaths. If you have a hard time balancing, try doing this with a nearby wall or chair for support.

WARRIOR POSE

What it does: Strengthens the arms and legs. Helps align the body and create balance. Improves concentration.

Especially good for: The balance in this pose is good for all Modes. The focus required can help anyone create change in her emotions, body, or energy level. Warrior is a pose that creates emotional strength— it's like making a statement in favor of your own personal empowerment. Try this pose if you are ready to take a stand for yourself in any area of your life.

How to do it: Begin in Mountain Pose and then jump the legs to about four feet apart. Stretch your arms out sideways and bend your right leg to a ninety-degree angle. Be sure as you perform this pose that the trunk of the body stays facing forward. Push the outside of the left foot hard against the ground as you bring the right side of the body out, over, and forward toward the right. Make sure that the right knee is turned and faces right. Stretch the arms long, extending from the tip of one hand to the other. The arms should be level and strong. Turn your head to look over the right arm. Focus on the middle finger of the right hand. Hold for about thirty seconds and breath normally. Inhale and return to a centered position, then slowly shift the body and perform the pose on the left side.

TRIANGLE POSE

What it does: This pose is a good one for overall stretching and strengthening. It works most of the body in both ways: strength and stretch. There is some internal compression of organs when performing this pose, which is great for stimulating the metabolism. Circulation in the lower body is improved.

Especially good for: All Modes.

How to do it: Stand with feet one leg-length apart. Legs are straight. The left foot stays straight or pivots to a forty-five-degree angle. The right foot pivots to a ninety-degree angle. The heels should line up on an imaginary line and your legs form an equilateral triangle with the floor. Stretch the arms out parallel to the ground, at shoulder height. Reach out and to the side with the right arm and gently press the hips to the left. Keep the right side of the chest long—don't fold. Lower the right arm toward the shinbone. Bring the left arm vertical. Depending on your level of ability, reach toward the knee, the foot, or the ground with the right arm. Hold and breathe for three complete breaths.

Repeat on other side.

THIGH STRETCH

What it does: This pose is good for the leg and hip muscles. It's great for circulation as well.

Especially good for: Mode One. This pose releases the muscles in the hip area, which are storage centers for all kinds of stress, anxiety, and even NECs! A feeling of well-being and calm can

result from proper performance of this pose, especially as you are able to go deeper into the pose. Also recommended for those with eating disorders or obsessive-compulsive behavior of any kind.

How to do it: Start with your feet comfortably apart. Turn, swiveling your feet, to face left and slowly bend out long over the leg, keeping your back as flat as possible. Place your hands on the floor on either side of your foot. Hold for three complete breaths. Slowly return to standing.

Repeat on the other side.

DOWN DOG POSE

What it does: This powerful pose covers a lot of ground. It limbers up the lower back and the hips. It's a great stretch for the hamstrings and entire back of the legs. It's a fantastic cardiovascular system strengthener, since it increases circulation to the head while it works the heart.

Especially good for: Fitness Mode Three, since it enlivens the entire body and creates energy and increased circulation.

How to do it: Get on your hands and knees. Place hands about shoulder-width apart and knees hip-width apart. Slowly come up into a V shape, keeping the hands and feet on the floor. If you can keep the heels on the ground, do so. If not, push the heels as close to the floor as comfortably possible. Drop the head away from the shoulders. Relax the back of the neck. Broaden the back by turning the armpits under. Lift up through the hips and push them back as much as possible, pushing back through the arms. Relax and breathe five complete breaths in this resting pose.

COBRA POSE

What it does: This is a boost for the digestive, reproductive, and respiratory systems. It stretches the entire spine. Cobra Pose is great for the complexion and, believe it or not, eyesight!

Especially good for: This pose works very well for all three fitness modes, but especially for Mode Threes because it equalizes the two sides of the body and creates balance, offsetting the yo-yo effect.

How to do it: Get in a push-up position on the floor. Hands are next to the chest. Squeeze the hips tight. Press the groin into the floor. Press the tops of the feet onto the floor. Keep the elbows in tight toward the body. Pull the shoulders back away from the ears. Take a deep breath and prepare to complete the pose.

Inhale and raise your torso away from the floor, squeezing the elbows inward. Your head and eyes should go back first, then the chest and stomach. Don't use your arm strength. Allow your back strength to pull you back, but keep your butt flexed so that you don't stress the lower back. Hold for three breaths, staring up toward the forehead. Try not to blink. Then exhale and release down, stomach first, then chest, then head and eyes.

This powerful pose increases blood flow and should not be performed after recent surgery or during your menstrual period.

BUTTERFLY POSE

What it does: This is good for loosening tight hip and groin muscles. It also helps to release back tension.

Especially good for: All Modes. This is a basic stretch that works equally well for all bodies and all personalities.

How to do it: Sit on the floor and bend your knees while touching the soles of your feet together. Grasp your feet or ankles with your hands. Hold and breathe. If you are limber in the hip area, exhale and lean forward slightly, keeping the spine as straight as possible.

SIDE LUNGE STRETCH

What it does: Releases the emotional "stuff" stored in the hips. Stretches and strengthens the back of the legs, calves, and Achilles tendon.

Especially good for: All Modes. This pose is great for anyone with a lot of NECs. It's almost like a physical trash compactor for them! Since this pose is also a balancing pose it benefits those seeking motivation as well as those needing to create moderation.

How to do it: Stand with legs together and jump them about four feet apart. Bend your left leg to a right angle and try to keep your trunk vertical. Lower the hips down, keeping the feet on the floor. Position your trunk over the bent left leg as you lower. Go as far down as you can without causing knee strain. Clasp the hands in front of your body and try to balance. Hold for three full breaths. When you're ready to go to the other side, move the hands along the floor for support and resume the position on the opposite leg.

INVERTED TRIANGLE

What it does: Good for lower body circulation and for creating strength in the hip joints while stretching the upper back. I've found that this pose is a great way to deal with depression. It seems to turn the emotions upside-down and reverse a bad mood.

Especially good for: Any inverted pose is great for calming and beneficial for Mode Ones.

How to do it: Place the feet comfortably apart, with the toes pointing forward. Inhale and raise your arms straight out to the sides, parallel to the floor. Breathe out and bend slowly forward. Grab each leg or ankle (wherever you can without feeling pain or discomfort) with the corresponding hand. Pull the head down gently with pressure from the hands on the legs, but don't force anything. Keep the back straight. Hold for three complete breaths. Inhale and slowly return to standing.

SEATED FORWARD BEND

What it does: This is excellent for the hamstrings and entire back of the leg. It's a terrific lower back stretch and it also massages internal organs, improving their functioning.

Especially good for: Mode Two. Can be stimulating and help generate motivation.

How to do it: Sit firmly on the floor with a straight back and both legs stretched out straight in front of you. Inhale and lift your arms high overhead. Stretch the entire spine out long and tall and slowly fold over your legs. Reach out past the feet with straight arms. If you are very limber and can touch your toes or calves, do so. Hold for three breaths. Release by breathing in and circling your arms to the sides and then back overhead. Exhale and release the arms.

BOW POSE

What it does: This pose is great for relieving stress and tension, so it's great for Mode Ones. It limbers up the shoulders and upper back, where Type A's typically store a lot of "stuff." Bow Pose will also help those with eating disorders, since it calms anxiety. Anyone who is obsessive-compulsive about anything should perform this simple pose a few times during the day.

Especially good for: This pose is good for all Modes and very good for Mode Twos because it will energize them.

How to do it: Lie facedown on the floor. Exhale a long, deep breath. Then inhale and stretch your arms in a wide circle to the sides, hands pointing toward your feet. Look up and backward as you try to grab your feet. Exhale and return to lying down. Repeat two more times.

SEATED SPINAL TWIST WITH BENT LEGS

What it does: Doing this pose is like giving your spine a big kiss. It enlivens the spine while improving digestion and strengthening the heart. It's great for helping alleviate constipation or bladder and prostate (for men) problems.

Especially good for: Moving the body out of its normal alignment is stimulating and will generate energy which is beneficial for Mode Twos.

How to do it: Sit with crossed legs. Lift top leg to a ninety-degree angle with the floor, keeping the foot on the floor. Wrap the opposite arm around the outside of that leg and pull the thigh toward the body. Keep both hips on the floor as you slowly twist to look over your opposite side. If your left leg is on top, place left arm on the floor beside you and, keeping it straight, use it to help push your torso into the twist. If right leg is on top, use straight right arm to assist the twist. Stare at a spot and try not to blink as you hold for several complete breaths. Slowly release and turn back forward. Repeat on opposite side.

SEATED SPINAL TWIST WITH STRAIGHT LEG

What it does: Same as the pose above. There is an added stretching benefit to the back of the straight leg.

Especially good for: Moving the body out of its normal alignment is stimulating and will generate energy which is beneficial for Mode Twos.

How to do it: This twist is a variation of the twist with bent legs. Repeat the moves, but allow the bottom leg to straighten before you perform the twist. Keep the straight leg "active" by flexing the foot hard and contracting the quadriceps. Remember to keep both hips on the ground. Hold the twist and breathe. Repeat for both sides.

CROSS-LEGGED OR HALF LOTUS POSE

What it does: Lotus balances the body. It's a way to get centered and focused, both physically and mentally.

Especially good for: It's great for all Modes, because it tends to bring the body and the mind into alignment.

How to do it: Sit with crossed legs. If you can perform a Half Lotus do so by folding one leg on top of the other by pulling the foot into the hip joint and allowing it to rest there. Hold either pose for ten long, complete breaths. Allow the benefits of your yoga workout to take effect as you further relax, breathing deeply.

thirteen
FOOD TRAPS AND TRICKS

Humans are the only animal who weaken themselves through choice. Think about it: lions, tigers, and bears become susceptible to illness, starvation, contaminated food, or congenital problems. We, on the other hand, process and pull the nutrition from our foods and feed our bodies junk. We have free choice about our foods, but that free choice has become the death of us. We make poor choices, when there are so many healthy ones available to us.

I believe God designed us all to be healthy. We're meant to have healthy immune systems and live long lives, yet our free choice has changed all that. We make unhealthy food choices that are killing us.

When I was a freshman at the University of Wisconsin I weighed a healthy 150 pounds and competed in track—the shot put, the high jump, the 800-meters. I'll never forget how hard I trained to improve my performance in each event. I was already doing pretty well in the shot put, but wanted to improve in the high jump and other events. I can remember to this day the moment when my coach told me that to improve in those events I needed to lose weight. "You're too heavy, Cory," he told me with what I perceived as disapproval and disappointment. Ever the overachiever (remember, I was a straight-A student as well as track star), I immediately set out to rectify the problem. In typical Cory fashion, I went way overboard. I started to eat as little—and train as hard—as possible. It was nothing for me to put in ten or twelve miles of running a day in addition to my training sessions with the team and everything else I was doing at the time.

The seed was sown: if I wanted to be "better" I needed to be thinner. That thought carried over into my budding bodybuilding career not long after. I had read somewhere that Tim Belknap, who was at that time Mr. Universe, and who also came from Illinois, stuck to a diet of egg whites, lettuce, grapes, and mustard. Well, if that diet was good enough for Tim, it was good enough for Cory. Except, of course, I improved upon Tim's combination by removing the grapes from the diet. Too much sugar! I was sure that I had stumbled upon the perfect training diet: egg whites, lettuce, and mustard.

As I cut way back on my caloric intake, I jacked up my training program. The quarterback on the Wisconsin team at that time was a nice guy named Dan Yourg. Someone told me that Dan ran around nearby Lake Mendota nearly every day. I began to join him on this twenty-six-mile "jog." Now Cory, the straight-A track team star/interior design student/bodybuilder/starving student, was working out even harder than ever and cutting back more and more on food. When I think about how I've burned the candle at both ends I'm sometimes surprised that I'm still alive!

During my first three years of competitive bodybuilding I weighed between 135 and 145 pounds, which is very low for me. But I wouldn't allow myself to gain any weight, since I wanted that ripped look so many of the women had. I'd take one look at them and think, "I need to starve myself harder and work out more." What happened, of course, was that as I starved myself, my muscles would go down and I'd look less muscular and ripped. Then I'd freak out some more, work out to the point of exhaustion, and eat less. I even got my sister Cameo on this crazy diet. She, too, began to put nothing more than lettuce, mustard, and egg whites into her mouth. I saw food as my enemy and starvation as my friend.

Remember, at that time we didn't know that in order to maintain muscle and lose body fat, you need to feed the body properly, not starve it. When I first started competing, bodybuilders had just come out of an era (the 1960s and early 1970s) when the typical bodybuilder was on the "any meat, any water" diet. The big guys (women hadn't invaded the sport yet!) of those early bodybuilding years ate up to two dozen eggs a day (often raw) and consumed huge quantities of red, fatty meats. They believed that by starving the body of all carbohydrates they'd build big gobs of muscle and burn off big buckets of fat. There was no such thing as a balanced approach to food.

By the early 1980s most bodybuilders were experimenting with their own personal versions of a competition diet. We didn't have all the perfectly balanced nutrition found in today's energy bars and meal replacement shakes. We were fitness guinea pigs willing to try anything to get that winning edge!

During that whole period of my life, food was not only the enemy, but a way of punishing myself. When my energy level was low and I hadn't trained what I considered hard enough, I'd punish myself by starving my body. I didn't understand that food should always be a positive thing, not a punishment. By *positive* I don't mean *reward*, either. You have to eat. You should enjoy eating. But food is basically fuel. You can't allow yourself a hot fudge sundae as reward after every good workout or career accomplishment or whatever it is you want to celebrate. You have to use your common sense and good judgment.

I can completely relate when I read the stories of anorectic Olympic gymnast hopefuls who deprive themselves of nutrition in their desire to remain light and springy. Recently I heard from someone who works with ballerinas today that a large number of these women are starving themselves on a diet of rice cakes and yogurt. It takes a lot of bad eating habits and rigid discipline in order to be thin like a Balanchine ballerina or skinny like an Olga Korbut gymnast. I know what it's like for these women who see food as an enemy, not an ally. They can each tell you the "good reasons" for their crazy eating habits. They see starvation as their only means to a very good end—dancing the lead in *Swan Lake* at Lincoln Center or winning a gold medal. The saddest part of all is that in many of today's sports and entertainment fields being ultrathin is more important than anything else—including well-being.

The "reason" for my food obsession was just as valid for me as it is for many overachievers. After all, I was competing in a field based solely on appearance. What's really sad is that in today's media-dominated society, more and more women find themselves competing to look like the waifish models seen every-where in print ads and on video and film.

THE BIG TRAP

Believing Weight Charts

LeeAnn N., of Indiana, fell into this trap and would try almost anything to lose weight to fit into the weight chart on the wall of her doctor's office.

"I about had a heart attack," LeeAnn explains. "I went to my doctor for help and when he lined me up with the measurements on the poster on his wall, I was literally off the chart!" Her height and weight didn't fit "the norm" and she was constantly waging a battle with food.

When a Harvard University research study came out several years ago, many women just like LeeAnn went into a panic. The study, published in *The New England Journal of Medicine,* reported on a sixteen-year study of 115,000 nurses. Basically, the report found that gaining twenty-two pounds or more after age eighteen raises a woman's chance of dying—especially from heart disease or cancer—in middle age. It stated that a five-foot-five-inch woman should not weigh more than 119 pounds. You can imagine the terror that struck the hearts of the thousands of women who fell outside those suggested guidelines. Not only did they feel like losers because of their weight, but now experts were telling them that they were likely to die because of it!

Rigid recommendations, without proper context, can cause a lot of damage.

It's no wonder that women who read guidelines for weight limits rush to the scale, fixate on the numbers, and begin to see food as the enemy. They never take into account variables like age, body type, body fat count, and medical health factors. No wonder most women would rather be thin than feel better and become more healthy. This is true not only of teenagers and very young women—who struggle to fit in with their peers—but of middle-aged women (and older) who battle the effects of an aging, slower metabolism.

The Body Mass Index is a better, more reliable way to determine if you are truly overweight.

The Body Mass Index

The Body Mass Index (BMI) is a calculation of height to weight that determines a person's health risk potential to diseases associated with excess weight. A BMI of 27 or higher puts one at risk for such illnesses as diabetes, heart disease, cancer, stroke, and high blood pressure. ("More than 20 percent of the residents in the nation's top 33 cities are obese and at increased risk for developing serious health problems such as heart disease, diabetes, cancer, and stroke," said Dr. Barbara Rolls, President of the North American Association for the Study of Obesity in a press release for the study. "Food is a powerful symbol of tradition and culture, which helps to explain the difficulty people have in making the commitment to long-term dietary changes that impact weight loss.")

The BMI, as opposed to other weight comparison systems, is a way for people to determine if they are at health risk due to excessive weight. It is a more realistic assessment than other methods and is an objective measurement that can be checked regularly, just like blood pressure or cholesterol screening. It is a more reliable predictor of health risk than body weight alone. (It is not applicable to competitive athletes or bodybuilders, since their high muscle weight will throw the rating off. Also, pregnant or lactating women, the frail and sedentary elderly, or growing children should use other methods.)

I like the BMI because I believe it measures "health" more than weight or even body fat. For those trying to create mind/body health and *life*Balance, the BMI is a way to help track results in a realistic, noncompetitive, healthy way.

I suggest that along with regular tracking of BMI, individuals should also have their physician check their blood pressure regularly, since high blood pressure can be an indicator of higher risk of stroke or heart problems. Total cholesterol should be measured on a regular basis. The "bad" cholesterol LDL and the "good" cholesterol HDL should total no more than 200, with an HDL count over 35. From time to time, it's also a good idea to check blood glucose levels. This measurement of the blood sugar in your body, usually taken at least eight hours after eating ("fasting glucose level") is a check for diabetes.

What is your Body Mass Index (BMI)?

BMI is a measure that can help determine if you are at risk for a weight-related illness. If your BMI is 27 or higher, you could be at risk for diabetes, heart disease, stroke, certain cancers, and high blood pressure.

To use this table, find your height in the left-hand column. Move across the row until you find your weight. The number at the top of the column is your BMI.

Talk to your physician to find out if you are at risk and learn about ways to lower your BMI.

BMI	25	26	27	28	30	32	34	36	38	40
			WEIGHT (IN POUNDS)							
4'10"	119	124	129	134	143	153	162	172	181	191
4'11"	124	128	133	138	148	158	168	178	188	198
5'	128	133	138	143	153	164	174	184	194	204
5'1"	132	137	143	148	158	169	180	190	201	211
5'2"	136	142	147	153	164	175	186	196	207	218
5'3"	141	146	152	158	169	180	192	203	214	225
5'4"	145	151	157	163	174	186	198	209	221	233
5'5"	150	156	162	168	180	192	204	216	228	240
5'6"	155	161	167	173	185	198	210	223	235	247
5'7"	159	166	172	178	191	204	217	229	242	255
5'8"	164	171	177	184	197	210	223	236	249	263
5'9"	169	176	182	189	203	216	230	243	257	270
5'10"	174	181	188	195	209	223	236	250	264	278
5'11"	179	186	193	200	215	229	243	258	272	286
6'	184	191	199	206	221	235	250	265	280	294
6'1"	189	197	204	212	227	242	257	272	287	303
6'2"	194	202	210	218	233	249	264	280	295	311
6'3"	200	208	216	224	240	255	271	287	303	319
6'4"	205	213	221	230	246	262	279	295	312	328

Column headed 27 labeled "AT RISK". Left column labeled HEIGHT.

THE COALITION FOR EXCESS WEIGHT RISK EDUCATION

MEMBERS: AMERICAN ASSOCIATION OF DIABETES EDUCATORS, AMERICAN DIABETES ASSOCIATION, AMERICAN SOCIETY FOR CLINICAL NUTRITION, NORTH AMERICAN ASSOCIATION FOR THE STUDY OF OBESITY **CORPORATE MEMBERS:** KNOLL PHARMACEUTICAL COMPANY, JOHNSON & JOHNSON (LIFESCAN, INC., MCNEIL SPECIALTY PRODUCTS COMPANY), AMGEN, INC., NOVARTIS PHARMACEUTICALS CORPORATION

MARCH 1997
USED WITH PERMISSION FROM
GEORGE BRAY, M.D.

OTHER TRAPS

Diets

Americans have seen their share of crazy eating plans. They continue to spend time and money looking for the perfect diet—the one that will deliver energy, weight loss, and more—despite the fact that leading medical experts continue to tell us that diets don't work! A recent study found that, in fact, diets "do more harm than good." This same study, like many others, reported that those who lost weight on diets regain as much as two-thirds of the weight back within the first year and almost all of the weight comes back within five years. Still, fortunes continue to be made and careers built upon the expectations and frustrations of Americans who are willing to try anything to lose weight.

Nutrition scientists now know that on a low-calorie diet (800–1,200 calories per day), up to 45 percent of the weight loss comes from the body cannibalizing its own muscle tissue. When you lose muscle tissue you lose one of the body's best fat-burners (muscle) and you build the body's fat reserves. Just the opposite of what you're trying to do!

Low-calorie diets aren't the only faulty fat-loss plans to find their way into the "diet" mainstream. We've gone to almost comical extremes in our efforts to be thin. For decades we've bought into the mania and madness of food fads that keep us off balance and do us, as the studies have proven, more harm than good. The 1930s' Hollywood Eighteen-Day (Grapefruit) Diet, the 1950 Gayelord Hauser "Look Younger, Live Longer" zero-carb diet, the 1964 Air Force (High Carb) Diet, and the mid-1960s' Milk and Banana Diet all captured our fancy—but little of our fat. The late '60s saw the advent of liquid diets, which have continued to enjoy some popularity to this day, but should be undertaken by only a very few and are certainly not to be undertaken by anyone without medical supervision. (Many of us saw the "before" Oprah when she was going on the liquid Optifast diet. Later we saw the "after"—after she put all her weight back on, only to have to lose it again!)

In the late '60s through the '70s, the Stillman Diet (high protein, high fat, very low carbs), the Atkins Diet (moderate protein, high fat, very low carb), and the Scarsdale Diet (high protein, moderate fat and carb) laid the foundation for some of the programs currently used. The Stillman Diet has returned in the form of the BodyBuilder's Diet or other high-protein, high-fat, low-carb programs. Remove the fat from the Atkins Diet and you've got the basis for any one of today's low-fat, moderate-carb, and moderate-to-high-protein diet plans. The Scarsdale Diet with its high protein and moderate fat and carb has been reincarnated in various forms today and continues to intrigue people, who initially lose weight, then plateau, and eventually regain the lost weight.

All of these early diets have been reworked, some with the addition of complicated theories about how to mix the correct portion size with the correct nutrient percentage to achieve a supposedly fantastic result. Even the popular "fat-burning Zone" diets of today are high-tech updates of earlier programs. Losing fat with these is too complicated, I believe, since eating the correct portion size and figuring the proper nutrient percentage can require a degree in math as well as a fancy slide rule. The Zone Drones, who have created quite a locker-room stir, claim that when the ratio of protein to fat to carb is in proper balance (30 percent protein, 30 percent fat, and 40 percent carb), an amazing euphoric, appetite-free, and energy-loaded zone can be reached. In the "Zone," its proponents claim, body fat, fatigue, and hunger are a thing of the past. If you're in the Zone and it works for you, great. I suspect that those who report good results on this type of diet are people who formerly had little balance in their daily eating plan. It's the relatively balanced approach to nutrition this type of diet espouses which I think accounts for the success of such diets, not any magical results they produce in the metabolism.

For many, however, figuring out how to get and stay in a zone of any kind is not only difficult, but impossible, and it's no wonder people turn to sillier but simpler extremes like the " 'miracle' fat-burning soup diets" featured in fashion magazines for men and women. The message is simple enough: "Eat soup and get slim!" The half-starved models in the magazine give mute support to these simple plans. These and other gimmick diets promise a weight loss of seven to ten pounds the first week, as they supposedly create a state in the body whereby it becomes more efficient at fat-burning. The fact is, the body can become more efficient at burning fat, but not by denying it sufficient nutrients. And as we saw with the extremely calorie-restricted diet fads described above, the initial weight loss is in valuable water and muscle, not fat. The body becomes not better at burning fat, but better at storing it. Since the basis of the miracle soup diets is usually broth, broth, and more broth, with a few straggly vegetables (usually cabbage or onions) added in, they are nutrient- and calorie-deficient. Can people lose weight on a diet of this kind? Yes. That first week, the needle on the scale will probably drop, but as it does, so does the body's metabolism, gradually slowing and storing fat. Clearly, fad diets don't work.

Diet Drugs

Many women have said to me, "Cory, why bother with all this training and diet stuff? Why not just take a diet pill and be done with it?" The biggest reason not to take diet pills is that once the patient goes off them, serotonin levels drop so dramatically that neurotoxicity (the killing of brain cells) occurs. The rebound effect is in full force for those who go off the pills. They not only gain back the weight they lost, but put on added pounds. This yo-yo swing is even worse than when coming off other weight loss plans. Obviously, the new wave of diet pills are no better at getting at the root of most women's weight issues. Only when one has inner balance—and not some outer, external quick fix or gimmick—can one safely get in shape and maintain the healthy results.

Pig-Outs

What really happens when you eat too much? To put it as simply as possible, when you eat one particle more fat than your body can use, it is immediately deposited into your fat cells. (You know the ones I'm talking about.) The stomach has receptors that send out "fullness" signals when you eat, but because the stomach can continue to stretch and expand, you continue to eat and don't listen to the signals given by the brain that you've had enough. These physiological cues are easily overridden and ignored by social cues of having a good time or by the needy demands of emotional feelings brought on by NECs or other negative inner messages.

The pleasures of eating can also override the signals of satiation. When you've achieved *life*Balance, you eat, enjoy the taste, and then stop before overeating. The person who has failed to create any *life*Balance often continues to overeat, looking for emotional as well as nutritional gratification from the food. That's when the real trouble can start.

Let's take a look at what happens to the various types of food during the metabolic process, so that we can better understand the importance of the smart food choices outlined fully in the next chapter.

Carbohydrates are burned first. They get converted first into glucose and burned to meet your body's energy requirements. If you eat more carbs at one sitting than your body needs, they get transformed into glycogen—a substance your body is able to store away in the liver and muscles to use later for energy needs.

Carbs don't get immediately transferred into fat. For that to happen you need to eat them in an overabundance for several days until you slip into carb overload.

People who are looking for emotional gratification in their food often eat an overabundance of simple sugars, which are empty calories that send your blood sugar into spikes. You can become shaky, hypoglycemic, and overly fatigued.

Protein is broken down into essential amino acids (the ingredients and building blocks needed to build muscle and maintain and repair body tissues). Amino acids are carried through the blood to tissues throughout the body.

When you eat more protein than the body immediately needs it's converted into carbs. As with carbs, you need to overeat protein for a number of days before it's transformed into fat.

Now fat—look out!—is the body's last choice for fuel. The body treats fat very differently from carbs and protein. It's only burned when there aren't enough carbs around to meet the body's energy needs. So if you eat more calories of fat at a single meal the fat just stays there to keep you warm and is taken via the bloodstream to cells throughout your body. Where does it go? That depends. If the fat you consumed is part of a balanced meal that contains no more calories than your body needs, the fat is delivered to muscle and other tissues that burn it right away. On the other hand, if you eat a load of fat, like a super cheesy pizza or triple chocolate ice cream, you store all the excess in your tissues. You can burn it over time, however, if you are consistently very active.

Muscles contain an enzyme that promotes fat-burning when a muscle is in use (especially over extended times: fifteen to twenty minutes plus). But if you sit around or go to bed or watch TV after a fat-loaded meal, the fat cells are activated and it only takes about four to eight hours for them to absorb most of the fatty stuff you just ate.

Although alcohol is fat-free, the body can transform it into storable form in the fat tissues. That makes matters worse, because drinking alcohol then reduces the total amount of fat that would have been burned. So when you have alcohol on top of a fat meal, you've reduced your calorie-burning potential by about one hundred calories. Every time you overload on fatty meals you inevitably store it on your butt and other body parts. And as your fat cells accommodate to more fat in your diet they expand—and so does your booty!

If for some crazy reason you are going to pig out, try calorie banking—by eating extremely little fat the night before and that day to create a fat deficit, so when you splurge a little, you bring the bank account back to zero. Again, balance is the key!

Too Much Alcohol

More than one or two glasses of alcohol a day have been shown to increase the risk of breast cancer. Too much alcohol is a problem for many of the body's systems, not the least of which is our emotions. Alcohol is a depressant and too much of it can be a major roadblock to finding *life*Balance. Have it in moderation. Again, balance is the key.

Too Much Caffeine

Caffeine makes you anxious when you indulge in more than a cup or two of caffeine-loaded liquid a day. For women, caffeine can be a double whammy because bone density is affected by having too much of it. Osteoporosis is and will continue to be even more of a problem for today's women. Too much caffeine is the enemy of any woman who wants to retain healthy bone mass.

Too Much Bread or Pasta

Too much bread, white rice, or pasta, even though low in fat, may cause the blood sugar level to spike. When that happens, the body starts overproducing insulin. More insulin in the bloodstream is a signal to the body to store calories as fat. But rice, whole grains, fruits, and veggies are better complex carbohydrate choices than breads and pastas.

Faulty Food Facts

If you've been eating religiously (and by that I don't mean ice cream at church socials!) and you're still not getting results, you may have fallen into the trap of believing Faulty Food Facts. These are common misconceptions to which many people mistakenly cling. The Faulty Facts include:

· Skipping meals will help you lose weight. *(Wrong!)*

Do you skip meals? If so, you've succeeded very well at one thing: slowing down your metabolism. Eating four to six small meals a day, and not starving, actually promotes fat loss, while skipping meals promotes fat storage.

· Fad diets *do* work. *(Wrong!)*

Do you frequently go on and off diets? Are you a charter member of the Diet-of-the-Month Club? Repeated bouts of dieting can and will lower your resting metabolic rate, which accounts for nearly three-quarters of your total daily caloric expenditure. Why would anyone knowingly do something that slows the metabolism down?

· Rapid weight loss is lasting weight loss. *(Wrong!)*

Do you try to lose too much weight, too fast? For long-term body fat loss (not just water weight loss) one to one and a half pounds per week is best and reasonable. Most experts don't recommend losing more than two pounds per week. Take it off slowly and make it last!

The Most Common Food Traps

Like the Faulty Food Facts, the Food Traps often disguise themselves as a dieter's friend.

Chicken

The Trap: Believing that chicken is always lower in fat than red meat.

· The average American has more relative fat than a hog.
· Most of us are eight pounds heavier than we were ten years ago.
· In 1994, people ate an average of 73 grams of fat per day, even though most of us have cut back.
· In 1949, the average daily caloric intake was 1,839 calories. That's amazingly low when you consider that some of today's fast food mega-sandwiches alone contain about half that.
· In the 1970s, one in five persons was overweight compared to one in three today.
· We eat like we did a century ago, although most of us are no longer farmers working the fields or workers doing heavy labor.
· In 1954 a small soda at Burger King was 8 ounces; in 1996 it had grown to 16 ounces. A large soda was 12 ounces; in 1996 it had grown to 32 ounces.
· A Double Gulp is 64 ounces—today equal to 5.3 cans of cola and with more calories than three Snickers bars.
· The largest popcorn today at Cineplex Odeon Theaters is 141 ounces—that's more than a gallon!
· One Triple Decker Pizza Hut pizza has more fat than a stick and a half of old-fashioned butter.

I can't tell you how many times I've passed on food I really wanted and opted for skinless chicken because I thought it was more lean. That's not always true. A skinless chicken thigh has more than twice the fat of an equal serving of eye of round roast. Skinless chicken breast, on the other hand, is low in fat and calories and a better choice than beef. Select or Good cuts of meat are lower in fat than Choice or Prime.

Natural Granola

The Trap: Believing that anything labeled "natural" has to be low-fat.

Would you believe that a half cup of many "100 percent natural" granolas has the same fat as a McDonald's hamburger? It's true. Read the labels and choose carefully. Low-fat, low-sugar, whole-grain products like Wheaties, Grape-Nuts, shredded wheat, and oatmeal are good choices.

Gourmet Ice Cream

The Trap: Not knowing that there's bad—and then there's *really* bad.

Cheating with ice cream is one thing, but cheating with one of the gourmet brands is another. Häagen-Dazs, for example, somehow manages to pack into its product twice the fat of regular ice cream. Some of its flavors have a whopping forty-six grams of fat! (That's equal to half a stick of butter.) Chocolate Chocolate Chip Häagen-Dazs has twenty-four grams of fat per cup. Three McDonald's Quarter-Pounders would not give you more fat than that! Find a low-fat ice cream with lots of flavor and cheat smart!

Donuts

The Trap: Not knowing how to cheat smart.

What could be so bad about having a donut once in a while? Everything! A chocolate-covered donut can have as much bad saturated fat (ten grams) as a Big Mac. To satisfy a sweet tooth, first check labels and cheat with lowered-fat donuts and sweets.

Noodle Cups

The Trap: Believing that something as seemingly innocent as noodles and water can't possibly be bad for you.

Many women take along noodle cups for lunch at work. They figure that these steaming, carbo-loaded quickie lunches are healthy. Wrong! Believe it or not, some of these cup o' noodle products are prefried and as salty as a small bag of potato chips. Some, like the Nissin brand, are fried in palm oil (a definite dietetic no-no because it's an artery-clogger!) and absolutely inundated with salt. Check the labels. Certain products are available which are much lower in fat and sodium.

Canned Soups

The Trap: Not knowing the hidden horrors that can lie in foods labeled "healthy."

Regular canned soup is mostly salt, salt, salt and fat, fat, fat (one thousand milligrams of sodium per half can and varying amounts of fat). Sometimes you have to look beyond those labeled "healthy," however. Try low-salt, low-fat versions like Pritikin Soups. They have even less of the bad stuff than Campbell's Healthy Request and others being promoted similarly.

Popcorn

The Trap: Believing that it's only butter that makes popcorn fattening.

Any popcorn popped in coconut oil, even though unbuttered, will load you up on fat. In fact, a large bucket of unbuttered popcorn at many theater houses can have as much as three days' worth of fat! If you order coconut oil–popped theater popcorn and add fake butter you're getting the same fat as eight McDonald's Big Macs! Whether at home or at the theater, choose popcorn popped in corn, sunflower, or other healthier oils. The unsaturated fat count may still be high, but at least you've kept the artery-clogging stuff to a minimum.

Breads

The Trap: Believing that all wheat or whole-grain breads are created equal.

Trying to eat healthier, whole-grain breads? Then look for more than just "wheat" or "enriched wheat" on the label. These are really just white flour. Check the label and make sure that the first ingredient is "whole wheat" or "whole oats" or the like. Otherwise, much of the high-fiber, vitamins, and minerals have been removed in processing.

Fruit Juice

The Trap: Believing that all fruit juices are created equal.

Fresh fruits and veggies are important additions to our daily food plan. Apple and grape juice, while tasty and popular, don't pack the nutritional punch of orange juice, however. Orange juice has fifty times more vitamin C, 170 percent more folic acid, and more potassium than apple juice.

Weenies

The Trap: Believing that turkey or chicken franks are always lower in fat than any other hot dogs.

Are you among the many who believe that "chicken" or "turkey" on the label of your favorite franks or hot dogs means healthy? Some turkey dogs contain as much as eleven grams of fat each. Healthy Choice Beef Franks, on the other hand, have only one and a half grams of fat per dog.

Tuna Salad versus Roast Beef

The Trap: Fish is always healthier than beef.

How many times have you seen a dieter ordering a tuna salad sandwich for lunch? Do you feel guilty having your deli favorite—a nice roast beef on rye? You shouldn't. Tuna salad with mayo contains more than a day's worth of fat. Roast beef with mustard, on the other hand, contains only a fifth of a day's allotment for both saturated and unsaturated fat.

Fat-Free Foods

The Trap: Believing that you can never eat too many fat-free foods and that all fats are bad for you.

First, let's get very clear about one important fact: We all need some dietary fat in order to be healthy. Our body requires about fourteen fat grams per day of essential fatty acids. It's when we put in much more than that that we begin to see health and weight problems. Fat put into the mouth does turn into fat deposited on the body faster than anything else you eat. The body burns 25 percent of the calories in carbohydrates just in converting them into a form that it can store. Only 3 percent of the calories in fat are burned in the same conversion to storage. Hot fudge sundaes travel virtually intact into your fat cells, while the calories from a medium-sized apple go from one hundred to seventy-five on their way to the storage depots in the body.

Going totally fat-free doesn't work, either, though. The signs of too little fat in the diet are not attractive: dry skin and dull and lifeless hair and skin. Fat is an important factor in many of the body's most important functions. Without it, you can't live with vitality and at your optimum. Most people don't need to obsess about eating only fat-free foods; they simply need to practice moderation. The average American is getting about 37 percent of his or her daily calories from fats; the American Heart Association recommends that fats account for only thirty percent of our daily calories.

It's also the type of fat we eat which is most important. We should eat unsaturated fats rather than the denser saturated fats. Saturated fats are solid at room temperature and often come from animal sources. Unsaturated fats are liquid at room temperature and are usually of vegetable origin. Peanut butter, fish, nuts, and avocados are good sources of unsaturated fats. They give your body the fat it needs without all the added cholesterol and saturated fats.

THE TRICKS

We've seen what the food traps are. Now let's take a look at some tricks that will enable your efforts to eat healthy.

Have What You Want—Just Less of It!

Chris Rosenbloom of the American Dietetic Association, in a television interview after the "fattest" cities in America were announced in 1997, said, "There's no such thing as good foods or bad foods, good diets or bad diets." I heartily concur. Another study showed that 55 percent of people surveyed thought that in order to eat more healthfully they'd have to give up their favorite foods. Again, we're back to the old dilemma of balance. No, you don't have to give up chocolate—even for a day!—in order to lose weight or be more healthy. You do have to learn to enjoy small portions, though, and not huge jumbo-size bars of the sweet and delicious stuff. Buy a bag of Hershey's Kisses and make them last a month or so. Eat one small Kiss—every day—to quell those chocaholic cravings. If you deny yourself completely, it's more likely that you'll go on a chocolate binge or be so discouraged and deprived that your motivation will fall by the wayside. Remember when we talked about control being a major factor in ridding stress and staying motivated? Start to take control in small steps and you'll start to see changes. (More about small steps and control in the next chapter when I discuss the 21-Day Break-the-Pattern Plan.)

*Life*Balance EXERCISE: "WHAT I REALLY WANT"

The next time you're really hungry—and not just nervous, anxious, or depressed—I want you to imagine the food that you really want to eat more than anything in the world. Take a minute and imagine yourself eating this fabulous meal. Imagine how it smells and tastes. Feel the texture of it on your tongue.

If, at the end of the visualization, you're still hungry for the imagined food—go for it! Eat what you want and as much of it as you like.

If, however, this little mental trick leaves you feeling unsatisfied, try again until you figure out just what it is you'd really like to have. In time, this visualization will lead you to the foods you really want and you will be able to make better choices and eat more appropriate portions of food.

Limit Fats and Cholesterol

Eat only lean meats, fish, and skinless chicken. Limit portions. Incorporate more pasta, rice, beans, and vegetables into your diet. If you can't imagine a main dish without meat, add small portions to pasta dishes.

Learn to prepare foods with little or no fat. That means boiling, baking, roasting, poaching, steaming, or stir-frying. If time is limited, microwave.

Trim the visible fat off all meats before cooking. When preparing soups, chill them after cooking so that you can remove the hardened fat that congeals in a layer at the top.

Remove whole milk from your shopping list. Substitute skim or low-fat milk.

Cut down on fatty foods and meats and increase your intake of fresh fruits and vegetables. Develop a liking for whole-grain cereals and breads rather than processed, nutrition-poor products.

> The American Heart Association recommends the following to help lower cholesterol and control your weight:
> · Total fat intake should account for less than 30 percent of calories.
> · Saturated fatty acid intake should account for less than 10 percent of calories.
> · Polyunsaturated fatty acid intake should account for no more than 10 percent of calories.
> · Monounsaturated fatty acids make up the rest of total fat intake, about 10 to 15 percent of total calories.
> · Cholesterol intake should be no more than 300 milligrams per day.
> · Sodium intake should be no more than 3,000 milligrams per day.

When baking or cooking, use two egg whites (or one egg white and two teaspoons of unsaturated oil) in place of one egg in recipes. Forget the old bodybuilder rule of eating raw eggs to build muscles. Cook your eggs and egg whites!

Drink Plenty of Water

The doctor examined the woman and began to write down the results on a piece of paper. After several minutes, she became alarmed, "What are you writing?" she asked.

"Oh, it's just your prescription. You have to take one of these red pills with two glasses of water in the morning. Then, at noon, take a blue pill with two and a half glasses of water. In the late afternoon take one of these yellow pills with two more glasses of water," he advised.

"What on earth is wrong with me that I have to take all these pills?" she asked.

"You don't drink enough water, ma'am," he replied.

I've got only one thing to say about amazing aqua: drink up and have plenty of it every day. We've all heard this ad nauseam and I'm not going to harp on this much more. Carry water with you in the car. Drink it in place of diet or regular soda. Give your body the ammunition it needs to perform its fat-burning functions. Allow your cells to have enough of the precious life-giving liquid. Just do it!

Eat Fewer Calories and Fat and Reduce Free Radicals

When you eat too many fatty, high-calorie foods, you set yourself up for disease, not health. Free radicals, caused by high levels of fat and calories in foods, are molecules that damage your cells, age you more rapidly, and help to cause diseases like high blood pressure, stroke, osteoporosis, and diabetes.

Eat cancer-killing foods. Oxygen-absorbing foods like broccoli, cauliflower, carrots, onions, garlic, and tofu help your body remove free radicals. Eat foods full of antioxidants like vitamins C, E, and selenium.

Eat More Fruits and Veggies and Less Meat

I don't ever eat red meat, but I'm a big fan of the bird. Chicken has been a part of my life for as long as I can remember. I know, however, that animal protein is a big contributor to disease. I'll give you an example that made me stop and take a good hard look at the amount of animal protein I ingest. In countries where the people don't eat much animal fat, there are fewer diseases of many types. In Japan, for example, the women rarely get breast cancer. The rate of breast cancer is 400 percent lower in Japan than it is in the United States! Japanese women don't have some special anti–breast cancer gene, either. When they move to the United States and start to eat like American women, they begin to develop breast cancer in the same higher ratio.

Cutting back on animal fat doesn't mean cutting protein out of the diet. Protein is an important part of the *life*Balance plan and there are great ways to get enough in the daily diet—without all the animal fat. One of the best ways to get enough nonanimal protein is by using soy, which is also so full of other good nutrients that it's truly a *life*Balance nutritional superstar.

Enjoy Soy!

What reduces cholesterol, relieves some side effects of menopause, helps fight osteoporosis, and can actually cut the risk for some forms of cancer? It's that healthful legume, the soybean. It's a neglected stepchild of American diets, but in countries where it is consumed regularly, heart disease and certain cancers are found in fewer members of the population. The average American's cholesterol level is about 200. Her counterpart in China has a level right around 165. United States inhabitants suffer from four times as many cases of breast cancer per capita as residents of Japan. As noted above, much of this is attributable to the smaller amounts of meat typically found in a soy-rich diet. Nonetheless, when soy was added to the diets of patients at the University of Milan, their LDL ("bad" cholesterol) levels fell about 21 percent in twenty-one days. In another study, at the University of Illinois in Champaign-Urbana, the women who volunteered added soy protein to their diets for six months. They used soy protein in each and every meal and their efforts paid off with many benefits, including stronger lumbar spines—which help prevent osteoporosis, which causes dowager's hump. For the women who ingested forty grams of soy each day, spine density increased by 2.2 percent over the course of the study.

There's a plant estrogen in soy (isoflavones) which is similar to human estrogen. These plant estrogens appear to replace a woman's own once they begin to deplete.

I suggest that women have at least twenty-five grams of soy protein a day. If you like the taste, which I do, you can have as much as forty grams a day. You don't have to be a total health food nut to enjoy soy, either. It comes in different forms and many of them are rich in isoflavones (which might be disease-fighters!) and are low in fat. Watch out, though, because some forms of soy are almost as high in fat as regular cheese. Here's how to enjoy soy:

Fresh soybeans: I love to order edamame (fresh soybeans) at my local sushi bar. They're green and served after boiling for fifteen minutes in salted or unsalted water. You can buy them in specialty, health, or gourmet grocery stores. They're sold frozen in the winter and can be found fresh in Asian groceries in the summer.

Dried soybeans: Use these in your bean and chili dishes. Just allow a little extra time for cooking. They usually take two to three hours.

Soy milk: Use it as you would nonfat, low-fat, or whole milk. Great in cereal. I love it with my coffee instead of milk. It gives it a really creamy, richer taste. This is sold at many supermarkets. I recommend the lowered-fat versions. The vanilla-flavored low-fat soy milk has a great taste!

Tofu (bean curd): This comes in several varieties, including soft, medium, firm, and low-fat. Tofu can be used in stir-fry dishes or added to pasta, and it makes a tasty soup or salad dressing base.

You can also buy soy protein powder at your health food or supplement store. This dissolves quickly in recipes or drinks, but it doesn't have the great taste and texture of other forms.

Eat Plenty of Complex Carbs

Complex carbohydrates are fantastic *life*Balance foods. The greater part of your nutrition—60 percent to 70 percent—should come from these. They are low in fat, fast-burning, and rich in vitamins and minerals. They are also high in bulk, which means you can feel full on fewer calories. Whole-grain cereals, rice, breads, pastas, beans, fruits, and vegetables should be consumed daily. Enjoy huge salads regularly. Heap your dinner plate with greens. The greener the better. Pile on the carrots, mushrooms, cauliflower, broccoli, alfalfa sprouts, tomatoes, purple cabbage, celery, onions, cucumber, and sweet red pepper. Add beans to your big dinner salads. Try kidney, garbanzo, and black beans.

Don't avoid bread completely—just be sure that it doesn't take the place of fruits and veggies, which should make up a large part of your daily food intake. Yes, you can eat English muffins, raisin bread, or white bread. Just limit the amounts. Hot dog and hamburger buns must be counted as two servings or more, depending on their size. Choose water bagels, not egg bagels. Tortillas can be included in your daily intake as long as they are not fried. Crackers and pretzels should be unsalted as much as possible. Pancakes, French toast, and waffles should be low-fat and must be counted according to size. Granola-type cereals can be very high in fat. Check the labels!

Make Fiber an Important Part of Your Diet

When you mention fiber to many people they imagine tall glasses of gooey, liquid "grout" to relieve constipation. Well, some commercial forms of fiber do resemble caulking substances and fiber can relieve constipation, but there's more to the fiber story than that. First of all, there are two types of fiber—soluble and insoluble—and both aid in fat loss by way of inhibition of calorie absorption along with decreased insulin output. Insoluble fiber swells in the stomach, helping to produce the feeling of fullness. Fiber can act as an appetite suppressant and increase and speed elimination. It can bind to fats and sugars and pull them through your system. Plus, fiber is low in calories and fills you up.

A high-fiber diet also helps prevent heart disease by lowering serum cholesterol levels; in addition, it reduces the risks of pancreatic and colorectal cancer, hemorrhoids, ulcers, and diverticulitis.

Foods high in fiber include carrots, whole grains, whole wheat pastas, fresh broccoli, peppers, celery, air-popped popcorn, beans, whole fruits, dried fruit, and unprocessed wheat bran.

I tend to get a bit constipated when I'm traveling and I make sure to eat extra fiber. Be sure to drink plenty of water, too, since that helps the fiber do its good work.

Know Your Oils and Dressings

Margarine does not contain fewer calories or less fat than butter. Both have over one hundred calories per tablespoon and are 100 percent fat! Fats—whether palm oil, coconut oil, or butter—all contain 9 calories per gram of fat. Whipped butter is generally less in calories and can give the illusion of much more buttery taste without all of the fat.

Use only vegetable oils and margarines that contain no more than two grams of saturated fat per tablespoon. Good choices are canola, corn, olive, safflower, sesame, soybean, and sunflower. Choose salad dressings and mayonnaises that have no more than one gram of saturated fat per tablespoon.

Read food labels carefully, particularly on products that contain coconut oils, palm oil, and palm kernel oil. Count the hidden fats in prepared baked goods. Ask for foods cooked with little or no oil when dining out.

Experiment!

Plenty of great low-fat cookbooks are out there, so you have no excuse not to enjoy low-fat eating. Begin to prepare new recipes and meals for yourself and your family.

These are some of my personal favorites. I've listed only a few, since these are intended as quick examples of what's possible to those who want to start eating—and enjoying—low-fat dishes. Consider this a starter kit. Have fun. I hope you like them.

MIND/BODY OATMEAL

Use any oatmeal that requires at least five minutes cooking time. Prepare exactly as specified in the directions, except: After you add the oatmeal to the boiling water, also add two egg whites per serving. Continue stirring the mixture for the duration of the cooking time. Add fresh fruit for the last thirty seconds of cooking, or frozen fruit for the last two minutes of cooking. Remove from heat and sweeten to taste with brown sugar or honey.

NO-FAT REFRIED BEANS
    1 or 2 16-oz. cans of no-fat refried beans.
    1 can each of no-salt-added black beans and pinto beans, rinsed and drained.
    1 large tomato, chopped
    Chopped onion (to taste)
    1 4-oz. can of diced green chilies
    1 15-oz. can of corn, rinsed and drained
    Spicy or hot sauce (to taste)
    Thick and chunky canned or bottled salsa (to taste)

Mix all ingredients together; store in refrigerator.

Serve one-half cup of this mixture over one corn tortilla. Cook three egg whites and serve over tortillas and beans. Add one or two tablespoons fat-free sour cream.

Or combine one-half cup of this bean mixture with one-half cup rice (measured after cooking); this tastes great served with a broiled skinless, boneless chicken breast.

BANANA BREAD

¾ cup honey

1 cup oatmeal

3 egg whites

2 cups flour

½ tsp salt

4 ripe bananas, mashed

½ cup low-fat margarine

1 teaspoon baking powder

½ teaspoon baking soda

1 cup applesauce

½ cup walnuts, chopped

1 cup skim milk

½ cup protein powder, Bricker's "Lean machine" in vanilla bean or natural or Next Nutrition's Designer Protein in vanilla or natural

Preheat oven to 350 degrees. Lightly grease two loaf pans. Combine honey and oatmeal and set aside. Combine egg whites, applesauce, and skim milk and set aside. Sift together flour, salt, baking powder, baking soda, and protein powder and set aside. Add honey and oatmeal mixture to the egg white mixture. Add mashed bananas. Slowly add in dry ingredients in two parts. Fold in nuts. Bake for 45–60 minutes or until a dry toothpick inserted into the center comes out clean. Keep one loaf for now and freeze one for later or give it to your training partner.

PANCAKES

3 or 4 egg whites

1 cup oatmeal

1 tablespoon cinnamon, vanilla, or almond extract

¼ cup water

1 tablespoon protein powder, Bricker's "Lean machine" in vanilla bean or natural or Next Nutrition's Designer Protein in vanilla or natural.

Mix all ingredients in blender for thirty seconds.
Cook as you would any other pancakes.

ENJOY SOY MUFFINS
(Each muffin has about 6 grams of soy protein!)

> 1½ cups all-purpose flour
> ¾ cup soy protein powder
> ½ cup sugar (less if juice is used instead of water)
> 2 teaspoons baking powder
> ½ teaspoon salt
> one whole egg or egg substitute
> 1 cup water (or try apple juice)
> 2½ tablespoons canola oil
> ½ cup blueberries

Preheat oven to 375 degrees. Spray twelve muffin cups with nonstick vegetable spray. In a medium bowl combine all the dry ingredients. In a smaller bowl combine one whole egg or egg substitute, water (or juice), and oil. Add wet mixture to dry mixture and stir until moist. Fold berries into batter. Fill muffin cups halfway. Bake for 20–25 minutes or until toothpick inserted in the center comes out clean.

*LIFE*BALANCE GRILLERS
(Grillers have 135 calories each, with 21 grams of carbs, 5 grams of protein, 5 grams of fat, and no cholesterol.)

MARINADE:
> ⅓ cup extra-virgin olive oil
> ¼ cup balsamic vinegar
> 1 tablespoon minced garlic
> Pepper (to taste)
>
> 4 ears of corn, husks removed
> 4 medium-sized zucchini, ends trimmed off
> 8 ripe plum tomatoes

Combine marinade ingredients in large bowl and set aside.

Cut corn and zucchini into two-inch lengths. Halve the tomatoes crosswise. Put all of the vegetables in the marinade and toss. Let marinate for 5 hours.

Use eight 12-inch skewers to thread corn, zucchini, tomato, zucchini, tomato, corn.

Place Grillers about four inches above hot coals. Grill five minutes on each of four sides, until veggies are thoroughly cooked. Use remaining marinade for basting.

Your body is always with you. It houses who you are, including all the facets of mind, body, and soul. Why not enrich and provide for it in a healthy way? The next chapter provides many keys for creating your body just the way you want it.

THE *LIFE*BALANCE SHOPPING LIST AND 21-DAY BREAK-THE-PATTERN PLAN

If you turned to this chapter hoping that it would teach you the latest, greatest quick-weight-loss fad, you're going to be very disappointed. This chapter *is* about food, but it's not about snazzy new food combinations or some complicated fat-to-calorie ratio diet plan or starvation secrets. It's about learning to look at food as an ally, not an enemy. The emphasis is on which foods create *life*Balance because they are loaded with nutrients that enable you to enjoy good health and vitality. You'll learn to consume nutrient-rich, tasty foods that will help you fight disease, depression, lethargy, ulcers, heart disease, obesity, colitis, asthma, and many more diseases that are the result of all the high-tech advances we've made, including those found in today's popular foods. Microwavable "lean meals" are loaded with salt and digestive pollutants and contain little that's nutritious, and fast foods can be shortcuts to sickness and disease. Many women eat what they shouldn't simply because they don't know what they *should* eat. They often go to complicated diet extremes because they haven't yet discovered the simplicity of healthy eating. Here's a joke I love, which I think perfectly illustrates the difference between complicated solutions and simple ones.

A woman suffers from severe headaches for what seems like an eternity. Finally, she can take the pain no longer and she goes to a brain tumor specialist, sure that she has some inoperable disease. Sure enough, upon examining her, the doctor has very bad news. "Tomorrow we have to begin very complicated radiation treatment. The next month is going to be extremely hard on you," he informs her. "Unless we operate immediately you will never get relief from the headaches."

Depressed, she leaves the office and goes straight to a fancy store. "If I have to suffer so much I'm going to treat myself to some beautiful new clothes," she tells herself.

At the store, the saleslady is quite helpful. "I can see that you wear a size seven shoe," the saleslady says. "I have only one pair left of gorgeous Chanel pumps in that size. Let me get them for you," she says.

The ailing woman is amazed. "How could you know what size shoe I wear?" she asks.

"I just know" is the saleslady's reply.

Next, the saleslady picks a fabulous designer suit off the rack and hands it to the woman. "Here you go," the saleslady offers. "This will fit you perfectly. It's just your size—a size ten."

Amazed, the woman with the horrible headaches says, "I do wear a size ten. You're amazing!"

Finally, the saleslady leads the woman to the lingerie department. "I'll get you a 36D bra to try on," she says.

"A-ha!" the woman exclaims. "At last I've got you. I'm a perfect 34B. You finally guessed wrong."

The saleslady looks at her with amusement. "No offense meant, ma'am, but you're so wrong. I'm more sure of this than I was of any of the other sizes. You are exactly a 36D."

The customer says with assurance, "I always buy a 34B."

The saleslady sighs, and says with resignation, "OK, but if you wear that size, I promise you'll get horrible headaches!"

We're always looking for extreme measures when small ones will often do just as well. Like the lady who needs only change bra sizes in order to get rid of her horrible headaches, we often need only make small adjustments in order to get our bodies back in balance. Small adjustments can also improve your diet dramatically.

*Life*Balance JOURNAL EXERCISE: THE COOKIE MONSTER

Get out your journal and your crayons. Imagine there's a little monster inside you who is ruining your healthy eating promises by munching away at all sorts of cookies, cakes, fatty foods, and junk food. He's a Cookie Monster who's totally out of control. Draw him with your dominant hand. Color him any color you'd like with crayons, but make him nasty looking.

Next, you're going to interview him. With a pen or pencil, jot down the following questions, being sure to leave room for answers:

Who are you?
How do you feel?
What makes you feel that way?
What can I do to help you?

Now, use your nondominant hand to answer the questions as though you are the Cookie Monster. What he has to say in answer to the questions will show up as thoughts in your mind. Write them down.

The answer to the last question can provide an opening for you and the Cookie Monster to become friends. For example, here's what this exercise looked like for one woman:

Q: Who are you?
CM: I'm the elf pig who lives inside you!
Q: How do you feel?
CM: Fat and nasty.
Q: What makes you feel that way?
CM: Who wants to know? Who cares?
Q: What can I do to help you?
CM: Go away!

She continued to "talk" to the Cookie Monster with her right (dominant) hand and had him "talk back" with her left (nondominant) hand. She chided him like a spoiled child and was able to get to a place where he opened up a bit more and was receptive to her positive input. She wrote: "I love you, little guy." He wrote back: "I don't care." She wrote: "I wish you'd stop what you're doing and go away." He: "I hear you and I'm not going to leave." She: "Then you have to listen to me." He: "Maybe. We'll see."

NO QUICK FIXES, JUST SMALL CHANGES

So many fall into the traps described in the previous chapter. These are typical of letters I receive every day:

Dear Cory,
I'm sorry, but by the time I get home from ten hours at work, the last thing I want to do is cook dinner. I usually eat whatever I can get my hands on: cheese and crackers, junk food, chips and dip. My diet is horrible, but I have no choice!

Dear Cory,
I'm a working mom with three kids. By the time I pick the kids up after sports practice, the four of us are irritable and starved. What can I say? McDonald's sounds like a good idea most of the time.

211

Dear Cory,

I know I should eat more fruits and vegetables, but I just can't seem to get to them before they rot in the fridge. It's a waste of money and nutrition. I do eat a lot of fat-free snacks, although that hasn't helped much.

Sound familiar? These problems are very real for many of us. The solution lies not in making drastic changes—but in finding balance. For example, in the second letter, the busy mother can help herself and her kids by creating a more balanced "meal load" throughout the day so that by early evening, the family members aren't all starving and suffering from low blood sugar, which makes them all more ravenous than need be. Busy moms and active kids need to make sure that they eat at regular intervals throughout the day. By holding off on adequate nutrition until it's too late, people have low resistance to foods like sweets, fats, and fast foods, and are less able to make good choices. By eating regularly throughout the day and "indulging" in healthy snacks at regular intervals, you can help stave off those ravenous, "gotta have it" food cravings. Then, the family can sit down and enjoy an evening meal that is relaxing and sociable.

In both the first and the second letters, the women are equating fast food with junk food. Increasingly, this is not the case in America. If you have to stop for fast foods, make sure that you have done your research and discovered the drive-ins in your area which serve salads and other healthy, low-fat foods. Check the nutrition guidelines that are now posted at these restaurants and make smart choices. A person who has a diet from which 30 percent or more of the calories come from fat stands a higher risk of heart disease and cancer. Typically, the fat comes from meats and dairy foods, so try to avoid the big, juicy burgers and thick, whole milk shakes. There are many and varying diets and eating plans, but they almost all agree on one thing: eating a diet with less fat means a lowered body fat count. The American Heart Association suggests limiting fat in our diet to less than 30 percent of our total daily calories. It's hard to stick to these recommendations if you make frequent stops for the wrong foods. You can have your fast foods, just make smart choices. Begin to nourish your soul as well as your body by ingesting healthy, nutritious foods.

In the third letter, the woman has overlooked a pretty good source of nutrition: frozen vegetables and fruits. Freezing protects a food's nutritional value and can end the problem of rotting fruits and vegetables. Frozen veggies can be microwaved for quick, healthy nutrition. Frozen broccoli, carrots, peas, and squash are nutrient-dense and perfect for those on the go. Also, if you've missed your fruits and veggies one day, rather than going on a guilty binge, remember that punishing yourself with more unhealthy behavior just upsets the scales further. Eat more of the healthy, nutritious stuff the next day. Remember, we're trying to achieve balance—and that means juggling nutrition needs from day to day so that over the course of time we are getting all we need of most nutrients.

Note: An important reason to eat fresh veggies is to get enough of an essential fat: linoleic acid. Too little of this fat has been linked to hardening of the arteries. Essential fatty acids (EFAs) like linoleic acid are found in green leafy veggies, certain nuts and seeds, fish, and canola and soybean oil.

Also, the woman who wrote the third letter has fallen into the fat-free food trap. Too many people overindulge by eating anything that is labeled "fat-free." I know one woman who actually thought she was going to lose weight by eating a diet of fat-free cookies. She reasoned that if there was no fat in her diet, she would lose tons of weight. Imagine her surprise when she gained five pounds during the first ten days of her fat-free diet. What she neglected to take into consideration was that her fat-free goodies were loaded with sugar!

Part of the problem with all the fat-free foods today is that they lull people into believing they are getting good, low-calorie nutrition. It used to be that the sugary foods we ate were loaded with fat and we knew they weren't great for us. That's not the case anymore, which can be confusing. Sugary fat-free stuff can be as bad as nonsugary fatty stuff. My friend on the fat-free diet loved French fries but never ate them, preferring to "stick to her diet" with lots of fat-free cakes and cookies. In fact, she would have been better off eating the fries she loved in moderation than too much of the fat-free stuff. The American Cancer Society did a study that linked sugary foods, not just fatty ones, to more deaths from breast and cervical cancer. Those with diabetes or hypoglycemia know the pitfalls of eating too many sugary foods.

I don't want you to rush into your kitchen and throw out all your favorite foods. I encourage you to allow yourself to have tasty, satisfying food in your house. Unhealthy old favorites will eventually lose their allure because we're taking away labels like "forbidden" or "tempting." Those labels have given them power over you, but food has no power—except to nourish and empower when eaten in healthy doses. Take back the control. Put your favorite foods back in the fridge and learn to control them, not vice versa. You can enjoy your "cheat" food favorites occasionally and still have the body you want.

*Life*Balance EXERCISE: SOAK UP THE HEALTH

Before you plan your next meal take a moment to use your mind as a built-in Healthy Food Sponge. Imagine your usual meal. Think about the foods you've just taken a mental picture of. Picture those that are loaded with good nutrition and imagine your body as a big sponge soaking up the nutrients and vitamins. Imagine the better health, energy, and confidence that spreads through the body from these foods. Think about how much better you will feel both mentally and physically.

Next, imagine those foods that are sugary, fatty, or just plain junky. These can't even be absorbed by the big sponge in your mental picture. They just accumulate and turn into a gooey, blubbery film that coats the sponge. Occasionally they provide a little bit of quick energy but this burst is negated by the bigger depletion of energy which occurs not long after.

For your Healthy Body Sponge to work properly and efficiently, when the bones and muscles call for good nutrition the good stuff can be wrung out and sent where needed. Then the sponge can go back to work collecting the good stuff once again. However, because the useless matter—the junk foods and sugary, nonnutritious desserts and cheat treats—form a greasy, slimy film that coats the outside of the sponge, slowing down the absorption of the good nutrients and making it harder for the sponge to soak up all the good health.

Once you start to use this nutrition visualization it may become harder and harder for you to eat junky foods. You may find that you want to fill up the Healthy Body Sponge with only those foods that can be absorbed by it and used to build better bones and fat-burning lean muscle mass.

SHOPPING LIST FOR *LIFE*BALANCE FOODS

I've put together a shopping list to make stocking up on all the right foods easy. Bring this book along with you to the store or tear out these pages and bring them along when you shop. It'll help take the guesswork out and help you to make smart, healthy, balanced choices at the grocery store.

I suggest that busy people set aside one day a week to shop for the days ahead. Pick a time when you're not hungry and stock up so that you have good foods on hand when you're in a hurry. A well-balanced meal doesn't have to be a cooked one, either, as long as you are careful to include at least three types of foods in each meal. Grab a glass of nonfat milk, a banana, and some nuts for lunch if time is limited. Make yourself a turkey and lettuce sandwich on whole-wheat bread and carry it with you when you know lunch time will be limited. Low-fat cheese, crackers, and an apple make a good carry-along lunch or late-afternoon snack.

Attending an after-work seminar and there's no time for dinner? Take along a bagel with a light peanut butter "schmear" and a non-fat yogurt. Allow yourself a little time before the seminar to sit in the lobby, your car, or entryway and eat your healthy snack. I've done this many times and, invariably, people who have stopped for fries and a greasy burger remark to me, "That's smart—I should have done that!"

A very expensive gourmet grocery store is having a sale. Sumptuous fruits, baked goods, and meats are all being sold at reduced prices. One particularly budget-conscious woman makes a mad dash for the meat and poultry department, where she sees a sign advertising skinless chicken breasts. When she looks into the refrigerated case, however, all she sees are skimpy, scrawny slivers of chicken packed in oversized containers. Dismayed, she approaches the butcher, who assures her that he will look in the back and package some more chicken for her. "By the time you reach the checkout counter, I'll have them for you," he tells her. "My name is Dave and I'm happy to serve you," he adds. The woman continues to shop and when she reaches the fruits and vegetables at the other end of the store, she hears a voice boom over the Muzak playing on the store's sound system: "Uh, this is Dave. Will the woman who wanted the bigger breasts meet me up front?"

OK, that's a little shopping humor for you. Now, let's take a look at what you should buy at the grocery store.

Veggies

Always think vegetables first. I eat a ton of carrots. They're a great source of vitamin C and antioxidants like beta-carotene. Best yet, they go right through your system and push stuff through along with them. They take more calories to break down than they even have to begin with! In other words, if you eat a thirty-four-calorie carrot—or other vegetable, such as broccoli or cauliflower—your body uses forty-plus calories to break it down. Vegetables have about 25 calories per serving and are high in soluble and insoluble fiber and water, all of which your body needs to eliminate fat from your system. Think of veggies as scrubber brushes pushing and pulling fats and sugars through your system twice a day.

The average person knows she should eat fresh veggies; she may even buy them and stick them in the fridge. She's got great intentions but forgets to eat the fresh vegetables just the same. Two weeks later something begins to smell in her refrigerator and she sees the spoiled spinach and peppers behind the milk and she throws them away. Sound familiar?

I suggest that when you go to the store you buy enough fruits and veggies to last exactly one week. Before you put them away to be hidden by the milk and pickles, wash them, cut and peel them, and store them in separate plastic bags as single servings or in larger plastic containers. Put broccoli in one bag, carrots in another, and so on. Stick the bags in front of the fridge so when you open the door it becomes a simple process to grab what you want, take it in your car, leave it on the passenger seat, and let it rot there. (Just kidding!) Take the bags into work with you and nibble during office hours instead of eating junk food. Eat them instead of the muffin from the local 7-Eleven store. This way, fresh veggies are also ready to throw into your salad at night and you'll be more likely to eat them than a higher-calorie food. Veggies (and fruits) survive very well without refrigeration for a day. Keep them within arm's reach at all times.

(Note: The only fruit or vegetable to be avoided is coconut. Olives and avocados are counted as fats. Potatoes and other starchy vegetables should be counted as breads.)

*LIFE*BALANCE SCORES FOR VEGGIES

Each vegetable's lifeBalance score is based on a serving of it having about 10 percent of the Daily Value of nutrients listed, in addition to healthy fiber and carotenoids. One asterisk (*) means negligible fiber; two asterisks (**) means negligible carotenoids. Each listing is for one-half cup, cooked, of each vegetable—whether fresh or canned—unless otherwise noted.

	KEY NUTRIENTS	*LIFE*BALANCE SCORE
Spinach	Vit. C, calcium, some potassium and iron	10
Red Bell Pepper (raw)	Vit. C	9
Sweet Potato (med.)	Vit. C, potassium, some folate	9
Carrots	Lots of fiber and carotenoids	9
Carrot (raw, med.)	Some vit. C and potassium, carotenoids, fiber	9
Broccoli	Vit. C, folate, some potassium	9
Romaine Lettuce* (1 c. shredded)	Vit. C, folate, some potassium	8
Baked Potato** (w/skin)	Vit. C, potassium, iron, some folate	8
Brussels Sprouts	Vit. C, folate, some potassium and iron	8
Spinach (raw, 1 c.)	Vit. C, folate, some potassium and iron	7
Green Peas	Vit. C, folate, some iron	7
Tomato* (raw, ½ med.)	Vit. C	7
Cauliflower**	Vit. C, some folate	6
Boston/Bibb Lettuce* (1 c. chopped)	Folate, some vit. C	6
Green Beans	Vit. C, Some folate and potassium	6
Celery (raw, 1 stalk)	Some vit. C	5
Corn	Folate, some vit. C and potassium	5
Cabbage**	Vit. C	5
Iceberg Lettuce** (1 c. chopped)	Some folate	5
Beets (sliced, canned)	Some vit. C, folate and iron	5
Mushrooms	Some vit. c, potassium, and iron	5
Onions, Radishes, Cucumbers, Alfalfa Sprouts (½ c. raw), Eggplant, Turnips, Garlic (1 clove)		3

Suggested daily total lifeBalance score from veggies: 30

Canned Veggies (and Fruits) Can Be Good for You!

As we've already noticed, it's often difficult for many women to keep fresh fruits and vegetables on hand for healthy meals and snacks. That doesn't mean that these types of food should be neglected. Stock up on canned fruits and vegetables if you can't eat fresh. They're higher in vitamin C and as high in carotene and iron as fruit right off the tree or vegetables right out of the garden. Food experts tells us that canned vegetables are at their nutritional peak when they're picked. Then, the canning process involves a heat treatment that locks in freshness. On the other hand, fresh fruits and veggies may be on the road for as long as seven to fourteen days before they appear on the supermarket shelf. Often, they spend a few more days in our home fridges before we get to them. During this travel and storage time they lose some nutritional content. For example, by the time you buy them, fresh green beans will have lost 60 percent of the vitamin C they started out with! Canned green beans will retain much more.

We all need to get our five servings of fruits and veggies per day, and canned varieties can be time-saving and nutritious as well. For those of you who were expending a lot of mind/body energy feeling guilty about serving your family too few fruits and veggies, take heart and buy some canned goods, which will always be on hand to provide good nutrition. (Note: When buying canned fruits and vegetables, check the sodium content so that you don't sabotage yourself with hidden sodium.)

Grains

Set aside one hour a week to precook your rice, pasta, and dry beans. Do what I do and store these complex carbohydrates in single-serving containers, just like your veggies. Then it becomes a simple process of sticking them in the microwave to reheat for the correct quantity at each meal. And what did it take—maybe five minutes?—to prepare a low-fat, healthy meal?

*LIFE*BALANCE SCORES FOR GRAINS

*The life*Balance *score for each of these listings was determined by evaluating the percentages of important nutrients listed, plus the fiber content of the grain. The values listed are for a five-ounce serving of cooked product.*

	KEY NUTRIENTS	*LIFE*BALANCE SCORE
Quinoa	Fiber, magnesium, vit. B_6, copper, iron	10
Whole Wheat Pastas	Magnesium, vit. B_6, zinc, copper, iron	9

	KEY NUTRIENTS	*LIFE*BALANCE SCORE
Buckwheat Groats	Magnesium, copper, iron, vit. B$_6$, zinc	9
Spinach Pasta	Magnesium, zinc, copper, some vit. B$_6$ and iron	8
Bulgur	Magnesium, some vit. B$_6$, zinc, copper and iron	7
Wild Rice	Magnesium, vit. B$_6$, zinc, some copper and iron	7
Brown Rice	Magnesium, vit. B$_6$, some zinc, copper, and iron	6
Spaghetti	Iron, some magnesium, zinc, and copper	6
Macaroni	Iron, some magnesium, zinc, and copper	5
Rolled Oats	Some magnesium, zinc, and iron	5
White Rice (converted)	Some copper and iron	4
White Rice (instant)	Some copper & iron	3
Couscous		4

Suggested daily total life*Balance score from grains: 20–25*

Fruits

Fruits are a terrific source of fiber and many different vitamins. They can also satisfy the sweet tooth of even the most sugar-crazed. Grab a piece of fresh fruit instead of a candy bar at snack time.

*LIFE*BALANCE SCORES FOR FRUITS

(These are listed in order of "power," and their life*Balance scores are based on having at least 10 percent USRDA of at least two important nutrients, as well as fiber content. Those marked with an asterisk also include folate!)*

	KEY NUTRIENTS	*LIFE*BALANCE SCORE
Papaya (½)	Vit. C, vit. A, potassium, fiber	10
Cantaloupe* (¼)	Vit. C, vit. A, potassium	10
Strawberries* (1 c.)	Vit. C, fiber	9
Orange* (one)	Vit. C, fiber	9
Kiwi (one)	Vit. C, fiber	8
Watermelons (2 c.)	Vit. C, vit. A, potassium	7
Pink Grapefruit (½)	Vit. C	7
Dried Apricots (10)	Vit. A, potassium, fiber	6
White Grapefruit (½)	Vit. C, potassium	6
Peaches (2)	Vit. A, vit. C, fiber	5
Blueberries (1 c.)	Vit. C, fiber	5
Banana* (one)	Vit. C, potassium	5
Apple (one w/skin)	Vit. C, fiber	5
Pear (one)	Vit. C, fiber	5

Raisins (¼ c.)	Some fiber and potassium	4
Dates (5)	Some fiber and potassium	3

Suggested daily total life*Balance score from fruits: 30*

Beans and Peas

These are a great source of healthy, nonanimal protein. The amino acids in legumes complement the ones in grains to form complete protein, so be sure to eat some of both regularly.

*LIFE*BALANCE SCORES FOR BEANS AND PEAS

Each life*Balance score here is based on a serving containing 25 percent to 50 percent or more of USRDA of important nutrients, plus healthy doses of fiber and protein. Each serving size is for one cup, cooked, of each legume listed.*

	KEY NUTRIENTS	*LIFE*BALANCE SCORE
Soybeans	Magnesium, iron, copper	10
Pinto Beans	Folate, magnesium, iron	10
Garbanzos	Folate, iron, copper	10
Lentils	Folate, iron	10
Black-eyed Peas	Folate, iron	9
Navy Beans	Folate, magnesium, iron, copper	9
White Beans	Folate, magnesium, iron	9
Lima Beans	Folate	8
Kidney Beans	Folate, iron	8
Peas	Folate	8
Tofu (raw, 4 oz.)	Magnesium, iron	7

Suggested daily total life*Balance score from beans and peas: 15–20*

Meats and Fish

First, a few words about protein. All living cells need protein. The body needs it on a daily basis for cell renewal and growth but cannot store it. Proteins are made up of twenty-two amino acids. Aminos are building blocks for protein. But there are two types of protein and unless you're a vegetarian you probably don't think of a meal as complete unless it contains meat protein. Complete proteins are found in meat, seafood, and dairy products like eggs, milk, and cheese. Incomplete proteins (like those found in nonanimal sources) are those that lack some essential amino acids. These incomplete proteins are not "productive" when eaten alone, but when you mix them with other proteins, they become productive again. In fact, mixing your protein types can be more effective than eating one source alone. Vegetarians become very adept at combining their rices, beans, peas, grains, and cheeses to create effective protein. If you're a vegetarian or simply want to cut down on your intake of animal fats, be sure to get your protein somewhere else, since too little of this important nutrient type can negatively affect your skin, hair, blood, hormone production, and the body's ability to fight infections.

Trim all visible fats from meats. (Remember, you can cook your chicken in the skin, but remove it before eating.) Choose meats that are high in protein, but low in fat. Buy lean cuts of meats.

*LIFE*BALANCE SCORES FOR MEATS AND FISH

The life*Balance scores listed are for four ounces of cooked, skinless poultry or cooked beef, pork, veal, or lamb with the fat trimmed off. The foods were evaluated for low saturated fat content, since experts recommend that most of us eat no more than eighteen grams of saturated fat per day.*

	SATURATED FAT (GRAMS)	TOTAL FAT (GRAMS)	*LIFE*BALANCE SCORE
Turkey Breast	0	1	1
Flounder	0	2	1
Chicken Breast	1	4	2
Turkey Wing	1	4	2
Turkey Leg	1	4	2
Pink Salmon	1	5	2
Beef Eye Round (Select)	2	5	3
Chicken Drumstick	2	5	3
Beef Top Round	2	6	3
Beef Bottom Round (Select)	2	7	4
Turkey Breast (w/skin)	2	8	5
Pork Tenderloin	3	7	5
Chicken Breast (w/skin)	3	9	6
Veal Shoulder, Arm	3	7	5
Chicken Wing	3	9	6
Lamb Shank	3	8	6
Beef Top Round (Choice)	3	8	6
Veal Loin	3	8	6
Lean Ground Turkey	3	11	8
Pork Top Loin	3	9	8
Ham, Leg	3	9	8
Beef Top Sirloin (Select)	3	9	8
Chicken Thigh	3	12	9
Chicken Drumstick (w/skin)	3	13	10

	SATURATED FAT (GRAMS)	TOTAL FAT (GRAMS)	*LIFE*BALANCE SCORE
Turkey Leg (w/skin)	4	11	10
Turkey Wing (w/skin)	4	14	10
Duck	5	13	11
Chicken Thigh (w/skin)	5	18	12
Beef Top Sirloin (Choice)	5	13	11
Chicken Wing (w/skin)	6	22	12
Pork Loin, Center Rib (untrimmed)	7	18	13
Ground Beef (17% fat)	7	19	13
Beef Chuck (Choice arm pot roast)	8	21	14
Ground Beef (20% fat)	8	21	14
Porterhouse Steak (Choice, untrimmed)	10	25	15
Beef Chuck (Choice arm pot roast, untrimmed)	12	29	15
Pork Spareribs (untrimmed)	13	34	20
Beef Short ribs (Choice, untrimmed)	20	47	20

Suggested daily total life Balance score from meats and fish: 20 maximum

Here's how the scoring for this category works: Your score should never total more than 20 from this category for any day. Also, your score of 20 must include no more than two items from the list. If any one item has a score of 20, then limit your choices from this list to only that one item for the day. For example, if you have a portion of your favorite beef short ribs, then limit your meat and fish selections for the rest of the day. If you love Porterhouse steak, then have it! Just be sure that you pick an item with a score of 5 or less for your second (and last) item from this list for the day.

*LIFE*BALANCE HERBS AND SUPPLEMENTS

Vitamins

The best place to buy vitamins is the grocery store—right off the produce shelves! The benefits of vitamins double when they come from natural, whole-food sources. But often we become nutritionally challenged persons (what we would formerly have called lousy eaters!). That's when supplementation from nonfood sources can be helpful.

Folic Acid

Studies have shown that adequate amounts of this vitamin can help prevent birth defects when taken prenatally. Doctors recommend 400mcg daily of folic acid before and during pregnancy.

B Vitamins

These keep our minds healthy and alert and our immune systems strong, help prevent disease, and are great for our skin, hair, nails, and more. B vitamins are also great for helping with stress and fatigue. Some studies have shown that people who are seriously depressed have signs of deficiencies in vitamin B_{12}.

These vitamins have had a positive effect in improving memory and concentration. A lack of B vitamins can cloud the mind. The body needs folic acid, B_6, and B_{12} to manufacture chemicals that control alertness and mood by speeding nerve signals through the brain. More than half of American adults get less than the RDA of vitamin B_6, which is only 2mg. Vegetarians often don't get enough B_{12} because they don't eat meat, fish, or dairy; they, in particular, should consider eating a fortified cereal with 100 percent of the RDA or taking a vitamin supplement.

B vitamins do wonders for increasing energy levels. They are natural energizers and aid in carbohydrate and protein metabolism.

B vitamins can be found in chicken, fish, potatoes, watermelon, green leafy vegetables, fruits, beans, and wheat germ.

Caffeine and alcohol cause the body to excrete B vitamins. The more of these you chug the more B vitamins you need. They are not time-released and need to be replenished throughout the day. Stress and smoking also diminish your B vitamin supply. If you smoke, drink, are under stress, don't eat right, lack energy, or burn the candle at both ends at work or home, be sure to take a B vitamin supplement.

Vitamin C

Vitamin C helps us fight off infections and repair damaged tissue. While dieting, it is important to get plenty of antioxidants. Remember, toxins and body wastes are stored in fatty tissue and will be released into the body as the fat is broken down through diet and exercise. These toxic substances must be neutralized before they get into the cells and cause damage. Another benefit of taking vitamin C is that it helps the body absorb iron. I don't recommend taking more than 1,000mg per day of vitamin C, since it may cause diarrhea. Women who are pregnant should *not* consume more than 5g a day. The RDA of vitamin C has been established at 60mg for people over fifteen years of age. I believe that the dosage should vary according to individual need. During flu season, for example, I take more than usual to help my body fight off disease. Also, I try to encourage people to get their C through natural sources like orange juice (120mg in each cup), broccoli (one stalk of broccoli, raw, contains 160mg of vitamin C), and other fruits and vegetables.

Other Life*Balance Supplements and Herbs*

Kelp

This family of seaweed grows in cool waters and is commonly harvested in Japan and increasingly in North America. These plants have large fronds that are rich in nutrients like carotene pigments, which are antioxidants. Most of us won't want to eat the leaves themselves, but will opt for the processed version sold in health food stores as pills and capsules. Seaweed contains mannitol, an ingredient that helps stabilize blood sugar. Sodium alginate, another component of this wonderful mermaid food, absorbs and holds water, making kelp a great natural laxative. The rich iodine content of seaweed makes it useful for increasing the metabolic rate by stimulating the thyroid hormone. (If you have high blood pressure or a thyroid problem, talk to your doctor before using kelp.)

I like the taste of kelp right out of the package as a "sweet" snack. You may grind it and sprinkle over foods as a condiment or seasoning.

Cleavers

This is a member of the same plant family as coffee and henna. The name comes from its prickly stems, which cause this plant to "cleave" to passing animals and people, allowing for the spread of seeds. This plant can be found at health food stores in capsule or tincture form and is used for tissue-cleansing and kidney-flushing. As it clears the kidneys and urine of toxins, it also has a slight stimulating effect on lymphatic flow. The lymph system helps further cleanse and detoxify the body of wastes.

Be careful when using the more common herbal diuretics like dandelion, buchu, juniper, and uva-ursi—all readily available in many herbal pills and natural weight loss products. Cleavers is nonirritating, but these other herbs actually force the kidneys to work harder, which can result in dehydration. Mental faculties are also affected by the other popular herbs' diuretic effect: coordination and judgment to name a few. I don't recommend diuretics as part of a healthy plan, but the nonirritating effects of cleavers can be very useful and safe when used occasionally for PMS bloat.

Garcinia Cambogia

The active ingredient in this dried fruit rind from India is called HCA, which blocks the enzyme ATP citrate-lyase. By doing so, this plant helps us to manufacture more glycogen, which gives us quick energy. Body fat is minimized and energy is maximized without the "buzz" from caffeine-based "natural" supplements. Since the body's engine is creating more energy, it is also revved up and burning hotter, which uses up more calories per hour.

Garcinia has been proven to have a mild appetite-suppressing effect also. It enables one to make more intelligent eating choices. It can be found in health food stores under different names. CitriMax, Citrin, and other products with like names all contain garcinia.

When chromium picolinate and L-carnitine are taken with garcinia, the fat-burning and appetite-suppressing qualities are amplified.

What about Popular Herbal Stimulants?

Numerous herbal, "natural" stimulants have become popular over the past few years. These promise everything from weight loss to energy gains to a fun, safe, and healthy "high." Often, these contain ma-huang (ephedra), kola nut, guarana, yerba maté, or camellia. These products, while indeed natural, all contain caffeine or caffeinelike substances and their purpose is to rev up the body by causing the sympathetic nervous system to release adrenaline. Safe when used in small amounts—like in your daily cup of coffee or tea—these same ingredients, when used excessively, can cause a variety of uncomfortable side effects. Anxiety, headaches, a racing heart, body sweats, and palpitations are the antithesis of the mind/body connection and I don't recommend these for anyone on a healthy weight-loss and fitness plan. I've seen many women try these and get pretty good initial results. They seemed able to train harder and longer and they reported a decrease in cravings. Eventually, however, most of the women who tried them discovered that they became jittery and nervous when they used these for any length of time. I know one woman who even started to eat more food as a way to calm the jittery feelings! She not only felt uncomfortable, but her body responded by needing more food and fat to even itself out!

Senna and Cascara Sagrada

These herbal laxatives are not harmful when taken occasionally, but, as with any diet "trick," using them over long periods of time is unhealthy. The result of laxative overuse is chronic diarrhea, poorly regulated bowels, possible inflammation of the colon, and electrolyte imbalance. Get your fiber from fruits, vegetables, and grains.

21-DAY BREAK-THE-PATTERN PLAN

People who study behavior have determined that it takes twenty-one days to make or break a habit. I suggest using this principle to begin to totally revamp the way you think about food. Make dietary changes easier on yourself and lock them in more permanently by trying one small change at a time, for twenty-one days, and then adding another small change for the next twenty-one days and so on until you have changed your eating patterns dramatically, but without a lot of stress and strain or seeming hardship. Remember, small steps lead to big change.

Yes, if you went on a drastic, starvation diet you'd get dramatic results the first week or so. But what do you think would happen to the *life*Balance you're trying to create? You guessed it—it wouldn't happen. You'd be in such a fight-or-flight mode that finding any inner (or outer!) calm would be next to impossible. How can you quiet your mind and get in touch with the Real You when your mind is screaming, "I'm starving!" all day long for weeks on end?

Losing ten pounds in a week or two on drugs or starvation dieting might indeed keep you motivated for a while, but your health and metabolism would suffer. Try the 21-Day Plan and use your journal or your buddy to help keep you motivated. Stay focused by creating a mind/body connection that will both calm and energize you in an empowering way.

From the 21-Day Plan Conversion List start with a level-one change. For the next twenty-one-day cycle choose a change from level two or three. In subsequent cycles, alternate between level-one changes and changes from level two or three.

21-DAY PLAN CONVERSION LIST

Level-One Changes

OLD	NEW
buttered toast	all-fruit jam on ½ bagel
oil or butter for cooking	nonstick spray
whole milk	nonfat or low-fat milk
sour cream on baked potato	salsa or nonfat sour cream on potato
junk breakfast cereals	Mind/Body Oatmeal (recipe on p. 205)

Level-Two Changes

OLD	NEW
French fries	baked potato wedge with salsa
cream cheese	nonfat cream cheese
sour cream	nonfat sour cream
cottage cheese	nonfat cottage cheese
ice cream	nonfat or sorbet
frozen yogurt	nonfat or sorbet
yogurt	nonfat yogurt
steak	turkey burger
fatty meats	lean cuts of beef
salty, buttery crackers	nonfat, lavash, or cracked wheat crackers
cakes, cookies, ice cream	fruit

225

Level-Three Changes

OLD	NEW
pudding or ice cream	Mind/Body Oatmeal, chilled
chili dog	turkey, chicken, or fat-free beef dog
fried chicken	grilled chicken breast without skin
meat-based meals	tofu, fish, or other protein source
pizza with cheese	nonfat cracker square with melted skim or nonfat cheese and a tomato slice
fancy pastries, desserts, cakes, croissants	whole wheat bagel with fruit jam

How to Cheat on This Program

I'm going to suggest something for which some of you will think I'm crazy. I want you to succeed in finding *life*Balance so much that I'm going to teach you how to cheat on the plan! I've been preaching the gospel of balance—and cheating is the flip side of all the good new habits you're learning. So let's balance the scales with a little cheating! By allowing yourself a cheat on a fairly regular basis, you'll find this program will continue to work for you, and you may find it works with even more ease.

Here's how the *life*Balance cheat works: Think of the sum total of your daily food intake as a pie chart. If you divided the amount of food eaten on any given day into eight pieces of mind's-eye pie, save space for one-half of one of those wedges to be composed of anything you want. Cheat. If you want a piece of cake and you've been strict on your plan for a few days, then have the cake. Just keep the portion small—no bigger than half of a mind's-eye pie wedge. Cheating with sinful foods or drinks, done in moderation, can help us enjoy life. Cheating of this kind can even act as a mood elevator and as long as its done in moderation, it does no permanent harm.

When you deprive the body of *certain* foods it often responds by rebelling and craving more of *all* foods.

Americans have gained weight since 1980. In the intervening years we've also upped our intake of sugary, low-nutrient foods. Most of us don't need to high-tech our diets. We need to become more low-tech and old-fashioned in our eating habits. We don't need to do more, we need to do less. By sticking to high-fiber, natural foods like fruits and vegetables and eating simple, easy whole foods that are fresh and nutritious, rather than overprocessed, high-tech modern stuff, we can return our bodies to their own healthy, naturally regulated state.

Give yourself permission to eat delicious, healthy foods. Feed yourself based on your real internal needs. Feed the Real You and not the one you think you need to be in order to match the media ideal or society fad.

Learn to Enjoy Healthy Eating

Use the ideas suggested in this chapter as part of a commitment to a healthier lifestyle and not as a temporary punishment to be endured for the next thirty (or however many) days. Look forward to your meals. This is not a restricted-calorie starvation plan. You can eat a fulfilling, low-fat meal and still lose weight if you learn to eat smarter. Use the recommended food substitutions, begin your 21-Day Plan, and make the small but important changes that will make a big difference in the long run. Do it for the health of it. Good health is your most precious possession. Eat right, eat light, exercise, and you'll feel the power of *life*Balance.

THE REAL YOU

When you make a decision for yourself and you own it, you are in control of your destiny. Once you make the decision to achieve *life*Balance, you begin to get in touch with many new feelings and thoughts about who you are and how you want to live your life. You enjoy your successes more, gain more self-esteem, and experience a sense of accomplishment. You begin to make choices to do things for yourself—and not according to other people's expectations of you. I've personally experienced "doing it for me" and "not doing it for me" and I know all too well just how unsatisfying life can be when you're living your life based on someone else's dreams or desires.

I used to get booked for guest posing seminar appearances around the world. I was pointed in the right direction, put on the right plane, picked up from the plane, pushed to the stage, helped to the seminar platform, and then pointed to the plane to return. I knew I was expected to pose, do seminars, and then go home. I did as I was told without question or complaint for about ten years because I thought that was who I was supposed to be and how I was supposed to act. It was also a big part of my yearly income during all those years. I was far from happy, however. I didn't really understand why it had to be like that, but I had no alternative goals of my own, so I just did what I was told to do. I wish I knew then that to "do it for me"—the Real Me—would have made me a much happier camper and would have changed my outlook. What eventually happened is that I got burnt out; I rebelled and didn't do any appearances for two years.

Gradually, I started to do my "job" again. But this time I traveled because I wanted to. This time *I* decided which plane to go on, at what time, and where. I took responsibility for the planning of my itinerary and made my own choices about which appearances to make. I had input about the direction my life took.

I did what I did for me and not because I felt I had to. Let me tell you, it felt fantastic. I now have a purpose and a goal and a mission—for me. They are the same seminars, the same planes, the same cities, and the same appearances, but there's one enormous difference—I now do it for me. I enjoy these experiences more than anything in the entire world because they enable me to be a better, more true me. I'm motivated and anxious to arrive in each city and proud as heck of what I accomplish.

What makes my career different today from what it was during those ten years of slavery is that I've come to know myself better. All the travel and speaking, instead of being pushed on me by others, is done because it serves the Real Me—the woman I truly am who wants to spread a positive fitness message to those who might otherwise miss it. I've gotten in touch with the Cory Everson of today and she's no longer the single-minded bodybuilder of yesterday. My goals have changed and my outlook is transformed. I can operate in the world in a more positive, self-empowering, and self-motivated way.

I still remember my friend Charlie Lindsay, who knew me both before and after I got in touch with the Real Me, saying to me, "Cory, whatever the heck got into you, girl, don't you ever get rid of it. You wear it well." I changed for the better and you can, too. When you get in touch with the Real You, you'll become more self-motivated, self-assertive, confident, and you'll enjoy the heck out of what you do.

*Life*Balance EXERCISE: "THE LIFE IN THE PICTURE"

Leaf through some magazine until you find a photo of a person, groups of people, or lifestyle experience that appeals to you. The photo could be of a woman at the prow of a ship sailing out to sea. It could be a picture of a family at a sporting event. There are no restrictions on the picture you choose, just be sure it's one that really stands out. Once you begin to look, you'll find that one photo will call out to you. Tear it from the magazine and study it. This picture can tell you much about the Real You. There's a "life" in the photo for which the Real You has an affinity. Trust the message in the photo and you can begin to get glimpses of the Real You from it.

For example, Jo picked a photo of a woman looking wistfully into the distance. She made up a story about the woman in the picture and gained some insights into her own inner feelings.

"She's mature, yet she has a youthful attitude about life. She's strong, intelligent, and wise-looking," Jo surmised.

After you've interpreted your magazine picture, save it and look at it from time to time to see what other information about the Real You it might contain.

WE'RE ALL CHANGING!

A recently published study released by the nonprofit Merck Family Fund found that a majority of Americans, alarmed by materialism and greed, rank among their deepest aspirations such nonmaterial things as more family time and less job stress. In the 1980s Americans became yuppified and shifted to high gear—working, buying, and doing more, more, more as winning the rat race became the new American Dream. We've become a society in which the workaholic who sleeps only four hours a night is revered, even when a society of overworked citizens compromises the collective health.

Now, as companies downsize and society undergoes radical changes, many of us want to learn how to downshift our lives. At these lower gears, all of us can get in touch with our real selves, while still achieving our goals. Using Power Connectors, defusing NECs, and finding *life*Balance isn't about letting go of everything that is part of you. They're tools for discovering the Real You.

Discovering the Real You means allowing the inner obstructions to drop out of focus as you key into what is important. When you throw away what isn't you, rid your mind of chatter and confusion, and allow yourself to just be still, you get in touch with who you really are. You give yourself permission to be authentic and then apply yourself to the business of living a fuller, freer life.

While the technique for finding the Real You can be used by anyone, the results will always vary, since no two people can ever turn out the same. You will develop in your own unique way. Your true inner self, when it comes forth, does so in a way different from any other!

The most important step in finding the Real You is to learn how to take care of your total self. You've already seen ways to empower yourself with proper nutrition and appropriate, effective exercise. But getting in touch with the Real You means more than just getting enough rest, taking the right vitamins, working out properly, and eating nutritious foods. It means spending time with yourself away from distractions, even though that concept often strikes fear in the hearts of women who are afraid to take quiet, reflective time.

"I don't want to get away from it all and spend time with myself," Pamela told me. "I'm not happy with what I've done with much of my life. Who wants to be reminded of their mistakes?"

I'll tell you what I told Pamela. Spending time with yourself isn't about wallowing in despair about the past. It's about celebrating the present and the future. No matter how damaged, discouraged, or depressed you may be, you're a survivor. You just don't know it yet! The Real You is waiting, deep inside, to take care of you and help you fulfill your dreams. The route you take may be different from that of others. You can choose from mind/body breathing, meditation, yoga, prayer, qi gong, or other mind/body connections. Each can help you get in touch with the Real You. For each of us the process will differ, but the results will be the same: self-discovery and self-empowerment.

LifeBalance EXERCISE: "MIND/BODY BREATHING EXERCISE"

Sit comfortably and quietly, where you won't be disturbed. Do a mental inventory of your body. What areas of your body call out for attention? Where do you feel tense or strained or heavy? Notice this and remember for later.

Then, touch your stomach about an inch below your navel. Push with a lot of pressure on that spot for about thirty seconds. Remove your finger and continue to focus on that spot. Picture the point where you applied pressure as a yellow balloon and allow it to expand until it fills the whole abdominal area, as well as the pelvis. Imagine filling in the sides as well as the front and back. Breathe in deeply through the nose and allow the belly to expand. Let it hang out. Think about filling the yellow balloon with the breath. Next, exhale through the mouth slowly. Allow the balloon to deflate and collapse. The abdomen should be flat once the air has all been exhaled. Wait for the next breath to start on its own, without forcing it to happen. Let go of your will and allow the body to tell you when the next breath is needed. Just wait for it to happen. Breathe like this for a few minutes.

What part of your body did you notice at the beginning of this exercise? It probably wasn't your abdominal area. Yet, this is the center of all mind/body work. It's where you can create balance and power in your body and mind by utilizing healthy belly breathing. Ironically, this powerful breathing is the opposite of what most of us have been taught. Most of us breathe backward and fight the natural tendency of the breath to expand the stomach area. We've been told to keep our chests out and our stomachs in. But this way of holding ourselves and breathing blocks our natural energy and emotional flow. We become unbalanced, out of touch with our feelings, and increasingly more aggressive. (No wonder there's so much road rage in this country!)

Practice this breathing by itself or in conjunction with meditation sessions. It helps you find the center and balances and relaxes the body. The moments between breathing out and breathing in can be used to free up creative ideas and feelings. These are fertile "free areas" during which exciting new thoughts and feelings can show up.

The Greek word for breath is *pneuma,* which means "spirit" or "soul." Use your breath to nurture your soul.

Are You Getting Enough Sleep?

The occasional bout of insomnia poses no threat to psychological health or mental or physical equilibrium. But regular insomnia can result in sleep deprivation, which causes major physical and mental problems. It has been estimated that one in four people suffers from frequent insomnia. Six million Americans rely on the use of prescription drugs—regularly—in their attempts to get a good night's sleep. Insomnia can be caused by anxiety, tension, and other emotional imbalances. Psychological factors are implicated in 50 percent of insomnia cases. One of the great side effects of the search for the Real You is discovering ways to mute the mental background noise that prevents many from getting their nightly dose of zzz's. Women suffer from insomnia more commonly than men and I think that's due to the fact that women have to keep it all together during the day, tending to so many and varied duties. When night falls, their minds, which have had to juggle so many different responsibilities and handle such a wide variety of problems, are unable to go into shutdown mode.

The Chinese attribute insomnia of this sort to a disturbed *shen qi* (mental spirit). By managing stress during the day with regular mind/body exercises and activities, the *shen qi* is in a much more relaxed state and sleep becomes easier. Whether you suffer from sleep-onset insomnia (it's hard for you to fall asleep) or maintenance insomnia (you wake up frequently during the night) you'll experience better sleep when you've begun to practice mind/body techniques.

Prayer

Prayer puts you in a meditative, reflective state of mind. Your metabolism slows down, as does your heart rate. Your blood pressure may lower. You consume less oxygen. Your immune system is refreshed. Guess what? Prayer is good for you physically! Scientific studies have proven that prayer does good things to the body as well as the mind.

Larry Dossey is a pioneer in mind/body healing. He graduated from Southwestern Medical School in Dallas in 1967 and later served as a battlefield surgeon in Vietnam. He completed residency work in internal medicine in Dallas and was chief of the Medical City Dallas Hospital in the 1970s. His book *Prayer Is Good Medicine* is dedicated to the idea that prayer is good therapy. His background includes studies in meditation, hypnosis, biofeedback, imagery, and visualization. In a magazine article in *Yoga Journal* published in 1996 he said, "[W]e know that when you pray for yourself certain things happen. You think *positively*. And positive thoughts aren't confined to your brain. They set in motion a chain of events that has been defined physiologically."

In his book, he mentions the more than 130 laboratory studies that show that in living things, healthy changes happen as a result of prayer. Recently, a study at Dartmouth Medical School studied the role of religious activity and feelings in 232 patients over the age of fifty-five who were to undergo surgery. Those with religious leanings were assessed as more likely to survive than those without such inclinations. Use prayer to make a healthy mind/body connection and create *life*Balance.

Meditation

Meditation, for many, conjures up mental pictures of people in pastel-colored robes seated on polished marble floors for hours on end, eyes closed and faces expressionless as incense fills the air. But meditation is many things to many people. Some people utilize walking as a moving meditation. Some people go into a meditative state when baking. Some find it easy to do while housecleaning! Meditation can help build a calm that is the opposite of the stressful state we live in so much of the time. It's a healthy form of self-care that can help us not only find inner calm, but improve our physical health through lower blood pressure and heart rate. It's an important addition to our daily program since we need to exercise not just our muscles and body parts, but our inner beings as well.

To try meditation, begin by setting aside a few minutes of your day. It's a great prelude to journaling. Let your family know that this is private time for you and ask for their assistance by allowing you this time to sit (or lie) undisturbed. Close your eyes. Relax. Do some mind/body breathing. Focus silently on your strongest Power Connector (or religious affirmation or a strongly desired goal) for anywhere from two to twenty minutes. The amount of time you spend with this meditation will depend on time constraints and your ability to stay focused, but just do what you can do and allow your body's defenses to relax. You may also want to explore taking a class in meditation. Check the schedule at your local Y or adult learning center. There are a variety of books and videos on the subject, also.

Hypnosis

Many people believe themselves incapable of being hypnotized, yet relatively few actually cannot go under. Each and every one of us performs a sort of self-hypnosis on ourselves every day. You hypnotize yourself when you drive on the freeway and arrive with no memory of how you got where you were going. You feel like you've been on autopilot. The fact that you arrive safely after one of these mindless drives is proof that during hypnosis the mind may seem to be shut down, but it still takes in whatever messages or information are being given it.

You are hypnotized daily by TV. Advertisers count on that. Ever notice that as soon as they start to advertise cough and cold medicines everyone around you gets sick?

Hypnosis and self-hypnosis are powerful avenues to the mind/body connection. Psychological counselors can work with your subconscious mind to rid it of clutter. They can also teach you self-hypnosis or make personalized tapes for you to work with at home.

Watering Holes

Clearing the mind of NECs, engaging in Mental Trash Compacting, creating Power Connectors, exercising, and eating right are all tools that enable you to tee up on the green and drive the ball down the fairway to a balanced life. Finding Watering Holes will enable you to sink the winning putt. Finding your own personal Watering Holes can make it easier for you to become more inwardly defined. They, as much as anything, can quiet your mind enough for you to discover what's already there. They're a great way to find the power within.

Everyone needs Watering Holes. Most people already have them but don't even know it. A Watering Hole is the place where you, like a traveler in a desert who must find replenishment at an oasis, can take a break from the stress and responsibility of everyday life and "drink" from your inner resources. A Watering Hole can be a hobby, a friend, a place, a style of music. I have a few. One of my best friends, Michelle LeMay, represents a cherished Watering Hole to me. No matter

An example of one of my Watering Holes.

what horrible situation comes up or how miserable I feel, no matter what tragedy befalls me, Michelle can always, without fail, give me a sense of safety. She has told me countless times, "Cory, everything always happens for a reason. You have to wait and see. This happened so something even better can show up. You should be thankful things are going the way they are because it's for your ultimate good. It might seem hard now, but you'll be happier later. Be patient and have faith." And she's right every time!

When I come up with ideas or need new ones, I spend time with Michelle and springboard thoughts back and forth from her. This becomes a relaxing and creative Watering Hole for me.

Another Watering Hole I use is a long walk. This one gives me no verbal communication, support, advice, or suggestions like Michelle, but it gives me more of a spiritual connection, a sense of being at ease, and a time to be grateful and acknowledge the gifts that I have in my life. It's a time for quiet relaxation and inner thought, a time to appreciate all that has been given to me, a time to look at my life from the outside and see it more clearly, and a time to connect and feel all those senses—sound, touch, sight, and smell.

Walking is a totally creative Watering Hole for me where I can either rejuvenate and regain energy, or generate ideas and concepts, and then go back and massage them into something I can create.

Some individuals use church or religious groups as their Watering Holes. Some use music, either listening quietly for soothing responses or driving music for generating excitement and energy and creativity. My fiancé, Steven, plays the

> **Healthy Mind/Body Habits for the Real You**
>
> 1. Practice your favorite mind/body connection exercise, whether it's yoga, mindful walking, or meditation. Do what works for you and do it regularly. Get in touch with the Real You and you'll lower your chances of having stress activate certain cancers in your body, particularly if you have a genetic predisposition to the disease.
> 2. Don't smoke.
> 3. Cut back on fat, but eat enough healthy fat.
> 4. Eat cancer-killing foods. Broccoli, cauliflower, carrots, onions, garlic, and tofu. Get plenty of antioxidants, like vitamins C and E and selenium.
> 5. Get mammograms.
> 6. Drink moderately. An oft-quoted "60 Minutes" segment several years ago reported the health benefits of fermented grapes, but several cancers, particularly of the liver, are linked to alcohol.
> 7. Go pale! Sunburn of any kind increases the risk of skin cancer. You can be too rich, too thin, and too tan!
> 8. Get Thee Fit! Yes, work out with weights and get your aerobic fat-burning session three to five times a week. Just don't go overboard!
> 9. Laugh. Norman Cousins told us in *Anatomy of an Illness as Perceived by the Patient* that laughing isn't just fun, it's healthy. This little luxury feeds the bloodstream with anticancer chemicals.
> 10. Enjoy. Live in the here and now and not in the when and then. Take time to appreciate any small daily progress and celebrate when you reach every goal.

piano after a hard day at work. The piano is his Watering Hole. Rollerblading by himself is another of his favorite Watering Holes, as is reading.

Painting is another Watering Hole for me; it makes me feel good. Basically, anything that brings about that good feeling—as if a weight has been lifted from your shoulders—can be considered a Watering Hole.

As I say, we can have more than one Watering Hole. It's good to have a few. I use exercise, art, and people. Steven uses the piano, rollerblading, and reading. Michelle, my good friend, uses dance, music, and people. Some use yoga. Watering Holes are personal and individual, different for each of us.

You probably already have them in your life, but you just haven't identified them and recognized them for the valuable tools they are. Find your Watering Holes and be grateful that they're in your life. They'll keep you sane. They help to relieve the mind of stress and become more balanced, and they provide a place to retreat and feel safe. They help you get in touch with your inner self and find out more about the Real You. Watering Holes allow you to feed your emotional needs. They support the best you.

Walk through the Fear

I still remember the first time I had to be in front of a TV camera. I was horrified. I was afraid I would look idiotic and when I opened my mouth I was sure I would say something unintelligible. I tried so hard to get out of that job. I used every excuse in the book. "Sorry, I'll be sick then." "My dog is having babies soon and I can't make it." "I think I have a big cold sore coming on, I'd better cancel." No one bought any of these excuses and the show had to go on.

Well, it wasn't that bad an experience, after all. I was pretty darn good, in fact. After the initial shock of being in front of a camera wore off I found myself enjoying the work! But what if I had let that fear control me? Then what? I might never have had the opportunity to have my TV show today. I still get nervous, but I've learned to take control of the fear and not let it control me.

Now I can honestly say that I'm proud of who I am, of what I do, of what I've accomplished, and of the Real Me.

If you're afraid, you'll never get anywhere; you'll just remain living with your self-inflicted wall of fear stopping you from any kind of action. Don't let excuses or fear dominate your actions.

Believe in Yourself—Believe in the Real You

Before you shut your eyes every single night and first thing every morning think about all the good things in your life and how fortunate you really are. I speak from experience. Nothing feels better than being grateful for who you *already* are.

Somebody sent this to me once on a card; I keep it with me at all times, in my wallet. It's by Collin McCarty. These are the twenty-four things to always remember, and one to never forget.

Your presence is a present to the world. You're unique and one of a kind. Your life can be what you want it to be. Take the days just one at a time. Count your blessings, not your troubles. You'll make it through whatever comes along. Within you are so many answers. Understand. Have courage. Be strong. Don't put limits on yourself. So many dreams are waiting to be realized. Decisions are too important to leave to chance. Reach for your peak, your goal, your prize. Nothing wastes more energy than worrying. The longer one carries a problem, the heavier it gets. Don't take things too seriously. Live a life of serenity, not a life of regrets. Remember that a little love goes a long way; remember that a lot goes forever. Remember that friendship is a wise investment. Life's treasures are people together. Realize that it's never too late to do ordinary things in an extraordinary way. Have health and hope and happiness. Take the time to wish upon a star. And don't ever forget for even a day how very special you are.

I love that.

RESOURCES

Here are some resources for services and for finding Cory's books, tapes, and videos:

MEDICAL/DENTAL

Carolyn M. Doherty, M.D.
Facial Plastic Surgery and Reconstructive
Surgery, Liposuction
Bedford Aesthetics
450 N. Bedford Ste. 110
Beverly Hills, CA 90210
310/859-1354

Steven Donia, DDS
Cosmetic Dentistry
16133 Ventura Blvd. Ste. 1045
Encino, CA 91436
818/772-1048

Garth Fisher, M.D.
Plastic Surgery
120 South Spalding Dr. Ste. 210
Beverly Hills, CA 90212
310/273-5995

MIND/BODY EXERCISE

Rolf Institute
205 Canyon Blvd.
Boulder, CO 80304
303/449-5903

For a worldwide listing of Certified Rolf
Practitioners on the Internet:
www.rolf.org

The Pilates Studio®
2121 Broadway, Suite 201
New York, NY 10023
800/474-5283

International Association of Yoga
Therapists
415/383-2478

Yoga International
717/253-4929

For yoga books and tapes, call
800/I-DO-YOGA

FITCAMP
18653 Ventura Blvd. Ste. 161
Tarzana, CA 91356
800/727-2888 (for a free brochure.)
3 and 5-day retreats for women featuring
mind/body work as well as weight training, aerobics and outdoor challenges for
every fitness mode.

SUPPLEMENTS AND NUTRITIONAL PRODUCTS

Bricker Labs
1/800-BRICKER
Call to order the Cory Fat Loss diet package, Lean Machine (protein powder), and other great supplements.

Wisconsin Pharmacal
This company makes a great vitamin designed for women by a female pharmacist and a physician. They also make terrific suncreens under the brand name Reflect.
414/677-4121

OTHER CORY PRODUCTS

Books

Fat Free and Fit
One-stop shopping to learn about the easiest way to lose body fat and keep it off permanently. Included are recipes, diets, weight-loss workouts, and tools for reprogramming your metabolism to boost calorie burn and train your mind to stick to a successful program.

Cory Everson's Workout
Once you achieve *life*Balance your energy levels will skyrocket and you might find yourself looking to expand your fitness interests. This book has workouts written specifically for forty-seven different sports, including tennis, golf, karate, body sculpting, inline skating, and more. It's like having your own personal sports training coach.

Audio

Commit to Be Fit
This three-part motivational audiotape series was written and recorded by Cory to help anyone pump up the mind and body. This goes hand-in-hand with many of the *life*Balance exercises. Listen to it on your walks or in your car on the way to work or school. "Listen to them," Cory says. "I guarantee you'll love them!"

Start Walking, Lose Fat
If you want a training partner to walk with, Cory is right there to help. Just plug in this tape and go! Cory takes you through two- to thirty-minute workout walks, starting out with a slow warm-up and gradually getting your heart rate into your fat-burning zone, not too slow, not too fast, just perfect. Too many people walk too fast

and don't get the full fat-burning benefit from walking workouts because they go beyond their fat-burning zone. "In this tape you'll meet interesting people along your journey," Cory promises. "Listen to it and you'll see what I'm talking about."

Photos

Six 5 × 7 glossies of Cory's bodybuilding victories, one for each of the following years: 1984, 1985, 1986, 1987, 1988, and 1989. This visual stimulation will keep you motivated. "My hint," Cory advises, "is to bombard yourself with visual, verbal, and written stimulation to help keep yourself on track."

Videos

Gotta Sweat Aerobics Series (five-tape series)
This series includes five of Cory's favorite aerobic workouts. Do a different twenty-minute workout every other day and you can see the fat begin to melt away.

Gotta Sweat Ab & Butt Solution (two videos)
Each tape gives you ten different three-minute workouts. Do just one every day to help get a sexy, flat stomach and slimmer, firmer hips, thighs, and butt. Cory asks, "You can give me three minutes a day, can't you?"

Get Hard Upper Body
Tone and sculpt your upper body using light weights. All you need are three-pound dumbbells and you can get rid of back-of-the-arm jiggle and other upper body areas needing more tone.

Best of Cory Video
If you're interested in Cory's Ms. Olympia history and routines, this is the tape for you. "This is a sort of *National Enquirer* of my life," Cory says. "I'm willing to share it with other women, even though it's very revealing."

To order any of the above Cory Everson products, call 402/384-6800 or, they can be found on the Internet at www.coryeverson.com.

THE POWER LIST

Following is a list of Power Connectors. Use them to facilitate your meditation, walking, or other mind/body activity. As you walk, sit quietly, or just go about your day, think about one of these and use it to help quiet your mind, center yourself, and get in touch with the Real You.

As we imagine, so we can create.

By setting small, realistic goals, I set myself up for big wins.

Finding quiet time enables me to get in touch with the Real Me.

Maintaining wellness is my greatest wealth.

I allow myself the little luxuries of quiet reflection and healthy moderation. By doing so, I feel happy.

I eat foods that nourish my body, mind, and soul.

Whenever I get down on myself, I practice Mental Trash Compacting.

I keep my mind clear and my body healthy so that the Real Me can show up.

I focus on my Power Connectors each and every day.

I keep my fitness program fun by trying new activities and allowing myself childlike curiosity.

I seek balance and stay away from extremes in my fitness program, my foods, and my thinking.

Eating nutritious foods makes me feel better, stronger, and more energetic.

A strong, healthy body is my most valuable asset.

Daily, I take the time to seek my inner direction. I trust it.

Today, I am at peace with myself.

I accept my body.

My goal today is to do the best that I can—in everything I undertake.

I can do it.

I can't change my ancestors . . . but I can greatly influence my descendants.

The person who wins might have been counted out many times . . . but he didn't listen to the referee.

Try not to base your actions on success . . . instead, focus them on *doing*.

My body reflects the amount of weeding done during the growing season.

Anyone can be enthusiastic for twenty minutes or twenty days . . . but the successful one is enthusiastic for twenty years.

Happiness depends upon what we are, not what we have: Your heart is the gold and your body is the mine . . . put them together and you have a gold mine!

I understand who I am . . . so I can be happy with what I have.

If I take care of my body, my body will take care of me.

When I choose a goal and commit to it, whatever I do will be enjoyable.

Since the taste of success is so sweet, you'll double your efforts to taste it again!

The ability to respect others is in direct proportion to one's own self-respect —if you have it, you can give it!

Don't waste precious time envying someone else's body . . . use that time to create your own.

You become successful the moment you take a step moving toward a goal.

It's not how many hours you put into a workout . . . but how much workout you put into those hours!

Choice, not chance, determines your body's destiny.
It is your choice to be fit . . . or fat!

We can turn grapes into wine . . . but we can't turn your whining into a healthy body. Get off your gluteus!

Some people dream about a beautiful, sexy body.
Others stay awake and create them.

Creating a more shapely body in the future starts with the ability to envision it in the present.

Even a woodpecker owes his success to the fact that he uses his head!
Train and eat smart!

Success comes in cans, failure comes in can'ts . . . feed yourself with only positive cans of food.

Most people get ahead during the time others waste . . . every little bit counts!

If the grass looks greener on the other side of the fence . . . you can bet they take better care of their lawn. Your body is your lawn . . . so manicure it!

If you always put in 100 percent at the present . . . you'll get 110 percent back in the future.

Rome wasn't built in a day, so why expect your body to be? Be patient, but persistent.

Knowing how to improve your health, but not doing it, is far worse than not knowing in the first place!

"To be fit or not to be fit"—that is the question only you can answer.

It is not what your *body* has done for you but what *you* have done for your body.

In the time it took to procrastinate . . . you could have finished a workout.

Put on a good face . . . it is like a mirror that reflects your attitude.

Motivation is when your dreams put on sweatpants—get dressed!

If you want to attain . . . then don't complain.

If you feel "dog tired" at night, perhaps you were growling all day. Workouts are a great attitude adjuster!

Fifteen percent of any workout is better than 100 percent of the workout you put off until tomorrow.

The greatest possession you have is the twenty-four hours directly ahead of you . . . use it or lose it!

Falling down doesn't make you a failure . . . but staying down does . . . just trying means you've already won!

To be upset over the body you don't have . . . is to waste the body you do have . . . be the best that *you* can be.

Procrastination about doing your workout takes just about as much energy as doing the workout itself!

Situations can stop you "temporarily," but only you can stop yourself permanently . . . keep positive momentum moving!

If you want to make an easy workout seem mighty difficult . . . just keep putting it off!

Sometimes we are so busy counting our problems . . . we forget to add up our blessings . . . be grateful.

Parking lot fitness: Park near and you'll keep your big rear . . .
park away and in shape you'll stay.

The smallest action is far better than the greatest intention . . . do it now!

Some people succeed because they are destined . . . but most because they are determined to.

Even your garbage disposal eats better than 30 percent of the people in the world.

Welcome obstacles as the stepping stones to the path of success.

The Tortoise and the Hare: Ultimate health is never won by the swiftest . . . but by the one with persistence!

The train of unhealthiness . . . usually runs on the tracks of laziness.

Your body is like a chunk of coal . . . with a little time it will become a diamond.

An artist creates a sculpture out of clay . . . you can create a body sculpted from workouts.

Developing your body and developing your self-esteem go hand in hand.

The goals you set are less important than the fact you are acting upon them!

It's not your *outlook,* but your *uplook* that counts . . . think positive. If you believe, you will achieve!

A winner makes commitments, a loser makes promises.

Always do your best at the present . . . and the results will take care of themselves!

Clarity of your purpose and direction, plus taking responsibility to act upon it, equals success!

Welcome whatever obstacles that confront you as opportunities . . . they are!

Set yourself increasingly more difficult goals and persevere until each one of them has been reached!

Be energy-oriented and see each day in terms of constant progress.

Cultivate the ability to concentrate and act upon whatever task you set yourself.

Start each day fresh, bright and with promise, and never define yourself in terms of past failures!

Your face is like a mirror . . . it reflects your attitude toward life!

The right angle to approach a difficult problem is the . . . *try-angle!*

The poorest of all people are not those without a cent . . . but those without a dream.

Laziness and Poverty are cousins . . . don't be part of their family. Energy and Persistence are cousins . . . be a part of theirs!

The difference between ordinary and extraordinary is putting in that little extra!

One thing you can learn from watching a clock is that it passes time by keeping its hands busy!

To forgive is to set a prisoner free . . . and discover the prisoner was you. Give yourself a break, you are only human!

Cherish your visions and your dreams, as they are the blueprints of your ultimate achievements!

Believe and you will succeed. The key to happiness is having dreams . . . the key to success is making dreams come true!

Opportunity always involves some risk—you can't steal second base and keep your foot on first . . . go for it if you want to get it!

Patience is a quality you admire in the driver behind you and scorn in the one ahead.

Your companions are like the buttons of an elevator. They will either take you up or they'll take you down . . . reinforce your healthy lifestyle by hanging around positive, healthy people!

You cannot win if you don't begin!

Start from scratch . . . and keep on scratching!

The secret to achievement is not to let what you are doing get to you before you get to it!

Without your health . . . you have no wealth . . . the richest man with poor health is worth less than a healthy poor man. There are some things money can't buy!

A professional is someone who will put out even when she doesn't feel like it . . . be a professional when it comes to your health!

Obstacles are those frightful things you see when you take your eyes off your goal . . . stay focused and you will achieve!

A diamond is a chunk of coal that under pressure became a gem . . . don't fear pressure, use it!

The smallest portion of a workout is far better than the greatest intention . . . quit babbling and just do it!

Do it now. You become successful the moment you start moving toward a worthwhile goal . . . take that first step!

There are two kinds of people in life. Those who *make* things happen, and those who *let* things happen to them. If it is a better body you want . . . you must go out and get it!

To achieve growth . . . you need attainable mini goals that have reasonable deadlines!

If you wait for all the lights to be green . . . you'll never get downtown. Don't wait for everything to be perfect before you start exercising. Start now!

When you become impatient, remind yourself that a few workouts won't remake your body . . . but the sum of all your workouts will!

Walk away your stress. It gives you a temporary reprieve from anxiety and stimulates your energy level!

There is nothing worse than hearing your mind close to an idea that can reshape your future . . . be willing to hear the possibilities. See you in the gym!

Have faith that for every problem there is an inherent solution!

Be grateful for what you have and get busy making you the best you can be!

Know that *you* are the final measure for everything you accomplish . . . or don't accomplish!

Put on a happy face and a happy attitude will follow . . . your face determines the mood that will follow!

Creating a more healthy beautiful body in the future starts with the ability to envision it in the present!

My fitness is in direct proportion to my commitment to improve my health!

My happiness is in the day-to-day journey, the effort expended on a daily basis . . . not only in the final destination!

We can't control our genetic makeup . . . but we can adjust the way it behaves. (Your family history of being overweight doesn't mean you have to be!)

Nothing succeeds like success. The best way to improve your self-image is to experience success in your fitness program!

The goals you set aren't as important as the fact that *you* are setting them and working toward achieving them!

Take responsibility for your actions. If it is to be . . . it is up to me!

The opportunity to shape up is here now—you'll always miss 100 percent of all the shots you don't take, so start shooting!

If the grass looks greener on the other side of the fence, you can bet the water bill is higher . . . be grateful for what you have!

Work with the construction gang, not the wrecking crew . . . create your body and don't destroy it!

Sandwich every ounce of criticism between two slices of praise!

You're not overweight, you are overfat . . . you're only inches away.

Dieting and stress mean that at some point you'll act like an idiot . . . ask your friends.

When you need an attitude adjustment . . . go for a workout!

Get out aggression in the gym . . . and leave it there!

You're in the gym to train your body . . . not your ego.

Your body fat percentage is a reliable barometer of . . . lean muscle versus *blubber.*

Believe and you'll achieve! That's the bottom line . . . and if you believe, your bottom line will recede!

INDEX